Everyday people's thoughts on Completing

William Curle
A story of life encounters growing up in Easterhou
transforming encounter with Jesus and a journey of discovering life to the full.
Written in Stuart's unique style. I found it difficult to put down.

Heather Hood
Fantastic book by Easterhouse boy Stuart Patterson! I kinda thought nah not my
thing n I already know the story ....was so wrong x once this is done I'll be giving it to
the English and Social Studies teachers in [local] High School. Nostalgic emotional
funny intelligent read. Heart-breaking at times ...if you can please give it a read it's
well worth it and guarantee you'll be talking or thinking about it for a good while!

Kay Johnston
Thank you, Stuart Patterson, for your book it's the first book I have read in a long
time and couldn't put it down. I laughed at some of it and cried. It was very
emotional at times... I gave it to my neighbour to read and she enjoyed it as well. The
girls are next on the list to read it so thank you very much for it.

Alice Fitzpatrick
I have just finished reading 'completing the tenner' and thoroughly enjoyed reading
it. I laughed and cried. I feel I have more understanding of why you 'chose' that path
although I'm sure nobody ever sets out to destroy their life in such a way, but once
on that road where's the way off for so many?

Sharon McGarr
Brilliant book to read.

Maggie McVey
A must read

John Spence
...a very thought-provoking book...that is a must read for anyone who needs a wee
bit of inspiration. Easterhouse has produced many good people and I am sure your
book will inspire folk to push through and achieve their dreams. I have been taken
back to my youth – the wall, the battles, territories, drugs, drink, Charlie's and the
days of no responsibilities. Every time I put it down I want to pick it up an read
another chapter.

Completing the tenner

How addiction smacked my education

Stuart Patterson

Other books available from this author:
Simply Jesus – Reflective poems from the twenty-eight-year-old me
ISBN: 9781097173167

Five weeks in May
ISBN: 9781099221019

These books are available on Amazon in Kindle and printed forms and are also available direct from the author.

Finally rounding up the dash of my life

for my wife, Tracy

and my daughters

Alisha, Zoë Ann and Naomi

Foreword

This book is a work in progress. Like all our lives the pages are still being written. As I go through it, I find better ways to express the events and so I edit them. I don't change the facts as, like our lives, the past cannot be rewritten. I don't have a company proof reading and editing for me, just you, the reader. If you come across any grammatical mistakes, please feel free to email and let me know. The funds raised for this book will go towards the continued work of Easterhouse Community Church, Teen Challenge – AND – me.

Stuart Patterson was born in Belvedere Hospital, Glasgow, 1970 to a Scots dad and an English mum. He grew up in the sprawling Easterhouse housing scheme (estate) but has lived in Wales, Dublin, Ballymena and now Paisley.

Now married to Tracy, they have three daughters and lead an Assemblies of God church in Easterhouse.

Stuart has overcome many challenges and adversities in his life since becoming a Christian in 1997. He cites Jesus as being his reason for living and the hope and strength for life.

"I was messed up before I met Jesus, now I am slightly less so. I have always enjoyed writing and am amazed that sometimes people enjoy reading my writing," says Stuart.

Stuart returned to Further Education in August 2017 through the Scottish Wider Access Programme. He won the Class Prize for the SWAP Access Humanities for Glasgow Kelvin College and also was a finalist in SQA Star Award for mature students.

Stuart spent most of his early life feeling like an outsider, even church he says that "he felt too bad to go in and thought they were too good to come out" whilst he was in the depth of heroin addiction.

Stuart is now a mature student, "people think I am mature because of my age...til they meet me" at the University of Strathclyde doing a BA in Humanities.

The following pages tell Stuart's story through moments, rather than a straight chronology. Using different writing techniques and styles, you will laugh, cry, love and hate as you walk those days through Stuart's eyes. It is not a full account, but it is an honest one. This is his – MY - story...

Contents

Foreword..v
1 - Heather did you know? (1970)..1
2 - Dragged kicking and screaming (1974) 4
3 - The hole in the wall (1977)...7
4 - Blairtummock Old Time Music Hall (1978)............12
5 - Family fun at Filey (1979)...13
6 - Bite Size (1980)..15
7 - Are you good enough (1981) 20
8 - Milk and a piece n Jam Part 1 (1981).......................23
9 - That first day (1981)..26
10 - Of Mice and Men (1982)..30
11 - Lochwood Farm (1979-85)..36
12 - Cairnbrook (1986)..43
13 - Sixteen Today Part2 (1986) 44
14 - The Lion's Den (1986) 48
15 - Hatchet Job (1986)..53
16 - Three step shuffle (1986) 57
17 - THAT first time (1986)...63
18 - Another First Time (1986) 65
19 - Flashbulb Memory (1987) 66
20 - Knives (1987) 70
21 - Weekend at Baird Street (1987)...............................73
22 - The road to nowhere (1988)......................................77
23 - Silver Fine (1988)...79
24 - The Fog (1989)...82
25 - Stewarding Stuart (1988, 1991) 85
26 - Innocent as Hell (1989)...88
27 - Milk n a piece n jam part 2 (1990).........................91
28 - The Great Escape (1990) 92
29 - Bittersweet Symphony (1992)..................................93
30 - That's handy (1993, I think)......................................95
31 - Vague recollections (1990's)..................................101
32 - Airplane Gaze part 1 (1997)...................................105
33 - An 'L' of a place (1997) 106
34 - Completing the Tenner (1997) 110
35 - The Phone Call (1997) 112
36 - Bus Service (1997) 115

37 – Don't Quit (1997)..118
38 - Your new life (1997) 121
39 - Ring of smoke (1997) 125
40 - Let's do this! (1997) 127
41 - Jailbreak (1997) 129
42 – Hands On (1997) 133
43 - The ghost of Christmas past (1997)..........................136
44 - Airplane Gaze part 2 (1998).....................................140
45 – Milk n a Piece n Chips (1998).................................144
46 - Lifted (1998) 146
47 - Talk to me mate (2000) 149
48 – Now it's Time to Say Goodbye (2000)...................154
49 – Dublin's Fair City (2000)..158
50 - Caledonia's calling me (2009)..................................164
51 – JP (2002) 167
52 – Milk n Another Piece n Jam (2003) 169
53 – Mother's Day (2010) 170
54 - Paddy (2014) 173
55 – Bored in the Winter (2017) 181
56 – The Road to Nowhere – Revisited (2017)..........183
57 – Fazed at Freshers (2018) 184
58 - We don't need no education (2019) 187

I Primary Education

1 - Heather did you know? (1970)
February 1970 - first day at, well everything...

Mary, did you know that your baby boy
will give sight to a blind man
Mary, did you know that your baby boy
will calm the storm with his hand
Did you know that your baby boy
has walked where angels trod?
When you kiss your little baby,
you kiss the face of God.
From the song *"Mary did you know"* by Mark Lowry 1991[i]

If I had been three weeks early, instead of three weeks late, I would have been a child of the sixties and Tracy - my wife - said that would have made me too old for her.

According to the United Nations Population Division there were an estimated 332,888 babies born worldwide on the 13th February 1970. I was one of them. Born at 6.55pm Belvedere hospital in Glasgow's east end. The fourth of what would be six children. It was Black Friday - 13th February. I'm not superstitious, but maybe my parents saw it coming.

1

Belvedere Hospital was just a stone's throw from Celtic Park, a place that would grow to hold fond memories for me in the coming years. It was part of the culture my brothers and I would grow into.

I don't really know much of the circumstances surrounding my mum - Heather - and dad – John - at that time. Other than my mum already had John, Gary and Yvonne and between the four of us there was an average of eighteen months. Darrin would arrive just over two years later, and my mum, at the tender age of 25, would have five kids aged from seven to new-born. How the heck did she manage? Mum and dad had met and were married fifteen days after her seventeenth birthday, (1964) and dad was just about to turn twenty.

Neil came along ten years after Darrin in 1982. By then, the mistakes had been learned, my parents were a wee bit older and he was spoiled. "As he should be" my mum used to chide us. She also demanded and commanded that we should be spoiling him as well. So, Neil grew up with a sense of entitlement that has served him well in all his endeavours. It's caused him to work extremely hard for what he has, because he believed that's how entitlement is worked out.

Anyway, this is not about him, it's about the little baby with the blue eyes making his way in this brave new world he had found himself in.

"Did you know that you were born three weeks late? You were not too keen to make an entrance into this world. The day your mum brought you home from hospital, I couldn't wait to hold you and remember her telling me that your skin was only dry because you were so late, and it would all clear up. At almost fourteen the shock of seeing a new baby with such flaking skin must have shown on my face. Isn't it strange the sort of things that stay in the corners of our minds?" Aunt Alice – one of mum's younger sisters, and my godmother - informed me as she recounted my birth.

My earliest memories all seem to involve people over at the house, socialising and drinking. Not in an abnormal way, it was just that parents loved company and people loved them. There was a close-knit group of friends - and their kids – that we shared our lives with. John and Betty Smith, Kay and John Johnstone, the McBrides, the Auld's, the McGarr's and so the list went on. If they weren't at our house, then we were all at one of theirs, that is how it went. This pattern followed through most of our lives while we all lived at home.

Friday nights were the main nights for the *social gatherings*. They were always full of laughter and fun. Singing and attempted singing and always went on into the wee small hours. These were our *aunties and uncles* whether we liked it or not – and me and my brothers didn't like it. We always protested, always in vain. Friday nights meant that, from a very young age, I would spend Saturday mornings clearing mountains of glasses, many with stale alcohol, and overflowing ashtrays. I never thought nothing of it, and probably even more surprising, I never tasted the alcohol, (well not that often).

It wasn't just the Friday nights though; they were for drinking. Through the week, the woman mostly, would be in and out for a cup of tea and a chat. It's mad to think that my parents were only in their twenties for much of these times – kids themselves. My mum was very sociable, and I think my love for networking stems from the way she got on with her friends. She was natural with people.

The first house I remember living in was in Baldinnie Road in Easterhouse, right across from the big playground gates at Blairtummock Primary School. We moved there when I was two. It was great.

Three bedrooms down the right-hand side as you came in the front door, with the kitchen, bathroom and living room at the front. All the rooms were a decent size. It was a bottom flat in a block of three up tenements (six in a block). We had a front and back garden and the space under the floorboards. This was a secret den (hideaway) in the end and smallest of the bedrooms. The boards in one part could be lifted and the space underneath was high enough to play under and hide things. Our own little world.

Our close (the name given to a block of flats) also backed onto a football pitch and Blairtummock Park with its bowling greens and the big old Blairtummock House where they showed movies to the kids on a Saturday morning, and aunt Alice had her office upstairs.

As I said, it was not uncommon for our house to be filled with mum and dad's friends in those days. And when friends were over, then drink was consumed. Lots of it. I even remember my dad having his own corner bar in our living room. Different days!

On those occasions I hated being put to bed. Mum and dad were quite disciplined with us, and bedtime was bedtime, no matter who was in the house. I used to sleep in a cot in mum and dad's room. I'm not sure what age I was, but I remember hearing people over. I would cry to be lifted out, and when mum and dad came in and asked what was wrong, I would say something stupid like, 'Can you fix the blanket?" Instead of asking them to let me join in. I hated missing out. I wanted to be involved in everything that was going on. They always seemed to be having so much fun and I was shut out of it, in a room on my own.

So much of what was to go on and go wrong in my life can probably be traced right back to those days, when I was unable to express myself properly. I always had a fear that if I said how I felt; people would not want to know me. It was a pattern that was to repeat throughout the years, resulting in me becoming a very withdrawn child who always struggled to make friends or even to get along with people.

I often wondered what my mum and dad thought when I arrived. What were the questions racing through this young couple's minds? What were their fears? The Christmas song *"Mary did you know?"* really does apply to all mothers. To cradle a new-born baby in your arms and wonder what kind of life is going to unfold through that tiny package. Scary thought.

Like the song, did mum and dad ever stare at this new-born child and know the joy, the despair, the heartache and the peace this little bundle would bring? Does any parent?

2 - Dragged kicking and screaming (1974)
August 1974 - first day at school

August 1974 saw Richard Nixon resign as US President; a coup in East Timor; the Turkish army attacking Nicosia in Cyprus; USSR, USA and France all testing nuclear weapons; 4000 Bangladeshis perish in a hurricane and subsequent flood; the Ramones perform their first concert and John Lennon is still seeing things in the sky, although this time it was not Lucy and there did not appear to be any diamonds. Inflation was at 17.2%! Tracy Ann Tormey – future wife - was five months old. The Rumble in the Jungle was a mere two months away and Germany had won the world Cup.

In August 1974 I was four and half years old and I did not know, or even care about any of those other events. I was forcibly removed from our ground floor flat, taken one hundred yards across the road, through the gates that would play a massive role in the next seven years of my life and dumped in a room full of other children that I had never met.

In August 1974, against my will, I started Blairtummock Primary School.

To make matters worse Darrin, my wee brother, was left at home. I did not like this. I remember vividly a day just prior to this when we were walking up to Rochs Store in Lochend Road. My nana worked there. I loved going up because Mr Roch always gave us sweets and my nana always gave us smiles.

This time stands out though, because I was extremely jealous that Darrin (just past his second birthday) was being pushed in our old metal pushchair and I had to walk. Just as we neared the shop I screamed and shouted and threw a massive tantrum, to the point my nana must have heard me. The normally loving caring smiling Nana Kiernan came out with her face on fire, took one look at my horrified mum and proceeded to tear me apart with her mouth for being a spoilt, selfish uncaring little boy. I stopped crying and looked at her bemused. Didn't she understand this bundle in the pushchair had hijacked my life and was getting all the attention?

Only weeks later August appeared. And my life was to change forever. I never went to Buchlyvie Nursery School (on Aberdalgie Road???) that my brothers and sister had went to. In fact, I didn't get to go to any nursery.

Don't know why. Never asked.

I had been told all summer how good this first day of school was going to be. Everyone was telling me I was going to enjoy what was coming.

Hmmm. To this day I am convinced they ALL meant they were going to enjoy it, not me. (Let me clarify who ALL refers to – EVERYONE – every single person that mum and dad knew, aunts, uncles, pretend aunts and uncles, nana and granda (mum's parents) and granny and granda (dad's parents) hope that clarifies the ALL).

Anyway, here we were -

My first day!

Primary one to primary three kids had to enter in via the Aberdalgie Road entrance. This was up the street from our house on Baldinnie Road, and around the corner and down Aberdalgie Road about a hundred yards. Our gate was just up a bit from what seemed like the massive St George's and St Peter's Church of Scotland, (now called Easterhouse Parish Church).

Mum and dad, entrusted by God to feed me, clothe me, give me food and shelter - to love me - abandoned me at the gates and left - WITH Darrin.

In I trudged to this strange, concrete prison yard, overshadowed by the monstrous, high roofed dining room, that seemed to tower over the much smaller primary 1 - 3 playground.

It really was quite an enclosed space, with the shelter attached to left hand side of the building. Next was the wall of the building, with the toilet windows being the prominent feature, and then that dining/assembly hall.

This was to be my recreational space for breaks and lunchtime for the next three years.

Abandoned!

We were in Miss Beck's (later to become Mrs Angus after being married) class. I had sobbed and cried all the way to school. When I was eventually brought into the class with all my classmates already seated, I got to sit in a chair at the front to make me feel special.

It didn't.

It made me the centre of attention (like the crying hadn't) and I did not like that.

Anyway, I soon got over the initial shock of my world suddenly changing and settled into the regimented regime of the class.

It was not long before I found that I loved class. We had a fantastic teacher, although even at that early age I had my questions, and I asked them.

My classmates were brilliant, forty-five years later, I still know and communicate with some of them. Now isn't that fantastic?

Others disappeared into the sands of time, and still I look and for news of them. My first day, though. The classroom itself always seemed dark, with not much natural sunlight coming in despite the big windows. This was because a large line of bushes ran along a slope outside the back of these classes. Primary one & two were on the ground floor, so hence the gloom.

In the midst of the dreary gloom, though, there were bright spots. The brightest for me, the most stand out moment from that first day was story time.

At story time we all gathered into a semi-circle and Miss Beck, (now seated on my chair at front of class) would read to us. She was great at it. I loved, even at that early age, of being transported to another world through books. As the words of the storyteller came out, I would instantly begin to visualise the scenes in my head. Sitting on that cold floor, I would be transported off to other worlds, right where I sat. Magical adventures, and thrills and drama and intrigue – and that was only the *Peter and Jane* books.

It is something that has stayed with me all my life. I believe it is because there is that part of us that knows we are something bigger than our physical experience.

Solomon says that God has placed eternity into the hearts of men, and in *Psalm 42* the writer urges us to the understanding that "*deep calls unto deep*". What we see with jus our physical eyes, can never be enough, whilst that deep rooted longing for eternity and our home with God beckons us.

This unlocking of my imagination that first day may have taken many years to hit home, but here we are.

Story time allowed my imagination to carry me off to places that my body could not go. It wasn't just novels either. I had an unquenchable thirst for general knowledge. News, papers, encyclopaedias, general knowledge books - like the character Jonny 5 from *Short Circuit*, (one of my favourite movie characters) and his incessant cry of "Need more input".

I did like football, and playing outside, and doing the jumps game (parkour before parkour was a thing) but I loved reading. I loved to feel the stimulation as even news pieces allowed my mind to explore what my ears were hearing and what my lips were reading. My eyes eager to move onto the next words as if each one was a secret code that unlocked another hidden destination.

Very quickly I settled into school because of this. The nightmare scenario of the prison gates, the concrete recreation area and the shame seat was replaced by the comfort zone of learning. What seemed a place of undeserved captivity became an infinite universe of possibilities.

School became the means to finding my voice and finding my place. I already mentioned the unknown kids all seated, witnesses to my private hell as I was escorted into my seat in the class at the start. As I became familiar and comfortable with the setting and the purpose, I also became familiar with the other pupils. One of my earliest memories is of David Alexander. He was the quiet, unassuming one that just got on with it. Always very good, always diligent. I never knew David to say or do anything unkind, never. I asked David if he remembers starting school, though, and he begged for mercy. "That's forty four years ago Stuart". Haha.

Another classmate was my cousin Caroline Dott. Caroline's dad was my dad's cousin, and I loved that we had family so close to us. Parents, Robert and Margaret, along with Lorraine, Evelyn, wee Robert and Caroline lived down Duntarvie Road in the early years and I used to be a regular visitor to their house.

Caroline was brilliant, attractive and popular - and my cousin- that was a good person to have in my class. She was also a very good friend to me whilst we shared a class. There were others, Todd Coster, Linda Shergold, Graham Keene and a whole class load that I was going to spend the bulk of the next seven years with. It is with great fondness and affection I remember that day - that day that started off so badly.

So here I am. All these years later and writing about vague impressions left in my memory cells, being dragged through the school gates, dragged to the class, sat in front of everyone, so much of that I did not want, I did not like and tried my hardest to make it not happen, and yet it unlocked the greatest treasure that my loving heavenly Father has given me. My imagination!

It wasn't long before we all settled into the routine of school life. I still kicked up a fuss most mornings on the way out of our close and across the road, up the hill, around the corner and down the hill to the school gates just up from St Georges and St Peters Church of Scotland. So much so that the lollipop lady, positioned at the street right outside our close for the school gates for the older kids, ended up giving me a wage envelope every second Friday with two pence in it, (don't laugh it was a lot of money to a four year old then. She paid me for going to school without annoying my mum – it worked.

Primaries one through three had their challenges. I was a bit of a slow starter when it came to reading (how funny is that, considering), and used to really struggle keeping up with the rest of the class. I also struggled with my pronunciation, and remember times when I was convinced in my own mind, I was saying words right, but couldn't have been as Miss Beck kept saying "No, like this -THE" in quite a frustrated manner.

Home life was good. We had our dog, Lady, and ferrets, (small stoat like animals used for hunting rabbits). Mum and dad's social nights happened through those years. Mum's brothers, Trevor and Vincent, and their families lived close by, and were also frequent visitors. Our twice weekly visits to nana's (my mum's mum) happened then as well. Every Tuesday and Saturday we would all make our way (all did not include dad). The rest of mum's family would all gather in those days and it was a good time for hanging out with our cousins.

"Whit you wantin?" would be the greeting from Granda Kiernan every time we walked through the living room door. We all loved it. The women would sit in nana's kitchen, whilst all the kids would be relegated to the living room with granda. We would sit and pretend shave him, and pull his hair, and generally annoy him. He never complained though. Just carried on watching his horse racing on the telly.

Life carried on like that, for a while.

3 - The hole in the wall (1977)
Time out in Tollcross

In 1977 Record company EMI sacks the controversial UK punk rock group the Sex Pistols. Star Wars opens in cinemas and film-goers line up for hours to see it. The TV Mini Series "Roots" is aired on ABC winning top audience figures, 9 Emmys and a Golden Globe. Never Mind The Bollocks Here's The Sex Pistols is released. The Clash release their first album "The Clash ". Jimmy Carter becomes president of the USA. The first Apple II computers go on sale, the first commercial flight of Concord happens, NASA space shuttle first test flight, UK Queen's silver Jubilee celebrations, Roman Polanski is arrested and Charged, Alaskan Oil Pipeline completed, New York City Blackout lasts for 25 hours. Jimmy Carter is elected as the President of United States . The precursor to the GPS system in use today is started by US Department of Defense. Elvis Presley Dies from a heart attack aged 42. And the Atari 2600 arrived in September - changing kids lives forever.

Stuart Patterson

Life is full of 'moments'. Incidents and circumstances that have the ability to alter the future course of your life. Some of them you know are coming, and others just sneak up on you. For the Patterson family that happened to us one night in 1977.

In 1977 we moved to a new house, well I say house, but what I mean is that we moved tenement flats. From the relative luxury of our 'front and back garden' bottom flat, with Blairtummock Park immediately behind it and Blairtummock Primary immediately in front, to an old Glasgow sandstone tenement in the old east end in Tollcross. One bedroom with four bunks in it and a living room with an alcove to the right-hand side as you came in the door. A close that opened straight onto the road, and a back 'garden' littered with rubble and rocks.

It felt like we had gone to sleep in Baldinnie Road and woke up in 1170 Tollcross Road. No explanations; no reasons – we just moved. That was it.

Bath time on a Sunday really was in a tin bath in the middle of the living room floor. There was no bathroom in the *house*. Mum and dad slept in a double bed squeezed into that tiny alcove in the so-called living room. All five of us were crowded into the bunks in the tiny bedroom. Two sets of bunks end to end with not much space between them and the walls.

What I remember clearest though, was on the middle of the wall in the lower bunk, nearest to the door, there was a hole in the wall. Not just a small hole either. It was big! Big enough to crawl through. Which was sort of the point, as probably whilst the tenement was empty before we moved in someone had tunnelled their way through to the wee newsagent's shop on the other side of the hole.

The hole was dark with only a few rough pieces of wood covered over it to 'stop' entry. It was bricked up at the newsagent side, but we did not know that then.

Our imagination led us to believe that all we had to do was remove the planks of wood over it and crawl through and help ourselves to the sweets.

Dad and the shopkeeper would constantly encourage us to believe that. Can you imagine, being seven years old and thinking you lived within touching distance of such a treasure trove? The nights I would lie awake and stare at those planks trying to work up the courage to 'just see what was really beyond' the other side.

Now and again I would say to JP and Gary, but they just laughed. I knew they were as scared of dad as me though so we never tried it. It would never have entered into my mind to suggest it to Yvonne, she was a girl.

The old tenement close opened immediately onto the much busier Tollcross Road. No front garden, no school gates just loads of people - and cars. Cars and vans and lorries and buses screaming and screeching by only three feet from the close. It was be quite intimidating at certain times of the day. Slowly though, I overcame my fear and would begin to explore the area around our *house*.

I had got a small scooter at some point, and I would use it to journey to unknown destinations miles from our *house* (the railway bridge a few hundred yards around the corner).

For the six months or so that we lived in Tollcross, I went to Wellshot Primary School. Another old sandstone building that seemed to be miles away from our house. Blairtummock Primary had been right outside our door, and my siblings and

8

I found ourselves having to navigate an environment so alien to the streets we knew only a sleep before.

I remember next to nothing about my classmates there. Considering how fresh so much seems to be, maybe the briefness of how long we were there and the distance in time have dulled those particular *files*. There are some memories though -vague memories. There are some of one guy I must have been pally with as we used to wander around the gigantic Tollcross Park (we were seven) at lunchtimes. In contrast to the much smaller Blairtummock Park, this was enormous. With trees and paths and flowers and the palace it was easy to go on many imaginative journeys there - we loved it!

One lunchtime , our time for going wandering, this old guy came alongside us. He seemed to be quite civilised and polite. He wore a sharp suit and tie, with an overcoat open. This man would fill us with wonder as he wandered through the paths with us. He would, speaking gently, inform us with all these 'facts' about the flowers and the foliage that surrounded us. My friend and I were amazed that a proper grown up would take the time to teach us all these things.

We came along one path and there were birds feeding on the grass at the side. Just a few of them. Our *teacher* rolled out a fountain of knowledge about the very rare birds we were seeing.

"These birds are almost never spotted in Glasgow," he said. "This is amazing, what an opportunity you have here." He continued to point things out to us, each new revelation guiding us further and further along the wooded paths, totally ,mesmerising. We were loving that he would take the time to tell us all about these wonders. He spoke with such knowledge. Every time one of the birds were spotted, (there seemed to be quite a few, for a bird so seemingly rare), he would again exclaim loudly how great this was.

We genuinely thought we were seeing something special and already chattered excitedly about telling our teacher and parents. He kept trying to lead and coax us along to see more. These rare birds were larger than the sparrows, black and had yellow beaks. It was years later I realised that these were blackbirds and anything but rare.

My friend and I were aware that we had to return to school. The *teacher* tried to coax us further on, for "just a few more minutes". We were more afraid of being in trouble in school, though than we were enthralled at his knowledge.

Lunchtime was over, and we had to go back to class. Hmmmm! I wonder.

Like most school playgrounds in those days, breaktime (playtime) were filled with the sounds of laughter and screaming. Children enjoying themselves with no thought or care of outside pressure. I joined in with these games, and love the running around that the games entailed. On one particular icy morning, whilst playing in the playground, I slipped and landed on my chin.

That awful, almost metallic, dull thud when your jaws are battered together filled my head, echoing around my skull. I could hardly open my mouth. The school were extremely worried about this, contacted my mum and got me to hospital. The usual questions about tetanus jags etc ensued and I got the full blast.

9

It seemed I had lockjaw. My mouth could hardly open, my head was killing me, and I had sore stomachs. Lockjaw is one of the symptoms of tetanus, but I was unaware of how serious this was, I just knew that soup and scrambled egg was all I was going to be able to eat for a while. I am sure, to this day, my parents thought that the symptoms were worth the scare - other than vain main mumblings and grunts, I was unable to speak!

Yet another incident from that short period involved my left knee. Our back court in Tollcross was full of very large boulders and rubble and some very, very old sheds. I used to love going out there to play. I remember one day, a boulder taller than me just looked so appealing. Action Man figures (not dolls, figures) were my preferred toy and I started off playing war games with my figure (not doll) climbing the rock. I got inspired though and wanted to be the hero myself – so I started climbing it.

Then I fell almost immediately and banged my knee off one of the many sharp edges. The blood was everywhere. The boulder seemed to be painting itself a deep shade of crimson - with MY blood. I screamed! (You would have as well if you had been me and seen the blood all over your leg AND the boulder and you were only seven). Then I picked myself up and made my way around up to the shadowy back door into the close.

Walking through our door I whimpered "mum I've cut myself" and stood sheepishly looking at all the blood.

"Whit noo?" as she turned as saw all the blood all over my leg – and my hands and clothes now. "Whit happened?"

"Ah wis playing oot the back and ah fell and banged ma knee."

"Ach ya stupid eejit!" she said. (This was a tender comment meant to reassure me). Off to the doctors again. Butterfly stitches over the wound. (I would have a lot of those in my childhood) and "Don't bend your knee" said the doctor.

I was seven years old so I took him at his word and would not bend my knee at all – for weeks. Even after the stitches were gone. When mum would protest with me that I could bend it now, I would defiantly reply with "But the doctor said…"

Whilst my wrecked knee was all stitched up, we visited aunt Margaret and Uncle Bertie's house in Rachan Street. My mum took this opportunity for me to have a proper bath. Now my knee is still stitched and bandaged, and the doc's instructions not to bend it is STILL ringing in my ears. "Ma, ah cannae get in the bath, right?" (For the grammar enthusiasts this is a question, me telling my mum I could not do something was me asking how to do it).

"How no?" she shouted through.

"Cos av no tae bend ma knee."

"Don't be stupid, ye kin bend it noo."

"Naw ah cannae, the doctor said."

I am sure I could hear howls of laughter coming through from the living room.

When, eventually, I did try and bend my knee, I couldn't. First my jaw, then my knee. Locked in place by the inaction. It took ages for it to bend properly again.

In fact, I have sort of limped on that leg most of my life, I wonder if it was because of that obedience. Hmm

Our time in Tollcross came to an end as abruptly as it begun. I recall coming home from school one dark teatime, with the rain pouring down outside. Mum told us to gather up our stuff (we had not been there long enough to have much). She kept anxiously switching between staring out the living room window and going through the front door to the close entrance, watching for something. If any of us asked what was wrong we would get the "nothing" reply.

She came hurrying in after one of her trips to the front door and shooed us and our stuff outside. All five of us grabbed and put us into the waiting van of family friend John Smith. I can still picture his van sitting parked up in the kerb, with the city traffic screeching and beeping by as we tried to avoid the pouring rain. It seemed to be even darker than usual. Mum and John kept rushing out and in carrying bags and boxes and forcing them into the back of the van. It felt like we were packed in the same way as our belongings. Squeezed in behind the seats.

Dad wasn't there, and it seemed important to mum that we were gone before he was. It was a horrible night. We all were crowded into that van in the heavy traffic, rain even heavier as we crawled through the east end streets and up through the city centre to another flat in an unfamiliar location.

It was actually a very large property on the top floor of a very large West End building. Ours was one large room with kitchen facilities and numerous beds all in it. There was a hallway with a bathroom, a proper large bathroom, to the right on the way to the main door. The ceiling was very high.

I don't think they called these particular 'multi floored' dwelling places were called tenements. They were built for an obviously more economically blessed people than those that currently occupied them.

Time would reveal that they were women's refuge flats. My dad hadn't been violent towards mum, she was hiding for other reasons though.

We were there for a wee while. Dad wasn't. It was weeks before we started going back up to Easterhouse and seeing dad.

On one trip, mum, dad and I were making our way from the shopping centre across the pitches. Dad was asking questions about where we were staying and if we were ok. I told him; the address was imprinted on my mind. He told mum. She was very angry with him.

Not long after that we moved into 26 Aberdalgie Road, back in Easterhouse, back across the road from Blairtummock Primary School. This time we were in a middle flat of a block of six. I also got to go back into my old class with my old friends. I liked that.

But the guilt of telling dad where we lived never left me. There would be times as I passed over the dirt path where Platform (Easterhouse Library and community theatre building) now stands that it would rise up. This was my 'traitor's spot'. The reality was, it was just one of the few times when people in my life were interested in, not just listening to me, but HEARING me, obviously for their own purposes though.

Hey, THIS is my life!

11

Stuart Patterson

4 - Blairtummock Old Time Music Hall (1978)
August 1978 – MC -me?

Daisy, Daisy Give me your answer do
I'm half-crazy over the love of you
It won't be a stylish marriage
I can't afford the carriage
But you'll look sweet upon the seat
Of a bicycle made for two[ii]
Edward M Favor *The Daisybell Song*

School shows! The end of year spectacular where your pride and joy, your offspring, your beloved children - all the pupils get to invite you - their parents in and show off their stage skills.

I was in primary four by this time, and our class were doing *Blairtummock Old Time Music Hall*. My role was to link the different parts of our show, and I knew I was good at it.

We were all excited by our show. Rehearsals went on for what seemed like months, but most probably was weeks. Quietly, the classes all competed on who was going to do the best show.

Considering I had only recently returned to Blairtummock, I was amazed when Miss Anderson (later that year to become Mrs Graham) my teacher suggested to Mr Ward, the headmaster, that I was able to MC the whole show – all primaries.

She felt that my ability in our show could be carried through to present the full school show. Mr Ward came along to one of our rehearsals, saw it and agreed.

This was a big moment, that foreshadowed life in future years. It was also weird that I was good at it, as I was already quite insecure and shy, and did not like to stand out. A pupil had never been Master of Ceremonies (MC) of the whole show, and a primary four pupil had never had such a prominent position at all.

Rehearsals went on, playground rivalries sparked up between classes about who was going to be better. Our show had old favourites like *Daisy Daisy,* and *My Old Man[iii]* as well as songs from a show called *Alvida and the Magician's Cape[iv]*. The whole class knew we were good at these, we also knew that what we were doing was different from anything any other class was doing. School rivalry at its finest. We enjoyed our rehearsals, as a class and we all looked forward to the big show.

When it arrived, we were all peeking out at our parents, and grandparents and neighbours and friends all piling into the vast hall, now filled with row after row of plastic seats. The buzz in the air got us even more excited, and nervous. People all seemed to be happy.

When it came time for the show to open, I got to stand in front of the 20' high curtains that hid the wonders of all the performances from the audience.

Mr Ward, towering next to me, kept whispering to me to relax and all would be ok. I was not worried; I knew what I was to do, and I was looking forward to it.

The curtains opened, and here was I standing next to the very tall Mr Ward. He seemed about eight feet tall (I think he was over six feet) balding silver hair, and distinguished moustache.

In front of us, the hall was packed. Every seat occupied, mums, dads, aunts, uncles, grandparents, brothers, sisters, neighbours filling every available space. People standing along the walls to the right-hand side. The floor to very high ceiling windows lined the right-hand side, and the school dinner serving hatches, (shutters now down) lined the rear wall.

I was excited.

"Good evening everyone, and welcome to Blairtummock Primary School show. "said Mr Ward. "It has been brilliant watching our pupils – your children – prepare for this evening. And we are excited. It also my honour to introduce one of our primary four pupils, Stuart Patterson…"

"Good evening everyone…" I said.

"Shh Stuart, haha, " said Mr Ward. "Your turn is coming. He is very eager to get on with the show."

I looked at him and wondered why he never got that I was just saying hello, as that was polite.

Mr Ward continued, going through some formalities and – eventually - handed over to me.

"Good evening everyone, and welcome to Blairtummock Primary School end of year show. It is my honour to be introducing each of the years and I'm sure you will be as pleased as we are at the amount of work, they have all put into their performances. (these lines memorised from a carefully written script, a copy also on a table just off stage behind the curtains), I have seen them all as we rehearsed this, and I have to say "Blairtummock Old Time Music Hall" is still my favourite. It is my class' show, but I am not biased.

Anyway, to open the evening please welcome Primary 1a and 1b…"

And that was it, my first ever time standing on a platform / stage and leading a meeting. Little did I know how big a part in my life that early preparation would play in the years to come.

5 - Family fun at Filey (1979)
We're ALL going on a summer holiday

Sony brings out its new 'Walkman", Nuclear accident on Three Mile Island
China starts the one-child rule, While Pink Floyd try bringing down 'The Wall'
The snowboard arrives as a sensation, Thatcher arrives with strikes and devastation
Hostages and terror run riot in Iran, 'Trivial Pursuit' is now in our hands
But for us, with friends and family, We're off to Butlins, in Yorkshire's Filey
by Stuart Patterson © 2019

I was nine years old, Neil Patterson was not a thing yet, nor a brother. It was the summer of 1979 and we were all on a coach on our way to Butlins'.

Not just any Butlins' mind you. Not even the one, at that time, not too far away from us.

No, we were going to Butlins' in Filey, Yorkshire. It used to stand on the site of the current Haven Primrose Valley Holiday Park[v]

Mum had been buzzing about this for ages, our first ever family holiday (well she would NEVER come camping with us).

Butlins, Red Coats, swimming pool, activities, chalets, sunshine. Mum, dad, and the other parents going talked all about these things in excited tones, but I didn't have a clue what they meant.

When we finally arrived there (my memory has hidden the torture of the coach trip in a dark, never to be accessed recess in my mind) it was a wee bit overcast. I might even have been a train we got, as when researching this chapter, I discovered that this particular Butlins' had its very own train station[vi].

The place was packed out with accents from all over waiting to register. It was surreal hearing all the different voices. Nine years in Easterhouse , the only non-Glasgow accent I had heard was my nana's. Originally from Malvern, her soft midlands accent was it.

Yet here we were surrounded by a cacophony of accents from all over. I was so enthralled by it all that – I got lost.

Yes, within minutes of our first ever family holiday at all, never mind in another country, and I was separated from them everyone I knew.

No matter how hard I tried I couldn't find mum and dad. I looked everywhere, (everywhere being just the registration area).

After what seemed like hours, but was probably no more than five minutes, I tearily made my way over to the desk.

"Excuse me missus, ahm loast."

"Pardon?" back at me.

"Ah cannae fun ma ma n da."

"Pardon, can you say that again?" the lady behind the desk looked at me, trying her best to smile, but obviously not understanding either what I was saying or how great my problem was. She turned to the guy sitting next to her and whispered something to him.

"Are you lost?" he asked.

"Aye ah um." Says I.

"Do you know what chalet you are in?"

"Naw" says I, "ah goat loast when ma maw wiz getting the key."

"What's your name?"

I gave my name and she told me to come sit behind the big desk. They had small packets of *Sunmaid Raisins* on the desk and the lady reached over, grabbed one and handed it to me.

It wasn't long before they had located mum and dad and I was collected. I got an *awful shirikin* for running away. ???? In retaliation I started greetin (that's crying, not welcoming people). As far as I remember I spent a lot of time on that holiday greetin. The few vague memories, and the photos we have bear witness to the fact that, for most of it, I was quite difficult.

I don't remember too much about Butlins, but one of the stand outs was being in the cavernous entertainments' venue, sitting with all the family and our jumpers, knitted by mum and one of the famous Butlins Red Coats coming sliding in for a pic. We still have it, the pic that is, not the knitted jumpers.

There are other pictures that fill in some of the blanks, of us and the McBride and Auld families. Those images do their best to squeeze information from long lost memory cells.

I also remember the final day, all the cases packed, we are checked out of the chalets and our Darrin pushed me into the pool. I got absolutely drenched. I cannot remember anything other than everybody thinking it was hilarious and telling me, as the cases were packed, that I would have to go home wet.

I don't think I did, but then again, I don't know if I didn't.

It was the first and only time that we all went away as a family for an overnight stay, never mind a week.

There were plenty of camping trips, loads of fishing and hunting with the dogs and ferrets – but never with the whole family.

As far as family holidays went this was it.

6 - Bite Size (1980)
Mr Stokes will see you now

"Mr Stokes will
see you now", she said,
as my mouth filled with dread.
The butcher was working
as a despot dental surgeon
and I had to visit him next.
I crawled through the door,
my teeth clenched the floor.
The needle leered over
as Mr Stokes said, "Come sit".
Stuart Patterson ©2018

26 Aberdalgie Road.

That's where we lived at the time. We had moved there after our brief sojourn out of Easterhouse, when we lived in Tollcross for six months.

Middle flat with the Woods family next door, Ross and McNeill's upstairs and the Rodgers family downstairs. We were surrounded by good neighbours, lived yards from my Primary School and life was pretty good.

I spent many a day playing out in the very large backs (backcourt) and there was always a wee game of football or jumps or kerbie or something going on.

I enjoyed playing with the others around my own age, although I was quite socially awkward.

Reading was my favourite past time though. Anytime I was sitting down, I was reading, mostly general knowledge books and I loved school.

Our class in Blairtummock had only two teachers for our whole seven years there. They were great and all these years later still stand out. Miss Beck (Mrs Angus) and Miss Anderson (Mrs Graham).

Probably the guys I hung out most within our class were Todd Coster (writing my blog reconnected us after all those years) David Alexander (thrilled that he has nearly always been around) and Graham Keen (no idea what has happened to Graham).

Stephen Parker was also a very good friend; his dad and my dad were also friends. We all got on well in our class. There were others like Jim Queen, Rab Martin, Stuart Campbell, Stuart Warren, William McGrath and, well I am gonna stop, as I will probably forget to mention the one person from my class that reads this book.

As a class we all gelled well and all sort of played together, but those guys were good at schoolwork and enjoyed it (not saying the others weren't). This meant we spent a great deal of time doing classwork as a group, especially as the years rolled on,

I have mentioned before that my wee cousin, Caroline, was in my class. She was great. Her gran and grandad were my dad's aunt and uncle and he was close to Uncle Robert and Aunty Greta, so we got on well as well.

Outside of school, I still hung out with Todd and the others from time to time, but John Ross and Tam McNeill lived above us and I loved to hang out with them as well. John's family was about the same size as ours and his brother James (Sauce, but my brother JP"s friends nicknames would make a great chapter all of their own). Tam was quiet but always great fun. I got on well with them (although I am sure it was more them tolerating me).

Anyway, one day sticks out. I was about ten or eleven years old. It was a very wet day outside, (I know normally when we remember our younger days it was always sunny, your mind is telling you lies). Tam and I were playing on the top landing, messing about. Tam shoved me, maybe I shoved him, and he pushed back) and I banged my mouth off the landing wall.

The top flat landing wall did not go all the way to the roof. I knew immediately my tooth was broken. As was the tile along the top landing wall. That dull skull thud that you get when you n=bang any part of your head left me a wee bit woozy.

Tam was very apologetic, but it was just boys being boys and one of those things.

Now I know what you are thinking, get straight to the dentist and get him to fix it. That would be the right thing to do. That would be what any half decent parent would do.

Here is the thing though, I had been attending the esteemed Mr Stokes' dental surgery on Easterhouse Road for root treatment. His surgery was no more than an oversized shed located just behind the doctor's 'surgery'

Six months I had been attending. Every two weeks for six months. My teeth were all squiggly and twisted and there were no braces, at least not for us schemers in those days.

It was all messing about with the gums.

Anyhow, as I was at the dentist every two weeks, we just assumed he would notice and deal with it so never really made an issue.

SIX MONTHS later (caps cos I am shouting) I was still attending the dentist. It was a very cold, dark and wet winters' day. It would have been just after 4pm as I had been in school. As I came out of his torture chamber (I mean treatment room) into a packed waiting room, where my mum sat waiting on me, he approached his receptionist all clandestine like, whispering in a LOUD voice.

"I cannot believe that boy's parents would let his tooth get THAT bad. We are going to have to extract it. They have totally neglected his teeth. It is atrocious"

Now as I said, I am only ten to eleven years old. I had had baby teeth removed. I did not like it. All I heard was EXTRACT. I could hear earth moving machines rumble and the diggers claws clutching and the pain screeching through my teeth as his whisper reverberated around the packed room.

Extract meant to pull a tooth out!!!!

Heather though. Heather heard an attack on her parenting skills. Heather saw a grown man slagging her in front of a whole waiting room. Heather also knew that MR Stokes was so far in the wrong and to blame for this that there was absolutely no way she was keeping her mouth shut and taking it.

When my mum stood up that day, she seemed about ten foot tall. There was an audible, collective gasp as every single person in that room recoiled and what they were witnessing

'Eh, excuse me. Whit did you just say?" MY mum said this in a voice so low that it was menacing, and she never spoke in a menacing tone. "Ma boy has been coming tae you every two weeks for six months fur his teeth. Did you not notice a broken front tooth in aw that time?"

"Excuse me, who are you?"

I am not joking that is what he said.

"Your son has NOT been attending here for six months and it is disgraceful that you have not brought him to get this sorted. He will have to get that tooth taken out and have a denture fitted."

I watched as my mum look around the room, biting her lip and turning white. At this point, even the receptionist was ashen faced as she knew Mr Stokes had to be aware, I had been there every two weeks. He was the only dentist in the surgery, and he had just finished another in a long line of appointments with me for root treatment. (Did I mention I had been there every two weeks for six months).

He stood there and smirked!

The condescending look that says, "I'm better than you," whilst all the while showing the opposite to be true.

My mum looked RIGHT back at him and said something that all my years I had never heard her say, "I'm gaun to get ma man, he'll sort ye oot. Yir no talkin to me like that in front a aw these people."

My dad had a reputation!

He could fight.

He took no nonsense or prisoners.

But I had never known my mum to have asked him to fight her battles.

She was well able.

She had never threatened anyone with him.

But this, this got to her. This made my mum feel so bad that she was going to get my dad.

Most people, sitting in that dental surgery waiting room knew my dad.

In all its ten foot by ten-foot strip light illuminated dullness, I don't think it had ever felt so many clenched teeth and stomachs (and bums).

They all thought they knew what would happen.

My mum grabbed me by the hand, and we marched out the door, down the path by the surgery, out into Easterhouse Road, across into Aberdalgie Road, down to 26, up the stairs and into the house.

Mum started crying.

Not a defeated cry, but just all the adrenaline all the emotion coming out.

Easterhouse women were made of good stuff. They had to put up with a lot of garbage and they did it well. Very rarely letting it get to them. My mum was one of the best. She was well liked. This day though, it got to her.

She told my dad that Mr Stokes had completely humiliated her and blamed her for my tooth.

My dad. He put his arm around her. Never looked full of the rage that by now everyone that knew him and knew what had happened (this was a scheme, news travels fast) would have expected.

My dad grabbed his coat, looked at mum and me and said: "c'mon let's go."

Off we went, out the door, down the stairs, up Aberdalgie, across Easterhouse Road, up the side of the docs, along the wee path, up the three steps, inside the door.

"Can I speak to Mr Stokes please?" said my dad, in the politest voice I had EVER heard him use.

"He is busy just now" replied the very nervous receptionist, addressing the still full waiting room (at least that is where she looked, avoiding Paddy's gaze).

"That's ok, I'll staun here an wait."

"Have a seat, Mr Patterson."

"Naw, its awright, ah'll staun here hen."

My mum, her eyes blazing defiantly stood at dad's side.

The receptionist stuck her head in the surgery door and whispered to Mr Stokes that someone was waiting to see him.

"I'm too busy" he called out, "You'll have to come back."

"I think you need tae come oot the noo" said my dad, still actually quietly spoken. That was unnerving. Nobody moved. Nobody spoke.

I think some were disappointed that Paddy had not come in and smashed the dentist and the surgery. I don't know what even my mum thought would happen. I don't think she wanted dad to get violent, she hated violence, even more, she hated my dad's violence with a passion. But this was a new, rare moment

I can remember as clear as the moment it happened. Flashbulb memory it's called. Mr Stokes trying to look all dignified and indignant walked through the door.

"Yes, can I help? I really am very busy as you can see."

What came next shocked both my mum and me. It was so out of character for Paddy Patterson.

"Kin ye check yir book an see the last time ma boy was here?"

As Mr Stokes, thinking of remonstrating, then thinking better of it began to urge the receptionist to do it, my dad again quietly said "Naw, ah want you tae check it"

"o o ok. What is his name?"

There, I saw it, I don't think anybody else did, but I did. My dad, hardly noticeable but inside his mouth moving his tongue to the side and gently biting on it, in the same way I do. He was composing himself and keeping his anger in check. That was a rare moment.

"You know his f$%^&*g name."

"Ah here it is here; it was two weeks ago."

"A before that, an then tell me when it wis before that?"

No menace. No growl. It looked so normal; it was terrifying.

Mr Stokes rattled off the dates, then asked if there was anything else.

He was white by this time. As white as an Arctic snowfall, and probably feeling as cold.

The room looked like it was frozen in anticipation, shocked into inaction. Anaesthetic wasn't the only smell in the room now.

"Naw that's aw!"

At this point can I take you back around twenty minutes in time and a few paragraphs before. Mr Stokes had publicly and loudly made a big deal out of my tooth being black and it is my mother's fault. At home, we had talked about it many times over the preceding six months but had always assumed that dentist knew what he was doing and would fix it in due time.

That was until twenty minutes ago.

Whereas he had publicly humiliated my mother in a very bad way, my dad had very quietly (and totally out of character for him, I have to say) showed Mr Stokes character up for what it was in a quite brilliant way.

As we walked out the door, my dad had his hand on my shoulder sort of urging me through. He opened the door, stopped and turned around.

"Apologise tae my wife now. And if you ever speak tae her like that again, I will be back, myself."

I am not quite sure what the look on my mum's face was at that moment.

The truth was I don't think my dad surprised her that often by holding himself in that way.

My dad adored my mum.

He loved her.

He just was not very good at ever acting in a way that showed it.

That day he did. That day the old school Glaswegian gave a university educated charlatan a lesson in manners.

The fact that my dad did it as Heather's husband and not as Paddy Patterson, has stayed with me long. I remember it vividly. He finished it with an implied threat. I don't think it was any in a way than most husbands would have. The difference was everyone in that room knew, there would be no second chance for humiliating my mum

It was a great feeling walking back down the road that day. It wasn't a march this time. Just a mum, dad and son making their way home.

How normal!

My mum had had her champion fight for her honour.

My dad had behaved totally out of character and shocked everyone, and it felt great.

Within a few weeks I had my dental impressions done, by Mr Stokes, and at the age of eleven I got my first denture. He was a perfect gentleman until he moved on.

I often wonder what Mr Stokes had to say after that day. He had a private practice in another area of Glasgow that he spent a lot of time in. Not long after that incident, he spent a lot more time there, and another dentist took over his surgery.

There are eight million stories about Paddy Patterson. This is just one of them.

7 - Are you good enough (1981)
It's a testing time

Are you good enough? Do you have what it takes
for primary exams, with no room for mistakes?
Are you good enough? Can you pass the test
for entry? Time, for no room for fakes.
Are you good enough? Can you stand the heat
in this question time, as your memory rakes?
Are you good enough? Do you have what it takes?
Stuart Patterson ©2019

"Paddy how do you think you will dae in the exam?" asked my classmate, Todd Coster.

"Whit exam?" I asked, bemused. The traditional end of year exams was next May, it was only around the end of September.

"The exams fir the private schools. Did ye no know we've bin pit forward for them? Maybe Mrs Angus just hisnae told ye yet."

We were walking up Aberdalgie Road, after a long day at school. Primary Seven seemed to be all about looking forward to Secondary School. Blairtummock pupils went to Westwood Secondary, only a few hundred yards along the road. I knew my mum would be delighted and I could not wait to tell her. This was a big honour.

That evening after dinner I told mum and dad what Todd had said about the exams. That he had been told he had been put forward for both Hutchesons' Grammar and the High School of Glasgow entrance exams. If passed then we would be up for both the school scholarships, and the city council ones. It was quite exciting.

Next morning, off I went to school, fully expecting Mrs Angus to have a word with me and tell me what she had told Todd. It was not long before I knew that Linda Shergold and David Alexander had also been put forward for the exams. I loved the idea of knowing a secret.

3.50pm came, the final bell rang, and off I went home, having been told nothing.

As I made my way up the one flight of steps at 26 Aberdalgie Road, I was a wee bit apprehensive about having nothing to tell mum. Those twelve concrete steps could feel like a mountain at times like these.

In through the door I went, and mum stepped out of the kitchen, immediately to the right, and was right in front of me.

"Well," she said, a big grin covering her whole face.

"She didnae say anything."

"Whit dae ye mean she didnae say anything?"

"That's whit a mean, she didnae say anything."

"Right, I'll go in the morra and ask."

Next day at school, I was nervous all day. 26 Aberdalgie Road was only yards from the main entrance to the school. I heard nothing, though, until I went home.

Mum said that the school used my position in the previous year's exams to justify not putting me forward. She argued that was ludicrous, (she used the word 'stupid'). In the six years completed so far in primary, I had been in the top three of the end of year exams five times. Linda Shergold and I had taken turns for the top two slots every year. Primary six I was fourth. David had managed third. Primary six exam time was also the beginning of my hero, granda Patterson taking unwell. It had affected me probably in ways I didn't know.

Mum was having none of that though. She challenged them that they were guilty of discrimination (this was 1980) on the grounds that the Patterson family just did not fit. Blairtummock had never put pupils forward for these exams, it was a big deal for them.

Mum wasn't letting them off the hook, year after year, Linda, Todd and I were told we were three of the highest achieving students they had ever had, yet they were allowing one exam result (I think I was fourth by about 2%) to deny me the opportunity. She threatened to take the story to the papers. The school relented but told my mum that she would have to apply for me herself.

I was put forward for the exams. From what I can remember David chose not to sit the exams. The whole year was then taken up with Linda, Todd and I doing extra study at every available opportunity.

Many times, I recall going along to the seemingly darker world of the P1-3 corridors and into a classroom there for teachers to set out extra revision for us to do.

The High School of Glasgow, Anniesland, exam was up first. I think it was a Monday, and I remember the building being new, but not much else. Nothing about the exam stood out to me. There was a day in between, then on Wednesday 11th February 1981, I went with Todd's mum and dad, and Todd in the car to Kingarth Street for the Hutchesons' Grammar School entrance exam.

Kingarth Street housed Kindergarten through to First Year at that time. An old building full of ornate touches and history. I remember we were running late.

At the time I did not know why Todd's mum and dad were bringing me. I was bursting for a pee as we ran up the stairs through the old building. Big wide stone steps with beautiful wooden handrails. We were ushered along to the first-floor class at the end of the corridor and I was pointed to a seat at the back.

It was one of those times where I wished I knew how to speak up. I was desperate for the toilet but was afraid to ask. This was an alien environment and I did not know anyone else in the class. Todd was in another classroom along the corridor.

We were told to turn over our papers, and all I remember is a question about a lawnmower, a slope, a piece of rope and how much grass could be cut. I had never seen any question like it, and as I spent time trying to work out what they were asking, I lost focus on trying to hold the pee in.

Yep, right in the middle of one of the most central days of my life in a class full of people I had never met before, in a part of Glasgow I had never been to before I peed myself.

All the way down my leg and onto the floor. I did the only thing I could, I carried on with the exam, hoping no one would notice.

It was halfway through first year when I was reminded that someone had – Alex Nagpal. "Stuart, it was you that peed yourself in the exam wasn't it?"

"No, I bust a carton of juice!"

After the exam, the Costers brought me home. I remember that Glasgow seemed darker than usual. As I trudged up the two flights of stairs in our flat in Duntarvie Quad and walked in the door I was aware that something was different.

Mum and dad took me into the kitchen, halfway down the hallway. "Stuart, your grandad passed away yesterday! He didnae want you to know cos of the exam. We wanted to wait til it was over."

All these years later I remember that moment as if it was today. The tears welled up and I ran out the door, down the stairs, up through the two Quads, around Easterhouse Road, into the corner close at Aberdalgie Road and straight to Todd's house.

I hammered on their door.

Mrs Coster opened and asked me what the matter was.

"Ma granda's deid and they didnae tell me."

"Come in, come in." They really were one of the nicest, and most genuine families you could ever hope to know.

Mr & Mrs Coster settled me down quite quickly. They were so comforting.

After a very short space of time, they brought me back around to ours. I was devastated. My granda really was my rock. I was so looking forward to going up to Belvedere Hospital to visit him that evening.

I spent the rest of that night sitting in my room crying. I did not understand why the hadn't told me. I was only ten, but I knew what death meant.

Granda Patterson that had taking me walks in the country, that had got me in helping on the farm, that had shown and taught me so much, was gone. I would never see him again.

At the age of almost eleven, **never** seemed like a very long time.

My eleventh birthday only two days later was not the happiest of occasions.

As a footnote to this chapter, I passed both exams and was given the Glasgow City Council bursary to attend Hutcheson's Grammar School.

As foreshadowing goes though, that day was a pretty good predictor of what Hutcheson's would come to mean to me.

8 - Milk and a piece n Jam Part 1 (1981)
Oh, I do like to be beside the seaside

In 1981 "Dynasty" debuts; John Hinckley Jr. attempts to assassinate President Reagan; The Space Shuttle Columbia is launched; Mehmet Ali Agca attempts to assassinate Pope John Paul II; Prince Charles marries Lady Diana Spencer; Elizabeth Jordan Carr, the first U.S. IVF baby, is born; AIDS recognized by the Centres for Disease Control and Prevention; MS-DOS released and the first IBM-PC is released. [vii]

During the summer of 1981 I could not contain my excitement. I was off to Seafield Residential School. This would be my second time staying in the big house on the Clyde coast. Two weeks of fun, adventure and activity. I had been there a couple of years before. This was my last chance to go as I started first year in Hutchesons' after the summer. I was so looking forward to it.

Mum and dad also seemed excited for me. As they helped pack my bag and got me ready for what seemed like an all-day coach trip to Ardrossan (even in 1981 it was less than one hour). They were buzzing; I don't think I had ever witnessed such happiness in them, on my behalf.

So, we got me all packed up and ready to go. This would be a great trip. I was still coming to terms with the loss of my granda that February.

All my spare time used to be spent in my granny and granda's. I loved my walks up the country road with granda. I loved sitting at the coal fire in their house. Instant recall of the newspaper against the fire with the metal plate in place, being told to stand back as they expertly light it. I loved the smell of coal, and who didn't enjoy the crackle and whizz of a real coal fire. Its flames dancing and leaping in its setting on the feature wall. I just loved being around them. They also used to make their own ginger. It was good.

My love for technology and gadgets was also built into me there, through my cousin Peter who had been brought up by them. He was the first person I knew to have a remote-control VCR, attached by a wire then, but still remote control. He was a music buff and would listen to groups like Orange Juice before anyone else did. Peter was also a very good guitarist and it was great sitting in his room, listening to him playing. He was one of the few people, it seemed, in my life that just treated me normal.

Anyway, back to the trip. A coach full of excited 11 and 12-year-old boys set out on a drive that seemed like hours long, it took an hour. I had been at Seafield a couple of years previously and loved it, so my expectation was really heightened. It was set in what seemed like an enormous old house on the Ardrossan seafront. Built in the 1800's and used as a military hospital in the second world war, I loved its high ceilings and long corridors. We slept in dorms of about eight or ten. Very well-lit dorms with the big scenic windows letting in tons of sunlight.

It was here that I probably really got to be, as a child, mostly me. Seafield was free of the pressures of home. I don't remember any issues with the other boys there. I only remember fun, although there was one night, where I had been particularly upset about my granda, and wet the bed. (Yep I did that, bed wetting became a very common theme in my life from then on and did not stop until the day after I left Hutchesons – the day after). The staff were brilliant, they acknowledged my grief and were good at talking and understanding it with me, BUT they also encouraged me to try and get on with it and throw myself into the activities.

So, I did.

Ardrossan Castle and its big slide. The assault course on the grounds. Football. Even shooting, imagine teaching boys from the schemes how to fire air guns. My studying Ailsa Craig and the classroom studies.

I felt at home here and loved it (did I mention that before).

Every morning in Seafield there was a small "church" service. We would sing a couple of hymns, one of the boys would read from the Bible and one of the staffs would share a story based on the verses read and give a wee bit of practical application to it.

What we call 'preaching'.

We all really enjoyed it, and the preach always seemed to be relevant to what we were going through with practical advice, from the Bible, on how to deal with it.

They always asked for volunteers for reading, but I never volunteered. Even at the age of eleven, I was aware that most of the boys could not read very well, which made me uncomfortable in how good I knew I was.

So, I said nothing until the last morning. I had wanted to read out. I always enjoyed it; I just did not want to showboat, or even worse – stand out in any way.

On our last morning, I was volunteered by the staff member on duty, "Stuart, you haven't ready yet, why don't you give it a go and see how you get on?"

What a great feeling for someone who was nearly always never chosen for stuff. I started reading publicly from the Bible surrounded by young guys my own age. I read well, very well.

The staff member leading us said, "Wow Stuart if we knew you were that good at reading, we would have had you doing it every morning." Yeah well, that is sort of why you didn't know.

In the evenings though, we had my favourite all time snack. A glass of milk and a piece n jam, (bread and jam sandwiches). The pieces were of course quartered. I loved those.

I loved the very relaxed evenings in Seafield. I could not even tell you what we did, just that it was peaceful, and it had milk pieces n jam.

Even now, all these years later, I like milk and pieces n jam. I think it has to do with the peace that I experienced there. The "out of body" or normal life experience that Seafield provided.

We had our last morning, packed our bags, sorted our stuff and got on to the coach.

Most of us were disappointed to be going home. This was such an escape.

As disappointed as I was that our time at Seafield was over, I thought about going home. I was looking forward to seeing mum, dad, John, Gary, Yvonne, and Darrin. I had missed them.

I had bought wee seaside gifts for everyone, and of course, all the crafts etc that we had done during our break. I looked forward to seeing all the excited faces when they saw what I had brought back.

Thirty-seven years after that last visit, I was talking to my friend, Craig who lives in Ardrossan. I mentioned Seafield to him and said how I loved going to the holiday home. "Ah Seafield," he says "the respite home! That's where hard to handle kids got sent so their parents got a break!"

Wow!

All these years I thought I had been sent there as a treat. I knew I was difficult as a child. Never intentional though. But I was a nightmare.

I knew what respite homes were, and I knew what respite care was, but cognitive dissonance had stopped me, all these years making the connection to my own past.

I smiled.

Then I smiled again, just a little bit broader the second time.

All these years later, I finally appreciated Seafield House meant that my mum and dad got a couple of weeks break from my behaviour.

25

I just sort of spent most of my life thinking that it was always the other way around.

This was it, though, this trip was the end of my life as a primary school pupil. It was now time to look forward to secondary school – coming fast after the summer.

II Secondary Education

9 – That first day (1981)
August 1981 Uniformly uniform

That first day, I never really noticed,
it just seemed to happen. Then it was gone.
Entrance to a new world, Old friends left behind.
Two buses and a goodbye, and Grammar on my mind.

New 'friends' new ways old money, to my dismay.
Old building, old desks one teacher had old specs.
Latin and French, English; history too, all this old was completely new.

Second day, dad gone only eleven, across the city
with the bus, on my own.
Not sure how I feel. Friends together in the Wood
But I'm in the library in a new neighbourhood.

The most memorable thing was Bertie and Margaret's,
with dad after school to see granny for photographs
they made me sit like 'the thinker'. Not knowing what lay ahead!
Stuart Patterson ©2019

In a recent radio interview with Stephen Jardine, (BBC Radio Scotland) he asked me about my first day at Hutchesons Grammar School. I could not answer him. I cannot recall walking through the doors of Hutchesons' Grammar School for the first time as a pupil. Funnily enough, when Stephen asked me about it, it was the first time anyone had. Even on the first day itself I don't think I was asked.

At that time, first year students were located on the school's Kingarth Street premises, along with Kindergarten right through to primary seven.

From second year onwards, it was the much more modern buildings in Beaton Road. Surrounded by the rugby and athletics fields, there, not the crowded sandstones of Kingarth Street.

As I have sat and tried to recall this day, I am surprised that it does not stand out more. Secondary school is a big move for most kids, never mind the fact that this was not just a newly structured day, but new teachers, new pupils, new method of getting there.

Apart from our sojourn to Tollcross, school had never been more than a couple of minutes' walks away, yet here I was now having to get two buses or two trains.

I remember bits and pieces of the first year. First day in one of my classes, English I think when we were all asked which primary school, we had come from the astonishment from my new teacher when I said "Blairtummock Primary".

"Blairtummock Primary? In Easterhouse!" said Mrs McCondachie. "I used to teach there."

How nice that was. An unexpected blessing in my new surroundings. Unfortunately for me, short lived. Mrs McCondachie was heavily pregnant and never returned to teach whilst I was there.

Another sort of humorous memory was in interaction between a nice young guy I was pally with, Geraint Jones from Paisley, and a French teacher whose name escapes me. Geraint was a tall guy, (well compared to me he was, but my nickname soon became *Tich* in Hutchesons' because of how small I was. Blond hair and friendly personality, Geraint was one day caught reading a book under the lid of his desk.

Mr Whatshisname yelled out "What are you reading boy?" Very old school, a part of my memory even recalls him in the old black gowns (although that may not be exact).

"A book on Yugoslavia, sir" replied Geraint sheepishly.

"What? So, we have a Scots boy with Welsh name reading a Yugoslavian book from an English library in a French class!!!"

The whole class, other than the very embarrassed Geraint, were in stitches. I don't think Mr Whatshisname intended it to be funny, but it was.

There were also the lunchtime clubs. I was in the modelling club, and the CB Radio club. How geeky was that. But one of the guys that headed them up was alright. His name was Iain Govan. There are other pupils that stood out to me from first year and all for good reasons. Some I got to be acquaintances with, lol, but I never really got too pally with any of them.

27

To be honest, from the start I was embarrassed and ashamed of where I came from. I was eleven years old, and I was now surrounded by (so it appeared) pupils whose families all had money and big houses and were more confident than me and went on skiing holidays and made friends easier than me and did not have to worry about loads of stuff.

I did not understand any or all of this, but I quickly began to tell wee fibs about where I lived. I didn't live in a top flat tenement, I lived in one of Lochwood Cottages.

I also practiced pronunciation in how I spoke. In Easterhouse we all spoke in Glasgow vernacular. Even in classes we mostly replied in that way, unless reading. Yet, without anyone ever commenting, I immediately began trying to *speak properly* because everyone else did.

I remember once or twice, in the city centre bumping into a friend from Easterhouse, Joseph JoJo Smith, whilst with a friend from Kilsyth, Stephen Baird. They were opposites in speech and mannerisms etc, JoJo proper Glasgow and Stephen, an almost accented proper pronunciation. And yet all these years later, both shared so many similar qualities despite opposite upbringings. Both were good friends to me. Both always seemed to look out for others. When getting the buses home, my second bus would always be from Buchanan Street Bus Station. Stephen got the bus from there as well.

As we approached the precinct entrance beside the car park to the bus station on a particularly sunny afternoon, I heard JoJo shout from a distance. I was mid-sentence in my *proper English,* and immediately I felt embarrassment. Not at JoJo, but at the fact that I could not talk to him whilst with Stephen. It was my inability to live both identities at the same time.

I hurriedly and nervously said bye to Stephen just as we approached JoJo.

"Did a hear ye talkin like a snob rerr Paddy?"

"Whit, naw don't be daft ya maddy. Whit ye up tae?" whilst looking around to make sure Stephen could not hear me speaking properly.

The next day Stephen asked me who it was at the bus station. "If that was one of your friends, I'd have loved to have said hello."

Nope, I was too insecure for my two worlds to meet.

It only seemed to be housing, and my speech that I lied over though, as I always said my dad was a steeplejack and fixed large chimneys, and that my mum worked in the Post Office.

On reflection, very strange. Very sad.

Dad collected me after school on the first day and we headed up to his brother Bertie's house on Rachan Street. Bertie and his wife Margaret had three kids, Scott, Sharon and Lorna and their vary large Alsatian dog. Granny Patterson was up there and that is why I was going. I recall sitting in the ground floor Rachan Street tenement, being told how to pose for pictures, and sitting with everyone individually. I have the still have the pics with myself and Bertie and Margaret, and one with me and granny. Later that evening it was off down to Cockenzie Street, Greenfield and my nana and granda Kiernan. Mum's mum and dad.

Nana hailed from the Malvern area and had met granda during WWII. The whole Kiernan side of the family and their tradition of going to nana's every Tuesday and Saturday. Nana's dish was spaghetti Bolognese, I loved it.

Most of the various cousins used to gather in nana's in those days as well. Whilst all the Kiernan sisters would sit in the decent sized kitchen in nana and grand's middle flor tenement, any of the kids would be in the sitting room with granda.

"Whit you wanting?" would be granda's customary and affectionate greeting for each of us when we walked through the sitting room door.

When we were younger, we used to sit and pretend shave him and pull his hair and generally annoy him while he tried to watch his horse racing and he never complained, never moaned.

That day I was there with me school uniform on and I felt proud. I loved getting my pictures taken in my uniform with my grandparents and I am glad they have survived down through the years.

I think each of my grandparents may have asked how the day went. I am sure they would have been met with an "Aye it wis awright."

The next day I was woken up at seven am, walked to the train station and – only on my second day at the age of eleven – began making my own way across the city to school.

I enjoyed first year at Hutchesons'. I enjoyed making some friends. Across the road was a mini sports field area with a football pitch and a running track. On the nicer days' lunchtimes would be spent over there. Darker, winter days would be spent in the school building.

Hutchesons' also had its own, much larger playing fields a coach ride away. Their main sports were rugby and cricket. I was made scrum half in the rugby games, as I was so small. I quickly discovered though, that If I pretended, I was even worse than I was then I got to go play football with the 'others'.

We, on occasion, would also take the twenty-minute walk over to the Beaton Road buildings as they had larger playing fields as well. One of the favourites of the PE teachers here was the cross country runs. Around the perimeter felt like it was about a mile long

Either first or second year I had the misfortune of leaving the very expensive PE uniform, with its reversible top, on my bus home.

Quick thinking mum sent me in to Mr Percy (Head of PE) with a note and some 'stand in' clothing.

Mr Percy made a big deal out of praising my mum in front of the whole class about how it wasn't used as an excuse to miss PE it. However, when weeks later mum still had not managed to buy replacement kit, it became a little bit sorer. I would be constantly pulled up over it, and told it needed to be sorted.

Many times, I would go home and have to annoy mum that it needed to be replaced. It took months of uncomfortable PE lessons before she was able to do that.

That was disappointing as I did enjoy the PE. I enjoyed the wide-open space and the circuit training and the team games. I even enjoyed trying, and failing miserably, at single wicket cricket and shot putt and discus and javelin. Manual dexterity is not my thing.

Overall first year was decent. Other than (I think) the PE kit, nothing major happened. We had good teachers and some good fellow pupils.

There was a good group in our teaching class. We were teaching group three. Of the near thirty students though, there are only a few that stand out – Geoff, Stephen, Lorna, Bruce, Clara, Robert and Vicky. Some of them I am still in touch with.

10 – Of Mice and Men (1982)
August 1982 Stuck in a moment I can't get out of

"As happens sometimes, a moment settled and hovered and remained for much more than a moment. And sound stopped and movement stopped for much, much more than a moment. Then gradually time awakened again and moved sluggishly on."
John Steinbeck, Of Mice and Men [viii]

"Mum, I need all the books now, we're supposed tae huv them for the start ae the year.

"Don't be stupid, will get them as ye need them." Said, my mum.

I was grimly aware that every penny was a prisoner. It was the summer of 1982, and I was getting ready to start second year at Hutchesons' Grammar School. My fees were paid via scholarship, but books etc had to be bought out of a relatively meagre household income. The average spend for mum and dad, for books and materials was around £300.

This was the eighties. We were an Easterhouse family. That was crazy money that we just did not have, so it was no wonder my mum was trying to spread the burden across the year. The problem was, I was right and within a couple of months, the issues over the book we had talked about would raise again. For me, it had life-defining results.

This moment hovered, waiting to find its mark.

I remember that day, a few months later. A Friday morning in Mr Strang's English class. Thirty-seven years later I still vividly recall the deep panic that arose within me as I heard, "Next week bring in your copy of "*Of Mice and Men*" as we are going to start looking at it.

It's hard to get across why it made me panic. I was a, supposedly, bright twelve-year-old, beginning second year in one of the best schools in Glasgow. I had done well in first year. Although my social awkwardness and even "shame" of where I came from had taken its toll.

This was it, though. I could not dare tell my mum I needed the book right away. There was no Amazon in those days, as hard as that seems to believe now. There was no money even if there had been.

I had two of the most dominant people in my life, my mum who did everything humanly possible to get her kids through life, and Mr Strang – a force of nature as a teacher. A real man's man. Fantastic teacher that we all loved, but we also feared. There was no messing about in his class. On the other side of all this, though, was the fact that I loved English. It was my favourite subject. And suddenly that moment from the summer came hovering back into view. Sound stopped and movement stopped as my heart took in what my brain tried to kick out.

What on earth was I going to do? How the heck could this be solved?

The sense of foreboding as I made my way home that day. The dread that locked my lips and clenched my fists. I sat on the bus, not even daring to breathe as my fear carried me across the city. I had spent the full journey going through various conversations in my head, (in hindsight, not the best idea since my head was already a fortress of insecurity and fear).

Foot off the bus at Aberdalgie, creeping along Duntarvie, caught up in my own prison of nightmare proportions, and eventually almost crawling up the two flights of steep tenement steps to our top floor flat.

As I pushed my way very slowly in the door, it was obvious that something was already going on. The atmosphere of argument hung thick in the air, and like the cold blast before a storm kicks in, I felt it.

Dad had been drinking. You did not need to hear him, never mind see him to know this. It was like he carried his own storm clouds around with him. A malevolent force of nature that made anyone that knew him take precautions. Mum and dad had been arguing over, you guessed it, money. Big Paddy had gone straight to the Brig after work, not an unusual happening, but this was one of those times when my mum had had enough. There was very little money in the house. It was very rare that my mom got much from him anyway but that was one of those days she had decided to face him down over it.
Moments!

My dad and his drinking in those days is another story. But on this day, every bit of courage I had spent an eternity travelling through Glasgow, building up to enable me to just come in and blurt out that I needed the book and I needed it now was blown away in the hurricane that was going on.

How on earth could I ask for that book when my mum was so skint and so fed up that she had chosen to face him down over it?
I went to my room, closed the door and cried.

The following Friday as I entered Glasgow Central Station to get the train to school, I saw the pay phones. In an instant, I knew what to do. I called the school, pretended to be my dad and said I would not be in as I was ill. Hutchesons' had probably never had to deal with this before so there was no suspicion and no questions asked.

The next six Fridays the same pattern repeated.

The Fridays then fed into other days of the week, as I tried to avoid being confronted.

The moment had settled and was now oh so much more than a moment. It had altered the course of my entire life.

> *"But Mousie, thou are no thy-lane,*
> *In proving foresight may be vain;*
> *The best laid schemes o' Mice an' Men,*
> *Gang aft alley,*
> *A' Lea's us nought but grief an' pain,*
> *For promis'd joy!*
>
> *Still, thou art blest, compar'd wi' me!*
> *The present only toucheth thee;*
> *But Och! I backward cast my e'e,*
> *On prospects drear!*
> *An' forward, tho' I canna see,*
> *I guess an fear!*
> Excerpt from "To a mouse" Robert Burns[ix]

After a few *months* Hutchesons' copped on to the fact that something wasn't right. I think they sent a letter to my parents. Anyway, by the time it was "being dealt with" I was an expert on the *Clockwork Orange* (Glasgow Underground) and the associated touristy bits around it.

I had extensively explored Kelvingrove Art Gallery and Museum, and I was an expert at hiding a change of clothes in my oversized school bag and getting changed in the toilets in Glasgow Central Station. Only once in all that time did anyone EVER challenge a very small boy (Tich remember) making the same journeys day after day.

"You ok, wee man?" said one of the Underground ticket inspectors.

"Aye, just on ma way home," I replied.

"But yir oan here nearly evry day. Should ye no be at school?"

And that was that!

After that, I used to go and play up in what is now West Maryston Woods, just at the M8 motorway bridge on Easterhouse Road. Then it was a hill, with no trees, just very long grass.

Hutchesons' answer to my problem was to assume the teaching was too difficult for me. Their answer was to move me from Teaching Group Three to Teaching Group Six.

No one at any point seriously asked me what was going on.

I'm not sure I would have answered, but this was too much. The classroom was the one place I was happy. I loved the class. I enjoyed working with other pupils and I enjoyed the challenge of learning. I also actually enjoyed that, despite coming from a much poorer background, I had managed to secure a place through my ability in one of the higher classes. Now they had assumed the exact opposite of the truth.

Now I was expected to walk amongst my peers with them all thinking I was too dumb for my teaching group. All because of a John Steinbeck's George and Lennie.

It was torture.

They did not ask me. I would probably not have told the truth if they did ask, but that wasn't the point – despite all the drama going on around me, I felt I wasn't being seen, never mind heard.

I moved back into my routine of just avoiding school.

I somehow, though, managed to start Third Year at Hutchesons.

Within three weeks it was obvious though, that despite the efforts of PE teachers like Mr Percy and others to try and help me (they still never asked what the problem was) I had to leave.

"Yir no going tae that Wessie," (Westwood Secondary School) was my parents' response to the reality of me going back to school in Easterhouse.

Westwood, the school of my older brothers and my sister did not enjoy a good reputation.

I wanted to go there, as my friends from Blairtummock went there.   By this time, outside of school hours, I had already been spending more time hanging out with some of the local guys in what was considered a gang. It was just the ones from the area that hung about the streets.

One of my "chores" in the evening, was to go to the video hire shops in either Duke Street or Shettleston. I had a travel card, so it did not cost me to go on the buses. I would make my way down there, pick out two or three videos that, normally dad, had told me to get, and head home.

Most of the time, either on the way to the bus or after the bus, I would seek out the gang, and see what they were up to. In those days it was smoking hash and drinking wine. Some of them would sniff glue, gas and or other solvents. I tried the solvents twice and didn't like them.

I would take enough of a puff on a joint to feel comfortable, but at no time was it pushed on me. In fact, most times I asked, I was normally told, "Don't be stupid ya eejit, you're too smart for this."

My friends really did not want me, at that stage getting involved.

Random walks for gang fights, and summer up the pitches in Lochend and Rogerfield were already part of my life.

And yet…

The decision was made for me. I was going to Lochend Secondary School.

For those of you not familiar with Easterhouse geography and gang territories, Lochend was in Drummy land, Lochend was populated by Drummy people. I was from Aggro. I think I would be the only person from my part of the scheme there that took part in the gangs. I also was NOT a very good fighter.

Lochend Secondary School was NOT a good option for me.

I had tried, unsuccessfully to remonstrate the unsuitableness of Lochend, but I did not mention the threat to my life, through my involvement in the gangs.

My parents at that point were blissfully unaware of it. I survived, and through the winter months and the dark nights, thrived in Lochend. For most of the lessons, I

33

was basically repeating what I had learned mostly in FIRST year in Hutchesons'. But I guess that is why parents pay them so much cash for their kids to learn there. The only exception was that Lochend did not do *Biology*. They did *Anatomy, Physiology and Health*. This was only about the human body, rather than the more general type I had done. I loved it because I was in a class learning new stuff.

In French I stood out above the rest of the class, as I was decent at it.

I remember a French intern coming in and repeatedly putting me out of the class as he thought I was showing off. I don't think I was.

English, I loved. Mr Don was the teacher, a wee tubby guy with a beard. He was the stereotypical English teacher though, all stern and serious.

I had left Hutchesons' because of issues in English, they weren't there in Lochend.

Unfortunately, though, as spring rolled in, so did the lighter evenings and street fights. Suddenly, I was fighting guys on a Saturday, I would have to avoid on the Monday.

I survived into the summer but begged to be allowed to leave and go to Westwood.

To no avail.

One incident in the summer of 1984 that I talk a wee bit more of later meant trouble for me after the summer.

The Drummy Milk Float.

On return to school in August of that year, within days a policeman had to be positioned at the school gates because of the rising amount of gang members hanging about.

They didn't know, and I didn't say initially, that they were all there to get me. I ran out of the girls doors for weeks, while they all hung out at the boys.

I would run across the arena, the rugby pitch (in Easterhouse right) the BMX course, through the fence and over Easterhouse Road back into our area – safe.

Many times, a group of guys from our area would come up and stand at the fence at the BMX course.

I stopped going to school. (notice a pattern here).

Meetings were called, parents were called, Mr Don fought my case and promised to do everything to make it possible for me to continue to study at Lochend.

"Nah" says I, nonchalantly "they'll murder me. Ahm gaun tae Wessie."

First day in Westwood Secondary School, September 1984, just over three years since I started Hutchesons' triumphantly.

I got to be a bit of class joker and troublemaker, for a while. The teachers assumed, as I was a new pupil, that I did not know anyone so could not be responsible for throwing stuff or making stupid noises etc, when their backs were turned.

I cannot remember my English teacher's name in Westwood nor anything about them.

I remember making a screwdriver and a hammer in *Technical*. My love for technology was sparked with the brand-new BBC Microcomputers that we got.

I passed my five O'Grades without really trying, I did not like exams.

Higher Geography, I had to do a paper that was to last the year. I chose *Sphere of Influence* for my topic. I chose to do it on Celtic Football Club – and I was allowed.

I spent time in the Celtic Supporters Association offices in the Celtic Club on London Road.

Gang fights in the corridors were not uncommon, even though our school was next door to Easterhouse Police Station.

Only difference was we fought the *Skinheads* from Wardie Road Easthall area, rather than the *Drummy.*

BUT

Westwood was in our gang's area. We were the predominant ones. We did the bullying etc.

I remember one day, a couple of guys from *Skinz* coming in and telling me I was getting stabbed at break. They pulled out wee boner (four-inch knives with wooden handles) and I laughed.

I genuinely did not care, even then.

I said to some of the guys from our gang what had happened. We gathered and got them at the shed at the main door of Westwood, overlooked by the staffroom and the headmaster's office.

It wasn't a big doing, but just enough.

That evening, when we were hanging about up the Quad, I happened to mention it to some of the guys.

Next day, I was sitting in my French Class. Mrs Organ or something like that. Again, I was good at French, so it was an easier class for me.

The door opens, big A and a couple of other guys come strolling into the class, bottles of either Elodorado or Old England under their arms, "We're here for Paddy" (I was Paddy) says A.

"Get out of this classroom right now."

"Naw, we're here for wir mate. Some bampots fae Skinz trying tae bam him up."

For a moment I did not know what to do. I recall Todd Coster whispering to me to tell them to go away.

I laughed, stood up with a "I'll be back shortly miss" and left.

Around that time, I had been attending guidance, and career guidance classes. In one of the guidance, my friend JS came with me, and we joked when asked what we wanted to do with our lives.

"Ah'm gonnae be a junkie." I said.

"An ahm gonnae be a dealer." Said JS. Both of us jokers, both of us foretelling our futures.

In guidance, I was warned during interviews not to say I was from Easterhouse. I was told that this would go against me when trying to get work. Way to go, Mrs, make me ashamed of where I grew up, as if I wasn't bad enough already.

Not long after that, sitting in my Geography class, I looked out the window and realised I could leave that Christmas. It was December 1985. It was now fifty-two months since I had walked through the doors of Hutchesons' Grammar School with a life full of purpose and six years of Secondary Education ahead of me.

It was over.

This was my LIFE?

11 – Lochwood Farm (1979-85)
Tribal Territories

"Everybody wants to protect their own tribe, whether they are right or wrong." [x] Charles Barclay

171 Lochend Road. The last close on the left-hand side, (none on the right) before the hill up to Drumpellier Loch. I knew it well because my granny and granda and our Peter lived there. I spent many a happy day therein my pre-teens, and then even in the first days of my teens, Peter would always be talking to me about music and electronics and stuff.

From 171, you crossed the wee bridge over the burn then walked up the hill. First on the left were the cottages, Benny's cottage (my dad's old pal Benny Gray used to live in one of them). As you turned the bend, there was the field through the hedge with all the old, rusting but fantastically magical farm machinery. From my earliest memories, these captivated me. I was always transfixed by these otherworldly metal beasts. Tantalisingly close to my young fingers through the gaps in the hedge and the fence, but not quite close enough.

My Granada Patterson was always taking me walks up to the loch (Drumpellier) and I loved them. Call it escapism, call it what you like, but I was just a wee boy that doted on his granda, and he doted on me. He would always be teaching me stuff and talking to me. It was brilliant.

I knew granny and granda were good friends with Jimmy and Mary Fyffe, the farmers. Many times, Jimmy and Mary had been up those never-ending flights of steps to the top floor tenement for a cup of tea, (or maybe another wee home-brewed drink from the kitchen cupboard).

I can still picture Jimmy and Mary's faces. They were always so kind to granny and granda. They were nice people.

Anyway, back to that field.

I will never forget the day, when, as a nine-year-old boy my granda asked me if I would like to help Jimmy on the farm. It was the summer holidays. (Actually, in retrospect I see a pattern devolving of my parents offloading me during the summer holidays, *respite* hmmmmmm).

I loved the days I would spend up there. I'd make my own way up in the bus. Off at the terminus. Around the corner looking up at granny and granda's window and ALWAYS stopping at the bridge over the burn before continuing up the hill. Past Benny's cottage, around the bend and up the driveway with the whitewashed wall one side and the "playfield" the other. At the end of the drive was a ninety degree turn with a hayshed on one side at the byre on the other. I loved it.

I loved the smells I loved the work I loved Mrs Fyffes cooking. I loved how nice their daughters were to me. I loved the fields, the milking the cows, being out on the tractor and more than all of this, I loved how Jimmy treated me the way my granda did - like a man. He expected me to be responsible, to do what I was asked and to ask if I needed help or didn't understand. No excuses accepted. Work hard and enjoy.

I did. Jimmy used to tell me stories about the farm. He was the first that talked about old bishops and Bishop Loch, but I never really processed that then. I would get to go out when baling hay, sitting on the tractor and wonder how the loose stuff went in and bales came out. I loved being out on the tractor when it was pulling the dung spreader and watching (and smelling) in awe as it spread its dung all over the fields.

And I even got to walk the cattle home.

I wanted to know how the machinery for milking the cows worked; why the dung spreader; how not to upset the bull and why the cows would follow Jimmy. I loved getting sent to collect the hens' eggs. They roamed free and you had to search the whole farm to find them. I loved being up in the grain loft, even though you had to wear a mask as the dust could be dangerous. I loved mucking out the byre - that heavy wheelbarrow full of dung (you know what dung is, right?) and then out to the dung heap just inside the whitewashed wall.

I loved it

I think I probably spent about three summers there helping until things began to go wrong elsewhere. I always missed it though.

Those were good days that, even when I look back, they make me smile. I love telling my daughters about the farm.

Fast forward just a couple of years. I'm up to my eyes in the early days of gang fighting and drugs. It's the summer of 1984. I had spent a year at Lochend (Secondary School in the Drummy's area) I had spent nearly the whole summer fighting them.

Mum says, "Stuart will you go up tae Kay's and get a lenny her rollers?" (Rollers were for the hair).

I know, big deal right. My mum wanted me to go to her friends and get something for her.

The problem was Kay is Kay Johnston. Her and John, wee John and David and Catherine and Lorraine were long time family friends. They used to live beside us, but now - NOW they lived in Canonbie Street which just happened to be in the hardest to reach part of the enemy territory.

So how do I deal with this? I can't tell mum that I can't go up their cos I was fighting the Drummy. My mum was more terrifying than them when she needed to be.

I knew there was no way out. I had to go.

I think I would have given the SAS a run for their money that day as I sneaked from back close through gable end to back close, worming my way through Den

37

Toi, Commonhead and finally that last stretch of Lochdochart Road. But that last bit was the worst. Kay and John lived right in the middle. Of course, they did.

I managed to get up to Kay's, find out she never had the rollers one of the other friends did. Can you believe it? I mean seriously I have risked life and limb for my mum's perm. Obviously never told Kay of either my fear of trying to get back to Aggro alive, never mind getting back to mum empty handed.

Words cannot describe the nervousness as I worked my way down the stairs. Every hair, every skin cell on edge. Had I been spotted?

Would I be? This was genuinely quite intimidating stuff.

Lochdochart Road. I made it up the first 100 yards.

"There's that wee b@#£@+* Paddy fae Aggro"

Seriously!

I mean, SERIOUSLY!!

TT and another face from the past. Not even two that would be considered hard or gangsters by any stretch. But there were two and I was one. Worse than that, I was one in their area. I knew this would happen!!!!!

Instincts kicked in. My brain kicked into survival mode, like a sat nav calculating my options for a route. Ahead through Commonhead - well they stood in between that route. Back through Canobie and Drumlanrig - you mad that's right through the whole of Drummy.

One option, what I knew. A route where I knew every step.

I turned and I ran. (At this point it is important to point out I never considered myself a gangster, hard man or even a competent fighter).

Run Paddy run was the right and only way to go.

Around the bend, over the bridge (still I glance very quickly though over it) and up the hill. For someone not noted for their speed, I was fast that day.

They are shouting at me. "Nowhere to run. We've got ye noo."

But they didn't know what I knew. I could go into Lochwood Farm.

And I did, up the hill, past Benny's cottage, round the bend and up the driveway. In through the turn, byre on left hayshed on right.

Jimmy was in the yard.

"Whits wrang with ye?"

I had to be honest. I told him that my mum had sent me for rollers and that two of the Drummy had chased me and were standing at the entrance to the driveway.

They were as well.

Jimmy knew a lot of stuff, but I don't know how aware he was of Easterhouse's gang problem.

He took me into the kitchen. Got me a drink of water. Let me catch my breath.

When the two had gone he said I best be making tracks, not quite what I was hoping to hear.

Again, with the internal sat nav.

There is no way I'm passing the bend and Benny's cottage and the bridge over the burn again.

For me.

Straight over the field, heading for the back of Commonhead and Den Toi.

A few hundred yards into the field the two from Drummy spotted me. They had been waiting at the bridge. I could not believe it as they started making their way up the hill via the field.

They were a distance away and I had an advantage. I had been in the field loads whilst helping on the farm. I knew the marshy bits.

Once again Run Paddy Run.

Commonhead. It had to be navigated carefully as they still considered themselves part of Drummy. The other two gave up at the first sign of marshland.

I made it. I was filthy. I was exhausted. But I made it. Back to the Quad. Up the two flights of stairs, in the door.

Breathless! Exhausted! Relieved!

But not willing or able to tell my mum what I had just gone through. I had no voice for that sort of honesty.

"Mum, Kay had already gied the rollers tae sumdy."

"Naw she's no" mum says. "She telt me she would hiv thum."

Mum turned can around. Seen how filthy I was and how out of breath I was.

"Ye never even went did ye? Look at ye, ye wir away messin insteed".

That's gratitude for you.!

NOTE:

The land around Lochwood has centuries-old history. Tracing back to the palatial home of the old bishops of Glasgow, the origin of the name of Bishop's Loch. Sandy Weddell, from Easterhouse Baptist Church has been praying over it for years. He has done a lot of studying on the area and is a fount of knowledge on it. The history is all part of Lochwood Farm. I've always been fascinated by it and prayed that one day God would move people there that would allow me to indulge my memories and make some new ones.

I have driven past many times. Many more than I needed to. Sad at the disrepair and yet each time my imagination kicked in and recreated it as it was for me. I would see, once again, the look over the bridge over the burn, up the hill, past Benny's cottage (now a newer house), around the bend, and I would be that little boy again every single time I pass the farmhouse and the "playfield" next to it.

Fast forward 34 years. It's now 2018. Easterhouse Community Church is on the go. Tracy, the girls and I were at morning service. Amongst the visitors that morning was an older Christian couple. Just moved up from England. Paul and Christine. We had a great time of praise and thanksgiving to God.

Blessing Him for always being with us during our circumstances and ALWAYS His love at work in our lives. After the meeting, we all decided to hang around for tea and coffee. On Sunday mornings we normally only do this before the short sixty-minute service.

I spent time chatting with Jim and Cathy Smith, AoG pastors from New Life Prestwick who had decided to join us on the first Sunday of their holiday. Then I spent some time chatting to Paul and Christine. It was fascinating. they were telling me all about why they moved to Scotland and how they had been visiting different churches in the area. They explained that they had bought an old farm in Gartcosh.

On we talked, me thinking this was a farm on the road through Gartcosh. Paul was happy that their sons were going to help them renovate the farm as there was a LOT to be done on it.

As the conversation moved on it became obvious that the old farm that they were talking about - the farm they had bought - was Lochwood Farm. Jimmy and Mary's farm (both sadly passed away). My farm! The scene of so many happy memories, and one scary one (although there are a couple about rats, roosters, and a goat I could share).

God had moved people in. I have already shared much of my love for the place and look forward to watching Paul and Christine building their own.

III Drugs (mis)Education

12 - Sixteen Today (1986)
Youth opportunities

YTS not a success, it gave me less and less;
magnified my inner stress. Kept me hopeless
yet just part of your chess with the youth, in a mess
you cut to excess for party correctness.
Your answer to the jobless whose futures you did possess
was to be gutless in your intolerableness
and scandalousness. So - thoughtless
and merciless you made it your business
in denying us access to keep us in darkness.
Living a life less in a scheme that was baseless,
so us you could oppress through your utterly hopeless,
completely useless YTS.

Thirty years later it's been part of my fate, eh
to remember that day your scheme came my way,
robbed my destiny by taking away
my right to a pay and some dignity
worth my working day.
All I've got to say!

Stuart Patterson ©2018

"Sixteen today, my feet are sore
trying to earn some pay
They close their doors and say
"I can't exploit you, try another day"
Youth opportunities Slave labour
Fight for proper jobs
Jobs not bombs we say
Youth in plight for brighter days"
From "Sixteen today" SchemeSongs

January 1986. I was a fifteen-year-old man. I no longer went to school. As I mentioned previously, halfway through the fifth year, just before Christmas, I decided that I was leaving because I could.

Spur of the moment. Annoyed in Geography. I had had enough, and I was gone. As I was due to turn sixteen that February I could. So, I did!

I did my first job interview in the Employment Training offices in December for a position in Fine Fare (now B&M). The morning of the interview I woke up to discover I was covered in chickenpox. I was fifteen. I did not really care about my appearance and, thinking nothing more of it, made my way to the interview.

The interviewer asked me if I had ever had any serious skin conditions, I looked him straight in the eyes and said "no".

Never having suffered acne, and not being the type of person that looks in the mirror in the morning when going out, (even before a job interview) I was oblivious to the condition of my face, covered in spots from the Chickenpox.

I didn't get the job. I had got the "job" as a YTS butcher after a successful interview with the Alex Munro/Dewhurst District Manager, Mr Guthrie. I remember him as being quite tall and old-fashioned looking with his handlebar moustache and sports jacket on.

Mr Guthrie was a pretty decent guy. He did what he could and what he had to. The job was in Alex Munro, in the middle of the shopping centre in Easterhouse. Just facing the back of the central stairs.

My friend from Westwood Secondary School, Gary Crawford, who had left school in the summer of 1985, was already serving his apprenticeship there. The Alex Munro interview came about because the broo said I had to go for it, OR ELSE I WOULD NOT GET ANY BROO MONEY (unemployment benefit).

So, I did. I started not long after it. My mum took £12.30 from my £27.30 a week training allowance, (well they could not really call it a wage).

I remember our John (JP), Yvonne and even my dad saying that taking it off my first wage was bit much. In fairness, she probably already knew my cash was going on drugs, or drink so thought she might minimise what I had.

41

Every Friday all the staff got a £5 parcel of meat as a bonus. I didn't as I was a YTS. This was my introduction to the working world of Britain in the 1980's.

The manager, Alan Vine, was normally a pretty decent guy. He said he wasn't allowed to give me the parcel. So, out of a staff of around twenty, the poorest paid was the only one that never got the Friday bonus. His daughter, Dawn, who only worked Saturday's, did get the parcel. The Assistant Manager, Graham Deeprose, was an even better guy and sort of took me under his wing and looked after me in there as much as he could.

I was good at my job. I did all the training modules that the YTS course involved. I worked all the extra hours I could. Obviously, I was not allowed to get paid for them, but I thought if I stick in there is a better chance I would get kept on. I thought this because the District Manager told me this.

The staff told me they had never retained either a YTS or a YOPper. I thought I would try anyway.

In the six months that the scheme lasted, I had to go away on two courses. Alex Munro was owned by Dewhurst Butcher's and the first one was in England. I had only ever been to England as a young boy on the Butlin's holiday I mentioned in an earlier chapter.

It was the end of January 1986. I was going out with MS. Diana Ross was number one in the charts with "Chain Reaction". Jon's men's clothes shop was part of the recently renamed Shandwick Square, situated where the Market Butcher is now. I know because I bought myself my first jacket out of there for going to Northampton. I got my hair cut in the Big Windae, only three doors down.

On the Monday, I and three other Scottish guys made our way together via train to Northampton. I had some hash with me, and some tablets, but the plan was to go there and do as well as I could. We joined with four English guys and very quickly a sort of friendly rivalry started between us.

Our first day in the training centre, us Scottish guys were shocked to discover that the English cut their beef forequarters different from us. It meant we were already at a disadvantage. We have been sent on a certified training course to cut meat in a way we had never been shown, and that we would never use when we went back.

The week away involved lots of classroom stuff as well. I even went to a Northampton Town vs Hartlepool local derby. Memorable because at one point during the game, a supporter, in disagreeing with a refereeing decision, called out "Away ref, that's Scottish football" to which my new friend from Airdrie replied, "There's nuffin wrang wae Scottish fitba!" All the surrounding supporters and the ref and the players burst out laughing. There were not many supporters there so you could hear everything.

Our group aced the presentation. (Our group being the four Scottish guys). The presentation involved having to prepare a unique sales pitch, highlighting the virtues of our chosen cut of meat. No PowerPoint or video graphics then. Our points hand drawn onto a flip chart sheet. Our pitch painstakingly drawn out over a quite enjoyable few hours with the other three and a few beers. We were determined we were going to beat the English team. National pride was at stake.

Our accommodation was a very smart Bed & Breakfast not far from the town centre. There was quite a large common room which we shared with a small group of senior Dewhurst managers, that were also staying in the BB. We annoyed them, but not half as much as their pompousness annoyed us. We drank beer in there, much to the annoyance of the landlady, who was sure as we were YTS trainees we must be too young to drink.

"No", we said, "we are managers as well." It was a great week. It was as. If I had been plucked out of the private hell of my life back in Easterhouse and been given a taste of what life could be.

It was different, and it was one of only two good "flashbulb" memories from my sixteenth year here on God's earth. When it was time to return home I did not want to go. I did NOT want to be on that train back up to Glasgow. I had tasted life outside of the drugs, gangs and scheme and I really enjoyed it. What's more, I was quite good at all the training stuff and excelled over the other guys.

I did not want to go back to MY life. Again, though, I did not know how to verbalise this to anyone. The train carried me back to Glasgow, and life led me down the only road I had ever known. I felt that I couldn't change, that my life wouldn't change, as if I was in a mould preparing another statistic to come out of Easterhouse.

THIS is MY life?

12 - Cairnbrook (1986)
Screaming cars and seeing stars

A wee bit of a different way to recall an incident in 1986, but here goes…

Walking up Cairn brook with the girlfriend on my arm.
It's a beautiful night, I'm not thinking of harm.
When out of the darkness comes a car screaming by;
they had it all planned, caught me on the fly.
Grabbed by the head and kicked to the ground
a few guys getting angry cos I was around.
Poor Maggie just standing, nothing she could do
but watch me get battered, up and down, black and blue.
The crime of the night, I'm on a street of their own
at midnight with Maggie, guys I'M WALKING HER HOME!
They did not feel I should be on their turf
I'm punched, kicked, bricks to the head, this is rough.

Ccovered in blood, bruised battered and sore
but I still think my pride is hurting much more.
With me crawling away, they shout out their threats.
My call one on one, none of them met.

43

I'm not a fighter, I'm not brave I'm not strong
man, this is too much, it went on for too long.
All because I did what mama said was right,
as I walked Maggie home in the dead of the night.

Then strange things happen when drugs are involved
and within a short time, I was friends with them all.
A common goal - get high and make cash
meant that their hatred for me wasn't destined to last.
Ready and willing to let it all go
for the sake of some acid, and other peoples' dough.
Up to Baldragon, soon a very normal sight
as I scored gear for others, night after night.
I stayed friends with some long into the future
even the one that caused me my sutures.

So, if you are caught up in the violence of the gangs
give thought to the morrow that in the present hangs.
Let go of the hold those guys have on you,
it might seem so cool, but the joke is on you.
The guy you are beating, might just be your friend
in the future, in who you might just need to depend.
The fighting, the gangs the hatred and ire
burns up your insides like Dante's cruel fire.
Think of the wee guy, walking his girlfriend that night;
caught up in a fracas that nearly switched off life's light.
Thirty years later, it's but a tale for a post -
but that night - in Cairn brook - I could have been toast
Stuart Patterson ©2018

13 – Sixteen Today Part2 (1986)
South to Southampton

"A horse is the projection of peoples' dreams about themselves — strong, powerful, beautiful —
and it has the capability of giving us escape from our mundane existence." Pam Brown [xi]

After having been to Northampton, I had felt as normal as it was possible to feel considering all the stuff that was going on in my real life.

I cannot remember much about my sixteenth birthday, except that it was on Thursday 13 February 1986. That's pretty much it. No great parties. No celebration. I would probably have avoided the house to be at TL's anyway.

The drugs got worse. I was taking all sorts of speed, acid and tablets now. In fact, as soon as my mum brought a prescription home from the doctors, I had tried her pills to see if I could get a kick out of them.

Wee TL's house was where I hung around with JJ and the guys. It was a bottom flat tenement right next to Duntarvie Road shops – our shops. Every day after work I would go home, get changed, then go straight to TL's.

I snorted speed at this point - that is, I inhaled it through my nostrils. I hated the taste of it and the feel of it on the back of my throat. We did an awful lot of snorting speed though.

And smoking hash. Joints, hot knives, bongs – whatever and whenever.

It would already be common for me, not quite sixteen, to be staying out nights. I would still be at work the next day though. That was important.

My mum and dad were already helpless at this point.

In denial over how bad I already was, but not over the fact that I was using drugs.

Many people try and blame the parents over how their kids turn out, and maybe sometimes that is true.

Me though, I was a product of my choices. My parents did the best they could under the circumstances. They loved us and they accepted us. My mum did whatever she could to try and provide a stable and happy home.

I was stubborn. I was screwed up. I made my choices. Now I am back.

My sixteenth birthday had been and gone with no fanfare or fuss.

Not long after my birthday I moved house.

I lived in my own council flat across Duntarvie quad from my parents.

Number 7, middle flat on the left as you looked up from outside. Fitzy's mum lived on the bottom right, and Fitzy and Lizzy lived above me on the top right. I had put in for it as soon as I turned 16 and was amazed to get it within a couple of weeks.

One of my dad's friend's had occupied it previously so I was well aware of the 'channel lining' on the living room fire place wall. For the six months that I lived there it never had floor coverings or any decorating done to it. I shared it with my ferret and my drugs, and sometimes my 'friends'.

I still worked in Alex Munro's and there were many incidents and scrapes I was involved in, both inside and outside the shopping centre.

After one such incident I had a scratch down my cheek from where a fight with a friend had resulted in me getting it hit with a rusty Stanley knife blade, and by some miracle, it not cutting deep enough in to leave a noticeable scar.

That tale is for another day. It is not a nice one and is still an episode I am deeply ashamed of.

As part of my YTS with Alex Munro I had another trip coming up in the spring. This one was more of an outward bound one. We were going to Southampton. It was Brockenhurst in the New Forest, but Southampton was the closest big town. We were going to spend a week outdoors and I could not wait. I had loved the Northampton trip. It was an escape, and without realising it - that was probably why I was so excited about this one.

It was the same guys that had been to Northampton that were going so that made it a wee bit easier. We also knew that we would be meeting up with the same four English guys. Off we all headed on the train to be picked up at Southampton and taken to our B&B at Brockenhurst.

This trip was to be a highlight of the first half of my life.

I loved it.

We did orienteering and long walks and a whole host of other stuff that was – apparently -normal behaviour for great swathes of British 16 - 18-year-olds.

I remember vaguely walking down next to all the yachts in Southampton, on a day trip there, and being blown away. I had never seen anything like it. All these different boats that people owned. And they weren't quite the pedal boats of the Glasgow park lochs either. Proper big, bold vessels designed for the open waters.

The highlight for me though, we were going horse riding. It just seemed ridiculously out there.

My closest experience to horses were the two in the field by Easterhouse train station (the field is, of course, now houses), that we used to pass on our way up to the garage at night to get munchies.

It was the same people that organised most of our activities that were organising the horse riding.

This may come as a surprise to those of you that know me, but I was mouthy.

Very mouthy.

Not in your face or anything like that, I just always had an opinion and insisted that my opinion was correct.

So, as a reward for being so wise and knowledgeable, they told me I was going on the biggest mare they had.

She, apparently, had the same attitude as me so that was a perfect fit.

After a brief prep session, we were assisted onto our horses and we set off around the beautiful New Forest.

At one point they even took us up to a fast gallop on the horses. It was brilliant. I remember my backside bumping up and down on the saddle, and even still recall the pain. But it was no match for the sheer joy and freedom of being on a saddle on a magnificent horse, in a line of horses galloping around such incredible scenery.

Then, one of the leaders called us all to a stop.

A band of wild horses had been spotted just up in one of the gentle hills.

It seemed that the stallion was taking an active interest in our horses, and either had taken a liking to one of them or had taken an exception to this encroachment of his territory.

Either was apparently bad for us.

Here we were 430 miles away from Easterhouse territorial gang fights, in the middle of one of the most beautiful places in England, and it seemed like I was about to be caught up in another territorial fight.

Who knows, maybe the Easterhouse gangs are closer to nature than many give them credit for.

The danger passed – but the moment – that didn't and hasn't.

As I am writing this in a Starbuck in Johnstone and there is a tear rolling down my cheek. I am back there in that moment. I can see it. Feel it. The moment is forever. And it is a good moment.

I loved the buzz of it. I loved the sense of apprehension on the leader's faces, and I loved the panic coming into the rest of the team. I was too ignorant to understand this could be serious. Apparently wild horses will behave like deer, for the most part, when they sense danger. That is that they will make their escape. The danger here was that the stallion was working his way closer towards us, and the rest of the gang was following. They were sizing us up, or maybe he was sizing up one of the females. Yeahhhh, right back in Easterhouse I was.

The decision was made to keep the horses in single file and very slowly keep trotting away. The hope was the stallion would lose interest.

He was a cracker. I can picture him slowly making his way towards us, head up, sizing us up. Wondering what his next move should be.

He played us - beautifully.

What a moment!

As we moved away, though, he got bored and turned back to his gang.   It really was just like Easterhouse. The rival gang left the territory and the danger subsided.

Moment over we continued for what seemed like many hours but was only two.

It was brilliant fun. The strange thing is to this day I have never managed to go horse riding again. I have taken our Naomi a couple of times and she has loved it.

It just hasn't happened.

Maybe, just maybe it's better that way.

Keep the memory as a flashbulb moment from my past rather than   sully it with a different experience here.

The week continued. Then it was over. I was now sixteen years old; I had managed to have two weeks of the past five months seeing what life should probably have been like.

Now, once again - I had to return to my real life.

Some time ago Tracy and I had dinner with two friends we had made at Port Ban.

Brenda and Adrian very kindly took us for a meal in Cumbernauld.

In the few years we had known them and enjoyed fellowship with them, there had never really been time to find out too much. So, it was with great amazement I learned that this wonderful older couple were from Southampton.

They had lived and served God in Scotland for a lot of years. Adrian used to work in one of the very first computer data analyst centres in the 60's and had been involved in that right up until his retirement.

We enjoyed a nice evening.

It was wonderful, though, for the first time since spring 1986 to share with locals of the New Forest, the tremendous experience I had in their area.

To have made a connection to the beautiful village of Brockenhurst.

47

I recounted my joy of discovering how good I was at orienteering, (no sat navs or Google Maps in 1986) a map, a compass and some cryptic clues.

We trashed the other team (yes it was Scots against English again) by almost two hours.

Our destination was a pub in the New Forest. We waited and waited on the English boys catching up, drinking cokes (honestly).

When they finally arrived, they insisted we had cheated.

We laughed.

It was simply down to me discovering I could navigate those clues and a map and my sense of direction so well.

Such a pity that I could not show the same inherent ability in my choices for navigating my life - my real life.

14 - The Lion's Den (1986)
Top flat torment

"You can take it from this skinny preacher from the hills of Pennsylvania; The cross is mightier than the switchblade."
From *"The Cross and the Switchblade"* by David Wilkerson

In Cairnbrook, I told of my experience at the hands of the guys from Baldragon. That was the beginning of a journey with these guys. I want to write about another experience. It was a few weeks later. I had, very nervously, being up to score acid tabs in a close in the middle of the square since a week after Cairn brook. I had got on well with them, after all, I was making them money. Some of the guys I got on well with and continued as friends for years.

One guy, HF, lived above my then girlfriend MS. He had said many times I should pop up to his house. For obvious reasons I did not think that was a great idea. It is important to remind you, dear reader, that I had spent a good part of the last few years fighting these guys. In all sorts of settings with all sorts of weapons. Let's go back in time to set the context a bit better.

One instance, for example, was the Drummy Milk float. I know, it sounds ridiculous, and maybe it was a bit. Anyway, the milk float was an actual milk float (electric vehicle) that delivered actual milk to actual people in actual houses. It was operated by one of the older guys from the Drummy area, but he always had some of the young team helping him. Part of the round was down through Aggro, but since it was early in the morning, nothing much usually happened.

As we were returning from some adventures there may at times have been the acknowledgement of "There's ra Drummy milk float!" But early morning was never the time to pick a gang fight.

This time though, for some reason it was down through Aggro in the middle of the afternoon. It was the weekend. We returned to school only a few days later so it was August 1984. I can place this accurately because of how events unfolded.

Anyway, that afternoon, it was travelling up Duntarvie Road, the heart of Aggro, and it was obvious they were up to no good. It always amazed me how quickly word spread in those days as in no time at all there was a large group of us all gathered ready for a fight. You see, driving through in the middle of the day was a provocation, a sort of act of war.

That's how it was.

There must have been, within minutes, about fifty of us on our way up through the Quads to cut off the milk float at Easterhouse Quad / Lochdochart Road.

I must give the guys in the float their due, though, when they saw us, they stopped right at the top of the Quad and jumped out.

Then commenced one of the largest gang fights on the streets there had been for quite some time.

It was bedlam.

Bricks.

Sticks.

Clashing metal.

Exploding glass.

Punches. Kicks.

It was so chaotic that we were even getting right to the float and grabbing crates of empty milk bottles off to use as weapons.

Remember, this was right on the doorstep of houses. There were kids in gardens and parents screaming at us. It was chaotic and mad, and everything was going on.

Twelve-year-olds right through to men in their twenties were battling like crazy. Swords and knives had been pulled and were flashing around.

I was running with a milk bottle in my, yet undamaged left hand, and a stick in my right hand. This is it, boys, this is war.

"Stuart, get oot a there ya eejit! You hiv to go tae school wi them oan Monday."

Eh?

The voice did not fit with the setting, and momentarily I was confused. Before I had time to think, I felt the hand on my shoulder dragging at me.

My mum had waded right into the middle of a chaotic gang fight to pull me out. She ignored everything that was going on around her, thinking only of getting me out of there.

She was right, of course. At that time, I still attended Lochend Secondary School. I had already had a few skirmishes in there, and there had been times I genuinely thought I was going to get killed. However, that Monday I was due to start the fourth year in a Secondary School (that is what they were called then).

I allowed myself to be dragged away out of the battlefield. It seemed that hell was ignorant of the nature of my humiliating departure, as it carried on raging against the hearts and minds of the boys and men.

It was a miracle that day that no one was seriously hurt. There were a few flesh wounds. I recall being banged on the back of the head myself, but not to any great hurt.

49

My mum was disgusted, with me and with the mayhem. She had watched her 14-year-old intelligent son racing to be involved in a fight that could end, so easily, in death.

So why is this relevant to the lion's den, you ask?

Most of the "passengers" on the float were later to be the same dealers that I would be scoring from in the *Drag*. There had been real animosity and hatred, not because of who we were, but because of where we lived.

Fate had conspired to provide natural boundaries in Easterhouse that resulted in several generations of young men being divided.

I was part of EYA, they were part of the DYT.

I hung about the *Quad*. They hung about the *Drag*. That was all it took.

So back to the current present that is the past, but it is what I am writing about kinda present.

One night I decided I was going to do it. I never really feared things, more of a practical outlook. When I decided I was going to do something though, I went ahead and did it. So, I did. I put my jacket on

With my mind set, my jacket on, I edged out the door and down the close stairs. I stopped at the shops to talk to some of the guys, but not for long. Making my way down Duntarvie Road, I heard a shout, it was my wee cousin, Paul Davidson. What was he doing here? Paul's mum and dad, my aunt June and uncle John, were my second home throughout most of my childhood. They stayed in, what we considered, the posh west end, in Whiteinch to be exact. Right next to the Clyde Tunnel entrance, that was so cool.

I knew that if I acknowledged Paul that I would be presented with two options - go with Paul or bring him with me. The latter was not an option, no way could I bring my wee cousin up to the Drag anything could happen.

I kept walking, faster. Down Duntarvie and up Duntarvie Place. Up through Dubton Path, along Lochend Road then around Baldragon, corner close, top flat.

I knocked on the door and it was not long before I heard Harry asking, "Who's there?"

"Paddy" I replied, quietly, almost convinced that if I said it out loud the whole of the Drummy would be there before I knew it.

"Paddy? Paddy who? Aw Paddy fae Aggro" as he began the process of unlocking the door.

HF opened his door. Even shorter than I was with dirty fair hair and a few years older, he looked a wee bit stoned - but a big bit shocked.

"You said tae come up some time, so here a um."

"Come in, come in," HF said. Grab a seat.

There was a small lamp on in the sitting room, just enough to let us see what was what. It was tidy and there was some drug paraphernalia on the table.

"Ah'm just expecting the boys up the noo" he said, and at the same time, I felt as someone grabbed my throat. I could hardly breathe, never mind speak. Here I was in a house deep in enemy territory and the enemy was due any second. HF himself was a genuinely nice guy, it was the reason I was here. It wasn't long though before there was a knock at the door and a shout for HF to open. I knew the voice, it was RM.

"Wait a minute Paddy" he said as he went to let them in. Nothing I could do but breathe and wait.

"Awright Paddy" said PT, the leader of the small group, "Got ye where we want ye noo, eh," he said with a big grin on his face.

"Whit ye daein up here ya maddy?" said PG. "Were ye lookin fur acid?"

"Naw, HF had said tae come up anytime I wanted, so here I am" as I said it, there was a part of me that wished I had turned around and went with my cousin, Paul when he called. However, I hadn't. Here I was, like it or not.

My mum wasn't coming in here and dragging me out.

Within seconds one of them was at the table rolling a joint. It was normal procedure, more normal than cigarette smoking. When the joint was being passed around, it was my turn, something inside me wanted to keep my head straight (in a flat with guys I had spent years fighting against, I wonder what that could have been). I refused the joint the first time. They were all like, "are you mad? you don't want a puff" so I took it, but barely inhaled.

There was some chit-chat, and to be honest the guys made me feel like we had been mates for years. The reality is that from that moment on, they pretty much were as much my mates as the guys from my own gang. In fact, there had been times when I was in Drummy that they had stepped in and stopped me from being seriously beaten up by other, quite hard guys from the area. I mean genuinely heavily beaten up.

In the Bible, there is the story of the young man Daniel. He was a captive in Babylon, but because he worshipped and feared God, he grew in favour and it wasn't long before he was used by King Darius.

This made the local leaders jealous and they conspired to have Daniel punished. He was thrown into a den of lions. The next morning, King Darius came, hoping against hope, that Daniel would be alive.

 Daniel was.

He said an angel had come and closed the mouth of the lions because he had done no wrong.

Now I am not saying that I was righteous or honourable or anything like it in those days, but there are similarities. My reasons for being there were, in a screwy sort of way, honourable. I did not want to be caught up in fighting these guys anymore. Even though that was so I could score from them, I saw that they were just normal guys.

I suppose, as I made my way up Baldragon that night, I was putting my trust, and, my reasons into the Hands of a God I did not yet know.

So up I went.

The next morning, I was still alive. Ridiculed a bit for not smoking the joint, but alive. More than that I had learned a valuable lesson. If I fought these guys, just because of where they lived, I could not get what I needed from them - however, if I got on with them and I could score, then I could benefit from it.

I am not saying that was right, I benefitted from getting drugs for others, it is not right, but I did make some great friends and it did let me see that freedom was important. Especially freedom of movement in a place like Easterhouse.

I ended up making friends all over the scheme, long before it was fashionable to do it, long before heroin made it necessary to do it.

Many of these friendships formed in those days still last - to this day.

The Lions' den team - well as we carried on doing what we did, we did drift apart a bit. As heroin took over most of our lives some of them, I was more friendly with than others.

As I grew through my twenties and on into my Teen Challenge days - those guys were never far from my mind. Many a prayer has gone up.

The last proper interaction though, was not long after I was back in Scotland living. Pete Gordon, one of those guys, and genuinely one of the nicest guys you could ever meet, had passed away.

I made my way, sombrely to his funeral service in St Clare's in Easterhouse. I cannot remember much of the funeral mass, other than noticing how much we had all aged in the years that had passed. It was obvious that some bore the scars of time and battle a lot worse than me.

At that moment I was thankful that God had spared me in the lions' den - but even more than that, I was thankful that for a time God had made these guys a big part of my life. Many looked on the outside and saw the hardness and the drugs and all that stuff, but I got a glimpse inside and saw that not every lion is a cold-blooded killer.

I knew even more at that moment than I did when I wrote *Role* that I wanted these guys to meet Jesus the way I had.

How I long to go back into the lion's den now, with the same intimate knowledge of God's love that Daniel had.

Pete Gordon was a good friend, as were most of the others, but Pete's funeral was one of the saddest (outside the family) that I have personally felt since coming to know Jesus. He was young, like so many from those days, too young.

As I sat after the funeral in the car of another friend from back in the day, AM, and spoke to him about faith and those days, it was heartbreakingly sad.

AM had also decided to follow Jesus. Both of us shared a desire to see more rescued before it was too late.

So often I feel completely ineffectual in that. As I attend funeral after funeral these days of those I grew up with, laughed with, cried with and got high with. I ask God to help me reach them with the ultimate Most High.

As David Wilkerson, the founder of Teen Challenge, says, "*Drugs, what a devil-inspired poison! It's death on the instalment plan.*"

15 - Hatchet Job (1986)
None of your lip, please!

"Some of you are so blind that you're heading for a ditch and you don't even know it."
from *'The Cross and the Switchblade'* by David Wilkerson

One of my drugs of choice from around sixteen to nineteen years old was LSD[xii] (acid).

Being on LSD made me do mad, crazy things. None of them was ever deliberate. None of them ever worked out. It was just the law of unintended consequences. I would act in the moment, but the problem with tripping out on LSD was the moment kind of looked different to you than it did for anyone else.

For instance, whilst walking down a street, you maybe see cracks in the pavement and the dirt.

Me?

I saw the pavement as covered in pure glass.

It was beautiful.

I was walking on the purest glass you had ever seen. That was my reality.

You maybe saw the weeds growing up through those cracks, but I would see the most incredible and lush vegetation you would ever think possible.

When I saw people, it was like a scene from *The Matrix* (except that was still a lot of years in the future). All numbers and stuff and my brain whirring away trying to figure out the purpose.

The problem?

Yeah, there were problems.

LSD did not like things out of order.

Everything had to fit into how the memory recalled it before.

One of those days when things were not quite normal left me with a gaping hole on my lip and the back of my head. It went something like this:

I was sixteen years old, (what an eventful sixteenth year I seemed to live).

I was on a bus heading back to Easterhouse from the city centre (or the toon).

It was a very cold, and horrifically wet November day.

The rain really was hammering down.

Anyway, I, GC and SS were upstairs on a bus, thick with the acrid smell of cigarette smoke and with our view obscured by the fog of 30 odd people calming themselves on its toxins.

I could not tell you where we had been and how we ended up on the bus, just where we were going.

We were on our way to Duntarvie Road shops. They were our shops, well I say shops, and they were, but they were also the centre of the Easterhouse Young Aggro (EYA, our gang) universe. The meeting point, the hanging point.

Where we got our alcohol and, sometimes our drugs.

As we were laughing and joking on the bus, we noticed PM.

He was from the Drummy, another gang area.

53

He was quite a no-nonsense young guy and had a reputation as a bit of a fighter.

We did as we all always did when a member of another gang was spotted. We started giving him it tight and shouting abuse at him. Telling him what we were going to do to him.

In fairness to PM, he never backed down or shrunk away (must be honest I would have) but instead, quite calmly said: "Come on then, aff the bus, here".

We looked and laughed. The bus was approaching the stop just facing Easterhouse Health Centre, and as I stood at the doorway watching PM with GC and SS behind me, I noticed he was carrying a holdall, and even more intriguing, his other hand was inside the bag.

That's when I clocked, he already had his hand on what looked like the shaft of a hammer.

"Look, guys," I said, mockingly, "he's tooled up".

The bus was absolutely crammed with people, it was teatime and it was dark and wet. As it rolled to a stop and the hiss of the hydraulic doors sounded like a fight bell, PM jumped off the bus and I immediately threw myself after him, grabbing the arm that was reaching into the bag at the same time.

We both fell onto the saturated pavement, rolling around getting even more wet fighting for control of what was obviously NOW an axe.

The adrenalin surged through me as the LSD seemed to give a superhuman strength, knowing the moment had various outcomes.

I gave an almighty pull on the axe, seemingly welded to the grim grip of PM, and as it swung free.

CLUNK!

The sound of the hatchet hitting me on the back of my head.

Momentarily my grip loosened as my thoughts seemed to bounce around with that horrific hollow clang that goes along with a bang to the head.

It seemed like an eternity, and as PM tried to rise and escape, I think, I grabbed for the hatchet again.

I was so good at this fighting with a weapon under the influence of drugs thing that I broke it away from his grasp and, with the axe suddenly free and moving under its own kinetic energy, came lurching towards my face.

CLANK!!! This time full on the mouth. We were back in a wrestling match.

GC and SS had, the whole time been trying to get PM, launching kicks at him and trying to pull us apart, but - understandably given the odds - he was like a man possessed. He was also a very good fighter.

Finally, I got to my feet and launched a kick at PM as he scrambled along on the river like pavement.

PM finally managed to scramble to his feet and made his escape. I think in the moment he just had the most sense out of the four of us.

I threw the axe after him, reminiscent of the many cowboy films I had seen as a youngster. The Indian's tomahawk chasing down the dark emptiness. It missed and landed on the grass at the side of the bus stop.

We picked ourselves up and I remember GC very clearly saying, "Your lip's cut,

Paddy." I put my hand to my mouth and checked for signs of blood, but there was none. So off we headed, thinking nothing more of it.

I know I have mentioned the rain, but for the next bit to work, I need you to know that it was almost torrential. In that rain it was like walking under a fire hose all the way back across the Buywell car park and the pitches, across Aberdalgie Road and all the way up Duntarvie Road.

We made our way into Charlies. (His actual name was Mohammed Hussain) and I shouted on Margaret, who was facing the myriad of sweet jars that 16-year-olds should have been buying and enjoying.

Margaret was Margaret Campbell. A local lady respected by most of us that hung around the shops. I got on well with Margaret.

"What is it Stuart?" (no Paddy from the adults) as she began to turn around and face me.

"Is ma face cut?" I asked, still oblivious to the actual damage as there seemed to be no blood.

"Let me look" she said as she turned around.

"Arrrrgggghhhhh" she screamed as she dropped the sweet jar she held. "What have you done, that's right through your lip?"

"Is it bad then?" I asked.

She grabbed a mirror, (I don't know, it was there) and showed me.

I looked at it, and shock, combined with the effects of the LSD made me burst out laughing as I saw my upper lift lip sliced right through and my teeth visible through the gap.

By this time the blood had begun to flow again as well, (or maybe there was just no rain to wash it away). I also felt the cold trickle down the back of my neck and asked Margaret to check my head as well.

Yep. That was wide open, and the blood was seeping out there as well.

Alternate reality!

Not thinking of the effect it would have on my mum and dad, I knew I had to go to hospital. I knew because Margaret's last words were "They need stitches, you need to go to the hospital, quick!"

Up I went to our top floor tenement. In the door. Along the hall to the kitchen halfway down. The smell of dinner was filling the house.

"Da I think I need to go to hospital!" I said with not a flicker of either remorse or pain.

"Whit fur noo?" He asked, as mimicking Margaret, he'd drifted from stirring the pot to facing me.

"Ya f@#$$g eejit, whit hiv ye done?"

"I fell." I lied.

As much as my dad was feared, and respected by anyone that knew him; as much as he would always be in fights and disagreements - he would not tolerate any of us being involved in anything like that and had very little patience for it.

"Heather come and see this idiot, his face is split wide open!!"

Sympathy?

It was surely self-inflicted and not deserving of sympathy.

My dad knew I hadn't gotten it falling.

My mum just shuddered when she saw it.

Got some material or other and put it over both war wounds.

We made our way to Glasgow Royal Infirmary – on the bus -where I was stitched up front and back.

Glasgow Royal Infirmary, on these occasions, would always ask how the wound happened as they were supposed to report any assaults etc to the police.

"I fell!" I lied.

Home I went, and I would love to say that I had learned my lesson and stayed in, suitably chaste.

I didn't. I went out, up to SS's sister's house. Got more LSD, them moaned when the guys would try and get me to go into fits of giggles because I knew it would burst the stitches.

PM.

I saw him a few weeks later in the Buywell. Remember I was now "friendly" with the guys from the Drag that patrolled the place. I scored most of my LSD from them and so it was not an issue to be walking around in there. Everyone knew of the fight with PM.

PT, this day says "There is PM, Paddy. You want to get him back. We'll back you up." They were just stirring it. PM was from their area and they were just looking to split the boredom.

As much as the half-filled bottle of Irn Bru in my hand was itching for payback, I couldn't be bothered. Also, I wasn't stoned, so I was able to think much clearer.

As we approached each other to pass, though, there was a visible tension. The stitches were gone from my lip and the back of my head, but there was still very much a visible wound on the front, and a bald patch with a red line on the back.

That split second when you wonder if something will be said.

"Alright P.." I said, taking the initiative that I just did not like fighting, so hopefully making the get out easier.

"Alright, Paddy" he replied.

We stood then and chatted for a few secs, tension and wariness still there, but each giving the other the opportunity to avoid conflict. The other guys disappointed that there was no entertainment to break the boredom of the afternoon.

So, what about PM?

In the gang fights that followed over the next decade, he would pop up. He was a fighter and really did not seem to hold much fear.

Then I went to Wales and Teen Challenge.

I think around 1999 I was with The Evidence (Teen Challenge ministry team) in Ystradgynlais AoG (Pastor Kerri Jenkins church, but more about him another time). We knew guys from Victory Outreach (another Christian Rehabilitation programme) were in the meeting, but never really thought that much of it.

As I stepped up to share my story of how Jesus had delivered me from and through addiction, I noticed a familiar face near the back of the small Welsh church.

It was PM.

I had not seen him up close in all those years, and it's funny how, for a split second, those old tensions arise. Alternate reality. Face from my past here in my present.

I composed myself and carried on.

After the meeting, I could not wait to chat with him. We swapped stories of how we had started out in rehab and ended up as God's kids. PM looked fantastic and said he had just had enough of it all one day and wanted out of it.

It was incredible.

It was probably the first real time the potential for old gang conflicted injected itself into the new Christian context. God showed Himself strong.

As the VO guys made to leave, PM and I hugged warmly and prayed God's best for each other.

Isn't it mad that that ridiculous rain-soaked blood washed episode that could have ended so badly 13 years before, when placed into the hands of Christ, created a love-soaked Blood washed episode that I remember fondly to this day.

Giving even my worst moments to Jesus, He can redeem them and give them a new meaning that neither LSD, gangs not intended hatchet violence could ever foresee.

I have no idea what has happened to PM since that moment, but many times I do pray that our paths would cross again.

"And we know that all things work together for good to those who love God, to those who are the called according to His purpose." Romans 8:28 NKJV

16 - Three step shuffle (1986)
Three days out

"So ask me if I am alright.
'I'm fine; I'm always fine.'
You see this look in my eyes.
'No, I'm fine. I am always fine.'
There is a corpse behind my smile.
'Listen, I am fine.
Always, always fine as fine can be.'
'Are you okay?'
'I am more than okay.
I am more than fine. I am wonderful!'[xiii]
Emma Rose Kraus, A Blue One

Fifty paracetamol tablets neatly stacked into five piles of ten lay on my carpet. The bits of oose distracting me for a moment as I thought that I needed to hoover, then laughed.

57

I stood up and moved to the door, once more making sure the latch was firmly closed so no one could come in and disturb me. Once again, I kneeled at the floor beside my medicine, and wondered. Earlier on I had been down at wee Bill's on Duntarvie Road. The sun had been shining outside, and I had intended heading back up to hang out at the shops.

"Ahm away up to the shoaps tae see who's there" as I made my way out the door. It was a normal refrain from most of our lot. Either you headed to the shops or to "the wall" up Duntarvie Quad. You would be sure to find someone.

"Awright Paddy, see ye later" came the response from inside. I made my way out to the front of the close and started up by the clinic on Duntarvie Road.

It was a nice spring evening, with the sun shining. and the shops, buzzing with life. I still felt the vague effects of the speed (Amphetamine Sulphate) that I had taken earlier in the day. I wasn't particularly stoned or anything, but I was thinking of what I could do for my next kick.

"Paddy ur ye comin o'er?" John screamed from outside Charlie's. Charlie's was the newsagent off sales, and Charlie himself was called Mohammed Hassan. I am not quite sure how he got the nickname, but it stuck.

"Ah'll be o'er in a wee bit." I replied, "Ah just need tae nip upstairs the noo."

"Awright, but don't be long."

I think the hope was to steal some more of the myriad of tablets my mum was already getting prescribed to her. My mum was only thirty nine years old at this time and she was having to deal with a large family, and all the issues I was already presenting in the midst of it.

Making my way up the stairs to our top flat tenement I could only think that I needed more tablets. The strange thing about substance abuse is how easily your brain – and your body – are tricked into thinking life cannot go on without more, there is ALWAYS a need for more. I wanted to mitigate the comedown (effects wearing off) of the speed on my body, so the hope was I would find a tablet to help.

As I went through the door, my ears strained for voices, it was my normal routine anytime I came home now. It was always easier if no one was in as that meant no questions about where I had been.

As it was at this point, I think I had been out for two nights. By out, I mean that I had not set foot in my mums for two days and two nights.

Safe in the knowledge that no one was home I made straight for the cupboard in the kitchen where all my mum's prescription medicine was kept.

Success!

A bottle with tablets that looked like *Upjohn 117s (Xanax)*. The thought that my mum would need these because of me never even entered my mind, but that's how self-centred I already was. I don't know how many I took, but I swallowed then made my way back down to the shops.

John was still standing at Charlie's off license door, going through the ritual of 'tapping'. That is, asking people for 'a lend of…' 10p, 20p, didn't matter. It was begging and it provided us with money for alcohol, dope or whatever. Most people would hand something over. Well wouldn't you if we stood in your way in and out of the shop.

John was a *Carlsberg (*Cally) drinker. I preferred *Old England.* Our shops, and Easterhouse in general was not a *Buckfast* haven. I stood and drunk with John, but for me it was blatant manipulation. If I stood with him long enough then John would make enough for me to get cash for more speed or hash. John was particularly good at getting cash.

After about an hour, and as it started to get dark, I made plans to go up to the house and get a wee bit of sleep. The *Upjohn's,* mixed with the alcohol were really beginning to kick in. No matter the volume of drugs I took, I always liked at least the pretence of being in control of my faculties and aware of what I was doing. I began to sense that I was losing that.

"Aye, **** aff ya dafty, get the money then bolt", moaned John when I said I was going up to the house.

"Ah'm tired, ah need a sleep." I had taken five pounds from the cash John had collected. I knew that I had enough for a bag of speed, but in the morning. I needed a sleep.

Our house in Duntarvie Quad was only a couple of hundred yards from the shops, and I hadn't seen my mum and dad returning. Chances were it would still be empty, and I would get to sleep before they came in.

As I put my key in the *Yale* lock, the empty silence greeted me. It always amazed me that houses possessed an empty and a full silence. You knew when you came through the door, even if there was no noise, if someone was in.

Success! No one was home. I went back into the kitchen, into the cupboard with the medicine, and I noticed the *paracetamol.*

For some strange reason an idea began to form in my mind. I wondered what would happen if I swallowed a load of them. My mind already doing the sums and figuring out what it meant by a load.

These were the days before sales were restricted to one or two boxes, and there were always loads that had been given on prescription.

Fifty! That seemed like enough. Fifty should do it.

Because I was a sneaky git, I took some out of the different bottles and packets though. I did not want anyone to notice a whole bottle or pack was missing so I accumulated them from all the different packs.

My room was directly across from the kitchen. I moved in quickly, ensuring the latch was closed over firmly.

Sitting down at my telephone table that doubled as a wee desk in my room, I began to separate into the piles of ten, on top of the newspaper cut-out of Pope John Paul II that was sellotaped to the bit designed for a phone to sit on.

Once I was happy that everything was in order, my mind all the time telling me this was a great idea, I moved the piles onto the carpet. Very neatly ensuring the five piles of ten were even. It was important, apparently, that I kept count of how many I had swallowed.

Now I am back to where I started this chapter, at the door, making sure the latch was closed. I remembered then that I had no water, and there was no way I could swallow that many tablets without water to wash them down.

Grasping at the latch to get over to the kitchen and back again before anyone came home, I caught my finger on a sharp bit.

"Ouch!!!!" it had cut right through the skin. Ah well now I had another reason for taking the tablets, they would dull the pain of the cut that I wasn't even feeling through the dulling of the *Xanax* and the alcohol.

Straight out, glass, water, tap, and straight back in locking the door. It had all taken about ten seconds. I sat myself down staring at the tablets and just thought, "right I better get started then."

The first ten I picked up and put in my mouth, gulping them down with a mouthful of water.

Second ten, rinse repeat.

Third ten, same again, but getting a wee bit more difficult to swallow now.

Fourth ten, I put them into my mouth two and three at a time. The way my mind worked was that the whole ten had to be swallowed, but I did feel the pull of sleep very strongly now.

I looked at the fifth and final pile and thought that I would just have a little rest and then swallow them. I had to take the fifty though, that was important.

Obsessive Compulsive Disorder, for me, reflected what being a 'speed freak' was like. Everything had to be done properly. I can remember spending hours lining up a pile of paper, as I could not quite get all the edges aligned.

I lay down where I was on the floor and drifted off to sleep. It was about ten pm.

Around two thirty am I abruptly awoke with the most ridiculous case of the munchies. I looked at the pile of ten still sitting there and thought that I still had to complete that. Pulling myself up from my now kneeling position, I never felt any ill effects, just a ravenous hunger normally associated with being stoned on cannabis.

As quietly as possible I opened the latch and crawled into the kitchen, remember at this point mum and dad had not seen me in a round three days. I got the bread out, good old Scottish plain bread, and took both heels, (outside slices) and buttered them.

Creeping back into my room, I latched the door as quietly as possible, and knelt at the pile of ten I had to complete. I ate my piece n butter first, though, then I looked at the pile. My eyes were heavy again though, and I just wanted to close them, so I did. Next thing I know, it is now around eight thirty am. I can hear noise of a house in full swing but could not really concentrate on it. My stomach was in agony. Extreme toothache type of agony, but deep in the pit of my stomach. It felt like someone had taken my intestines and twisted and twisted them until as tight as a guitar string – but this was no sweet lullaby they were playing.

As I made to stand up, I discovered that even this action multiplied the pain. I was in trouble, and I knew it.

And yet – as I looked on the last pile of ten paracetamol, I knew I had to hide the evidence. It would not do to let anyone see WHY I was in so much pain. I gingerly gathered them up and hid them at the bottom of the waste bin (it was actually a carrier bag for rubbish). I knew already no one would scoop through that, terrified of what they might find.

My mind was resolved that I had to go to the doctors, my problem was, its distance from our TOP FLOOR tenement.

I waited until there were no noises to be heard outside my door and began to, once again, quietly unlatch it. The pain in my gut now matched by the tension in the rest of my body as I strained to hear the slightest signs of life coming from elsewhere.

As I made my way to the outside door it was obvious walking was going to be difficult, each step matched by excruciating pain from my groin all the way up my chest. I got down the landing stairs, sneaking a look around from the front of the close to make sure no one was around and began to make my way out into the Quad.

Three steps – stop and rest.

Three steps – stop and rest.

Three steps – stop and rest.

All the way down by the shops, thankfully and unusually quiet, down Duntarvie by the clinic on the left and Donna's on the right. On down hoping no one would come out any of the closes. Passing by wee Bill's for the second time in twelve hours. The three storey high tenements on either side of Duntarvie towering above me like a canyon. The walls feeling, they were closing in. I honest thought I was going to pass out the pain was so severe.

At last I was at the end of Duntarvie and facing Westwood pitches. They seemed ten times longer than they ever had done though.

Three steps – stop and rest.

Three steps – stop and rest.

Three steps – stop and rest.

I got to just before the slope at the end of the red blaise and had to rest even longer, stopping and staring up at the sky. Nope. No help coming from there.

I had to get up though. On I travelled, through the shopping centre car park though, rather than the centre itself, hoping to avoid people. I was in agony, and yet the last thing I wanted to do was ask for help.

Eventually I found myself at Doctor Tobias' reception. Doctor Tobias had been our family doctor forever. His two children had attended Hutchesons (a few years ahead of me) and I always felt that he was kinder to me because of that. In my Hutchie days he would always be asking me how I was enjoying it. I had lied of course.

I found myself begging Gwen to let me in. Obviously, I did not have an appointment, but I hoped that she would relent. Gwen was and continued to be receptionist for Doctor Tobias, then his successor, Dr Dahmi for many years.

She got me in. "Yes Stuart, what can I do for you?"

"Ah've got a really bad sore stomach doctor."

"Oh really, do you know what happened?"

"Naw, ah just woke up this morning and it was killing me. It took me aboot an hour tae get here so it did. A hid tae stoap every three steps (that was true)."

Doctor Tobias checked me over and then asked me to pee into a bottle for him. At no point did I tell this wonderful doctor that I was in agony because I had swallowed forty paracetamol tablets. How ridiculously stupid was that?

Doctor Tobias, after a few moments prodding around again told me that I would just have to take it easy. He said that he would send the urine away to get tested and that I was to call back in two weeks.

That was it!

I made my way home, once again taking about ninety minutes to get there.

Still no one was at home, so I had a drink of water and crawled into bed.

When my mum returned home later that day, she saw my room door open and came in.

"Whit ye daein in bed? Ye awright?"

"Naw mum, ma stomach is killin me."

"Why? Where huv ye been? Three days you've been away fur. Nae word or nothing."

"Ah wis just oot ma, ah wisnae daein nothin. A went tae the doctors, he told me to pee in a bottle and then go hame and get some rest."

"Where hiv ye been?"

"Nae where, just oot."

"For three days!" tears rolling down her face.

"Aye."

It never occurred to me that my parents would think I was dead. It never occurred to me that I should have showed my face and let them know I was ok. In fact, it never occurred to me to think of anyone other than myself and what I wanted. I stayed in bed for about three days, and gradually by some miracle got better. I never let on to anyone what I had done.

Two weeks later I went to the doctors to get my results. This time the walk took all of ten minutes. I was very apprehensive about it. I was expecting to be confronted about that vast amount of paracetamol that showed in my urine.

"Stuart, nothing showed. There was nothing in your urine to explain why you felt so ill."

He went on to ask about how I had been and how long it took me to recover. I was convinced that he knew what I had done but could not be bothered dealing with it. Convinced!

I left the health centre quite annoyed that I had no reason for sympathy, and annoyed that he never acknowledges what I had done. I determined in my heart at that moment in time to not give a stuff about anyone.

As if I was doing anyway? Two years after leaving Hutchesons my life was already so badly messed up.

As a postscript to this chapter, not long after this moment, Doctor Tobias' daughters both graduated University. He celebrated, after devoting his whole professional life to giving his daughters the best education possible, by buying himself a small Jaguar convertible. Two weeks after this, Doctor Tobias died from a heart attack. No one knows what tomorrow will bring.

17 – THAT first time (1986)
Tiered Destruction

"For innocence lost, the same is the cost
The ride of your life, but you can never get off"
Oliver Oyanadel, Little Arson Annie: Short Stories [xiv]

"Paddy, gies a lennae a fiver, wee P has Tems and ah've only got a score (£20)."

K was very matter of fact. She knew I worked, she knew it was payday and she knew I would give her the fiver. I was like that. If I had it, you got it. I seriously thought though, that I would get the fiver back later.

I was 16, working in Alex Munro Butchers in the Buywell (Shandwick Square), and already hooked on speed and acid. In fact, anything at that point that would give me a buzz. J and the guys I mostly hung out with were speed freaks, with the odd acid tab and plenty of hash thrown in, but I had my feet firmly planted in both camps.

Another bunch of the locals were already mainline users. I was fascinated with my mates that injected, and I was very, very curious to try it. J (our very own Morten Harkett lookalike) for his part was constantly trying to persuade me to lose interest in it.

But I was always looking for excuses to leave wee T's house to go find them.

This night the excuse was to get my fiver back "so we can put it towards a deal" I lied. Not sure if I was even convinced by this. I had my own house at this point. K lived with her mum, just outside Easterhouse, but pretty much always hung about our area. When I hunted K down, to my very real surprise she handed me two of the little white tablets and said, "here is your fiver back". I protested, but not very much. As I said I was curious and wanted to try it.

So, I took them, and we went off searching for someone to give me my first "hit". We found P and up we went to my house. It was a proper mad situation. As we stood and put the tier around my left arm at the elbow (remember as curious as I was, I had never actually done this) I was looking at my arm like some passive witness instead of the owner.

"You've got great veins Paddy, this'll be easy". Of course, it wasn't and at one point we stood on my bare living room floor with blood spurting out of a hole in my arm. I mean seriously this was a fountain.

It took her a good six or seven attempts to get the holy grail of a "show of blood" in the needle. And the needle, man it wasn't the 1ml syringes I finished my addiction with, no this was a monster 10ml set with a proper spear on the end of it.

As I finally got the mixture in my veins, I don't know what I was expecting, but what I got was a big fat nothing. I was so disappointed! What was all the fuss about? All the others kept going on about the rush and the stone and the buzz. All I got was annoyed. I headed back down to T's to connect with the others. "Couldn't find her." I lied, as I never had the fiver, I said I had gone to get.

But J knew. At that point in my life, he was the closest I had to a real friend, as I didn't make friends easily.

I could see the disappointment in his eyes as he shook his head and walked back into the sitting room.

I remember waking up the next day and heading straight down to S's house. I knew he knew where to get more tems. And I was very stubborn. I wanted to experience what the others said they had experienced. S lived with his wife in her mother's house. Which happened to be next door to my sister. S laughed at me when I told him what I wanted.

"Don't be stupid ya eejit." He said. "You're better than that. You don't need them."

The more people tried to dissuade me from stuff, the more determined I was to do it. How stupid is that?

I finally found out where I could score. I made the long walk over to Provvy to where I knew these stubborn little tablets could be found.

I wanted so badly for them to unlock their secrets in me.

As I made my way back to my flat after scoring, I wondered how I was going to get those white chalky lumps inside my veins. Who could I trust that would not moan, or even worse, ask me to share? I hunted P down, and we made our way up the stairs. The dried blood staining the floor from the previous night's attempt was a forewarning of the future.

I paid nothing more than a passing glance and "I better clean that later." As we sat and went through the ritual of preparation all I could think was "This better be good!" No thought to what I might be beginning. No thought to the future. Just the immediate.

Tems in the works, add the hot water, shake till dissolved.

Tier on my left arm, just above the elbow.

Prepare the vein.

Grit the teeth.

Needle in.

Just the merest hint of red as the blood revealed that P had been on target this time.

As she gently began to push the plunger in, each mil of liquid pushing its way into my vein, my circulatory system, and finally my brain, it never occurred to me that each drop was wiping away the next 11 years of my life in a haze of opiate addiction.

All I was aware of was my heightened expectation as my whole consciousness focussed hard on the now. There it was, I could feel it. I could feel the rush of the drugs working their way through my system. I could feel the fog of opiate stone beginning to take over, and my body going limp under the sheer, counterfeit, bliss of it all.

As the last drop was pushed in, my first thought was, "How can I get more?"

18 – Another First Time (1986)
I feel sick

'The only person you are destined to become is the person you decide to be.'
Ralph Waldo Emerson

I had been taken *Temgesic*[xv] injections for a couple of weeks. My dogged pursuit of getting the rush had made me oblivious to the obvious dangers I knew I was placing myself in.

And yet I carried on doing it. Getting up, going out looking to score, sneaking back into the house (if I got in without being noticed I could sneak into my room and have a fix in peace.)

I learned very quickly to inject myself. I had good veins. Easy to inject into. I ended up being the one that would give a lot of our crew their injections.

That was life. One day after only a couple of weeks, I remember waking up and just not feeling right. I had the sweats. It didn't feel like a cold, but it did. My body had a real restlessness going on in it as well. My nose was running, and almost as soon as I was out of bed I needed to run to the loo.

I couldn't think straight. I couldn't settle.

Then the thought came rushing into my head - "I need a fix!".

I had been around guys hitting up long enough to know what withdrawal felt like. I had heard their stories, now I knew personally. Within weeks of my first injection, I had moved from a psychological craving - I wanted it because I wanted it - to a physiological one. As soon as I realised, I was strung out, it was like every cell and every thought now centred on that one thing - I needed a fix.

I knew I had some change in my pocket, but would it be enough to go and score a "*Tem*"? They weren't expensive in the bigger picture of drug abuse - £2 - but if you never had it then it might as well have been a million pounds.

I fumbled around the jumbled clothes on my floor looking for my jeans and pulling them over, I reached into the pocket. The sweats now increasing with the nervous hope and anxious fear that there would be enough to score.

Success!!!!

I had just over £2. I had enough. It was funny how, over the years, completing the £2 would change to the £2.50 (also early price for *LSD*) as inflation hit the drugs market – then £5 (price of a bag of *Amphetamine Sulphate – speed*) and eventually £10 (completing the tenner) as I graduated onto *heroin*.

The nervous hope and the anxious fear though, would soon be replaced by trying to ensure the morning's medication was always under my pillow the night before.

That was the struggle I had thrown myself into by petulant disregard for the warnings.

"It won't happen to me; I know what I'm doing!" The refrain of almost every addict the first time or two they take their poison.

I got up, got ready and sneaked out the door, not even aware if anyone else was in the house or even what time it was. I was sixteen years old, and I was on my way around the corner to score because I was strung out and I needed a fix.

The nervous chap at the door, followed by the "Ye gote any?"

"Aye, how many ye wantin?"

"Jist wan, but ah'll get some cash then in be back fur mair. Will ye have them?" (This was an important question that could save much anxiety later).

"Aye, how many dae ye think? Ah'll keep them by fur ye?"

"Don't know but at least wan."

That was a quick escalation, up to this point I had only been taking one a day, because I wanted to, yet the first day I was aware I needed to I immediately wanted at least two, just in case one wasn't enough to keep the withdrawals away.

As I made my way back around Duntarvie Road, up Duntarvie Quad, around the path in front of our block, in the close and up both flights of stairs I became aware of an incredible phenomenon - actually having the drug in my possession - almost feeling its power rushing through my veins - the withdrawals already began to wane a bit.

It was surreal. It heightened the expectation of the rush I was about to get. All I could focus on was getting that beautiful little white tablet dissolved in the massive hypodermic I used in those days and seeing the blood and pushing the plunger

Minutes later, as I lay on my bed enjoying the sensation mixed with relief, the thought began to creep into my head - I need around £1.50 for another *Tem*. I need to hurry because he might run out of them.

At that moment the swirling rush, the opiate intoxication is, whilst not pushed away, balanced out by the rush of thoughts as my brain computes ways in which I can manage to complete the £2.

Like a sat nav calculating all the different ways to a destination, on my brain went - every possible scenario that would include me chapping that door to get another - and back here on my bed.

Today! Now! Stuart - this NOW is your life! Welcome!

19 – Flashbulb Memory (1987)
A wee snapshot

Flashbulb memory is a special kind of emotional memory, which refers to vivid and detailed memories of highly emotional events that appear to be recorded in the brain as a picture taken by camera.

I have struggled to write moments from my life. I wondered at the ability for others to seemingly do it quite easily, and yet I can't. So much of the past is disconnected. Memories are vague snapshots seen through the fog of time. Glimpsed neurological stimulations that flash momentarily as electricity prods them, looking for something to stir me.

In this wee chapter I want to try and give a sort of collective memory – a snapshot – of life growing up in Easterhouse – or more specifically – the Quad.

There is the beginning of the walk up to Calderpark Zoo, my dad, the very young Neil and me.

I am holding Neil and vaguely remember having him on my shoulder, but that is it.

No memories of lions or tigers or anything else. Just a glimpse of a walk-through Baillieston to the back gate. The back gate being synonymous with East End life itself, why pay in when you could go through the back gate?

Then the family walk with our good friends, the Johnston's. Somehow ending up at a place with two Rolls Royce cars parked outside and the two dads claiming one as their own. Probably nostalgically stoked by Bruce Springsteen's "*Our pa's each own one of the World Trade Centres…*" from the song Glory Days. How pertinent.

Then my old buddy Michelle, as we were late teens talking about the song "*Holding Back the Years*" and how we wished we could all go back to the long gone innocent days of our early teens in the Quad.

We were still teenagers!!!!

Out of that emotional trigger comes the Quad itself. Alive and vibrant with all the gang.

Don's ghetto blaster blasting out in the ghetto. All of us hanging at the wall. Doing nothing and yet at the same time doing everything. We were a pretty decent crowd, most of the time. Don himself then appears. One of the nicest guys you could ever meet. That reminds me of Dons Mum, Mrs Weaver was awesome. Big lady with a big heart.

To get to Don's from the Quad, you had to pass Duntarvie shops. Our shops. Stuck up a side street. For most of us that was an echo of how our lives would be.

My earliest memory of the shops was the giant billboard advertisement for UB40's "*Signing Off*". An image of a UB40 (Unemployment signing on card). Strange place to see it, but then Duntarvie was always a strange place to see everything.

I will come back to the shops, I want to hang out in the Quad for a wee while again. I could not tell you what any of our conversations used to be about. But I loved that we were there.

The wee wall that we all sat around. The gathering point. Even our parents did not really mind as they all knew where we were.

My mum could see me from our top flat tenement window only 100 yards away, and in those days even she did not really mind.

Still, this does then take me down to the doorway marked "STUUAARRTT" that would cry out at the most awkward and embarrassing times.

For dinner, to come up at night, or even the Drummy Milk Float adventure (another story).

Each of us was a victim of the parent call at one time or another, but when it was someone else's turn we laughed and slagged mercilessly.

The Quad then wakens the two-man hunt memories. These were brilliant. Started off as two of us having to hunt everyone else down and catch the others, sometimes there were a LOT of others. Then they would join the chase.

Absolutely brilliant fun. Exciting days of youth with no boundaries. No worries. No cares. Just fun.

Then there were the dens! How we loved these towering edifices we built at the back of Fitzy's. We took great delight in them and we were very selective over who could come in.

Building materials were gathered from a variety of empty tenement flats. The former shutters of plywood sheets were the perfect material for us. As the city council devised new ways to keep us out, we devised new ways to bypass them. I remember Andy being the first to remove the big fibreglass boards with the metal tension bands.

The sheer joy of removing doors, and then talking about how we were going to build them.

We were a tight group. We didn't really think about how wrong it was to break into the empty tenement's, only that we needed the doors etc. When we were bored with the dens, they became a bonfire. We were so proud when, one den, took days to burn out. As far as we were concerned that was a sign of our (mostly Fitzy's) craftsmanship.

Dens at Fitzys then reminds me of music at the McGills. They lived in a bottom flat at Easterhouse Quad, and one of the brothers, Donald, used to blare music out the window. He wasn't part of our gang, as in he didn't hang about with us or anything.

He had music though. Loud music, and requests too at that back window. Our own private disco. We all would hang about there at daytime when he did that.

We really did spend a lot of time hanging about. Donald had quite an eclectic taste in music, so we really could expect to hear anything.

Music then reminds me of Paula. Paula Mulligan's family lived in the flat beneath us in the Quad. When it was only Paula and her gang that were in, then U2 was blasted out. I didn't mind, I liked U2. Maybe I should leave a pause here before I get stuck in a moment I can't get out of.

Paula, Lizzy, Joyce, Alison, Joanne others too. They were a great bunch. Always involved in community stuff. Never up to anything "too bad".

A large portion of our evenings were always spent walking around the block. For us, for the most part, this would be up through the two Quads, around Easterhouse Road, down Aberdalgie to Duntarvie and then back up the Quad.

As the Quad Young Team (QYT), this was our turf. At other times we would walk all the way around Easterhouse Road to the opposite end of Aberdalgie at Westwood Secondary and back up to Duntarvie and the Quad that way.

Taking in most of Aggro, the larger gang area we were from. It would not be uncommon for up to twenty of us to be doing this. Just talking and walking, as it would also be not uncommon for the police to stop us and tell us we could only walking groups of two or three.

So, a group of two or three, ten yards behind, another group, ten yards behind..., you get the picture, funnily enough, the police never had a problem when we did that.

I spoke in another chapter about God's gift of the imagination. Fuelled by the most incredible supercomputer the world has ever, (or will ever) see – our brain. As I sit here, it's mind-blowing that I can picture these scenes and be transported back in time to them.

Easterhouse really was a concrete jungle in those says. For the most part, the tenements might only have been three storeys high, but there was a lot of them.

They never seemed too far away from the roads, separated only by smallish front gardens, alternating award-winning 'landscaping' and overgrown jungles. That gave the impression of pebble-dashed canyons, having to be navigated through to get from where you are to where you wanted to be.

Our area circled around Blairtummock Primary and the pitches, so we had a wee bit more open space than most. Blairtummock Primary, ah the memories. In my teenage years, we would climb the roof, (not during school hours) as part of our jump games. Seeing who could do the most outrageous jumps. Some of the guys were very good at it. The jumps would also take us over all manner of gable ends and fences. By today's standards of parkour probably tame, but we were wild and carefree and had nothing to compare it to, so it was pure dead brilliant.

Then there were the pitches and that meant - football. On every bit of grass or open street, there would be a ball getting kicked. One on one, two aside, three aside, beat the goalie whatever. Two jackets and a ball were all you needed. But when there was enough to get a proper game, it would either be the grass on Aberdalgie, or the pitches. That wonderfully beautiful, torturous red blaise!

It seemed like it was designed in the tortured mind of some adult who was always last picked in school or at football and saw this as his revenge. Wee red stones in their millions, that if you were a victim in a scheme tackle, not only grazed open your knees but ground in the dust of the red blaise, just for full effect.

Ah, how I miss those injuries. He really must have had some grudge. Some of our "enough for a full game" games were about 20 a side. You couldn't leave anyone out.

They were wonderfully reflective of all that was great about scheme life. Nearly all the local youth (or so it seemed) playing a very competitive type of football. But all together. They were normally 'up to 21' but it wasn't uncommon to hear the cry of "next goal is the winner".

Then it was up to the house for a gallon of water, and back out to the Quad, or whatever street you hung out on. Disappearing, once again into the memory cells of time.

This chapter is just very brief snapshots of a wander down my own memories. It is hard to do justice to the rich vibrancy our brains can bring to these moments. The smells, the tastes, the laughter and even the tragic tears are all as real now as they were then.

I hope you have enjoyed this all to brief time out from my normal chapter type.

20 – Knives (1987)
CHAP! CHAP! CHAP!

"During the 70s, 80s, 90s and 00s the same gangs would remain, young men would be confined to their own area like a jail, scared to walk 10 minutes into a different street for fear of being attacked." Peter Cassidy *Glasgow Live*[xvi]

When writing your life story, it is usual to share from your past. Some of the horror – yes; shame – absolutely. However, the goal is to elicit sympathy, to make the readers want to read more and keep them onside.

But is that really a true retelling? By this time, I was already a thoroughly unlikeable person. I hope that you are getting that, reader? I did what suited me. I acted in ways, already, that only benefitted me.

Yes, I obviously had issues – but let's face it – who didn't. This chapter opens with a quote from a 2018 article on the *Glasgow Live* website. It talks about the gangs etc. in the 70's, 80's and 90's.

That's me!

I am one of those nameless people referred to. Whilst most of the youth in Easterhouse were making the most of the life they had and trying their best, I was one of the anti-social worst.

Unless I can get across to you how thoroughly negative a person I was in these next ten or so years, then I have failed. The normal is though, that unless you are a well-known personality, a media massive figure, then you do not want to go too far in being truthful.

Sometimes though, things are just so topical, and you have experience in them, that you have to share the things that may make people dislike you.

On the streets of Easterhouse, when I ran with the gang (Easterhouse Young Aggro) I carried knives. This is an easily verifiable fact as my second and third criminal charges were for carrying a concealed weapon. Both times the weapons I was charged with carrying were steak knives. Not the smaller ones dished out in a restaurant, but larger carving knives. I have used a knife, and I have been the victim of knife (and other weapons) crime.

The reality is that if you carry a knife you are 100% more likely to use it than if you didn't. I was seventeen years old. Not everyone in the gang jumped about 'carrying' but a few of us did. The only reason I can give you is – that we did.

Not because of defensive reasons or anything like that, but just because that is what we did. I cannot even remember how I was caught the first time. It was probably one of the random stops and searches that the Police carried out on us in those days. The second though, that stands out for many reasons.

A lot of the times it would have been a smaller lock back knife I would have carried. Some of my friends and I used to take great delight in carrying butterfly knives, so called because of their double handles that closed over the blade. You could show off your handling of these.

Picture the scene, it's a late in the year evening (I know this because it was dark). A few of us were hanging about at 2 Duntarvie Quad, a grey tenement block next to where I lived.

As well as being a part of Easterhouse Young Aggro, we also identified as Young Quad Team, as that is where we hung about. EYA and YQT were territorially marked in almost every close and street in our area.

Anyway, we were all hanging about the front entrance of the six flat tenement block – two on each floor – three storeys high. The Docherty's lived on the bottom left, and beyond that I cannot quite remember. Next thing two beat cops appeared from nowhere. I panicked as I knew I had the knife on me. I was the only one that night. I ran to the back of the close and, unusually, the back door was locked.

Running back to the front looking for somewhere to hide the knife, I panicked and placed it on top of the relatively high fuse box.

The two policeman walked in and started firing questions at us, "Whit ye up tae?" The first one said.

"Nowt!" says F. "Staunin here cos wur bored."

"Really?" Says number 2. "Then whit did he run away fir then?" Obviously pointing straight at me.

"Ah couldnae be annoyed." I said. "Ma da would have a fit if ah goat in any mair trouble." (Prophetic statement alert.)

They made us all stand with our hands out, they had already called for a car. Searching us one by one and then, searching the close. If I hadn't run that night, I would probably have got away with it. But run I did, and they knew enough to know that we only tried to run if we had something to hide. They searched even more intently. One of the younger guys looked anxiously at fuse box.

"Yah numpty" I screamed inside my head. "Yah 4444444 numpty" as obviously as soon as he looked up, the two policemen looked up.

"Ah wonder who this belangs tae?" says number 1 while reaching up and pulling down my wooden handled steak knife. All twelve inches of it, with the blade being about eight. Turning around and looking straight at me.

"Right own up or yir aw getting the jail."

"Nane ae us hid that." says F.

"Well yir aw coming tae the station then."

"It's mine. Ah pit it thair."

"Why you cairyin this aboot wi ye then?"

"Ah need it tae defend masel." I replied. (As previously stated, I did not need it. There was no one after me. We were in the middle of our area, but it was the stock answer),

"The rest aw yis, beat it." And they did. Whilst giving me stupid looks for being stupid enough to get caught with a knife. I wasn't the only one that usually carried one out of that group – but I was the only one that night.

"That's Paddy's boy." says number 2. Even some of the Police called my dad by his nickname. "Ah know whit tae dae wi him." They put the handcuffs on me, hands behind my back style. Made me walk down the path, turn to the left, thirty

71

yards turn left again, up the close, two flights of steps, with our door being right at the top of the stairs of 4 Duntarvie Quad.

CHAP! CHAP! CHAP! That unmistakable police chap of the door.

What seemed like eternity, but in reality, about twenty seconds later, the door was answered by my incensed mum.

One look at them, then at me then back to them. Not a word !

"Is MR Patterson in?" says number 1.

"John, somebody at the door."

"Who is it?"

"Ye better come oot."

"Ah fur 4444 sake," was all I could hear.

It is impossible to write how I was feeling. I am sure you understand that this was NOT normal Police procedure.

BUT

For me this was the worst possible thing they could have done. My dad came to the door, his face turning purple when he saw 5'7" of me between two very tall (over 6' police officers, it was the 80's).

"Whit the 4444 dae yous want? Whits he done noo?" Without saying a word, number one unfolded the concealed steak knife from behind his right forearm into full view. The grin on his face.

"Yah stupid we 88888888. Whit ye daein wae that?" Way to go dad. Vote of confidence. Guilt assumed.

"He has been cautioned and will have to come up to the station tomorrow to be formally charged, but can we leave him with you this evening?"

"Get in ya eejit." as he dragged me in the door and walloped me on the back of my head.

This was a triple blow. Not only had I been carrying a knife, something my dad, quite hypocritically thought I shouldn't be, I had got caught – and the worst of all – I had brought the Police to the door.

Of all three that is probably the worst. The unpardonable sin was bringing the police to the door.

Everything else could be skelped out of you. I knew I was in trouble.

The justice side of the trouble was eventually a £150 fine and eighteen months' probation. (I saw my probation officer at the beginning and the end, that was it).

The worse side was my dad telling me to get into my room. He was ashamed of me. Expecting a tirade – I got silence. If you knew Paddy Patterson, then you knew that was worse. Much worse.

Unfortunately for me I was too stupid to learn. I also worked in the butchers' shop at that time and had access to some bad knives. I had a couple of other serious incidents with knives, of which I am not sure even now I am ready to talk about.

Again, though, if you carry a knife you are one hundred per cent more likely to use it than if you didn't.

21 - Weekend at Baird Street (1987)
Not quite doon the watter

Making time stand still. Now there's a gift. The ability to actually make time seem like it has been halted and that you truly are paused in the moment.

Bank holiday weekends can seem like that. You know, when you finish on a Friday and you KNOW that there is now work until Tuesday. And then when you start back on Tuesday you know that your week is shorter because you now have a four day week. Now that is controlling time.

The weekend is just so much more enjoyable because of it. Who knows, you may even plan a weekend away - different accommodation - different sights - rest!!!.It's great, isn't it? Your Sunday is extended until Tuesday, because (and let's be honest here) the reality of a long weekend does not really kick in until you realise that you do not have to go to work the next day (or uni).Then...BLISS...waking up on Monday morning, about to drag your lifeless corpse out of bed and it hits you, in your sleep-deprived mind..........BANK HOLIDAYYYYYYYYYAnd turn over and go back to sleep.NOWWWWW!

In the Bible, Joshua managed it, (Joshua 10:12-14 NKJV). It was for help whilst he battled against five kingdoms at the same time (and you thought you had problems). He was pretty much showing off as to how God was on his side, and he could drag out time for the infliction of misery on his foes. He knew how to 'show off' his God's power.

But I don't want to talk about either work bank holidays making time stand still, or (SHOCK HORROR) Biblical leaders making time standing still.I want to talk about another authority that, seemingly, had the power to make the sun stand still, time come to a pause, and basically, inflict torture on you for no other reason than, well, they could.

Let me set the scene, in my youth I would have had outstanding warrants, that is, I may not have paid fines or Strathclyde Police (in the days before the joining of the forces into Police Scotland), may have wanted to bring me in for a nice polite chat about some things they wanted to talk about.

I might have been a suspect in an unsolved crime, they thought I was guilty, they wanted to charge me. In the lead up to a bank holiday weekend, whilst all you of a non-criminal disposition were excited about it, those of us that knew Scotland's finest wanted a word with us, were extra careful after midnight on a Thursday, (or is that Friday). That was the magic hour when Strathclyde Police and every other

73

Stuart Patterson

police authority knew that they could hold us over until Monday, or on especially looong bank holidays - Tuesday. This was one of those especially loooong bank holidays.

It was called a long weekender!!!!!!!!!! We all hated them.

The sign of a police car, especially when you had outstanding warrants, after midnight on a Thursday (or was it Friday) caused all sorts of fight or flight notions to rise up. (Note to non-lawbreaking reader - flight was always better in these instances).

Let me try and explain why that was important. It's after midnight. Even in summertime Scotland it is dark at this time. For whatever reason, you find yourself in the back seat of a police car, whilst they are doing a warrants check on you. For the most part, they already knew you had one, and that is why they decided to stop YOU. This was all about prolonging the agony of what was to come.

If (when) arrested you would be brought to your local police station to be interviewed, or if a warrant for arrest had been issued, to be thrown in a cell. In my case that would be Easterhouse police station, next door to my old (well my final out of three) secondary (not high) school - Westwood.

The police car parked in their high-security car park (the wall was at least eight feet) and taken out with the handcuffs on, you were marched up to the very strong and safe back door. Entry was sought from those that were inside via intercom, and obviously, granted.

Marched around to the charge desk, and presented to the custody sergeant (as he was about to take legal ownership of you) "Do you have any sharp objects or anything else in your pocket that we should know about?" "State your full name" (I am making most of the questions up now, as I don't really remember them all, but it was along these lines)."Stuart Patterson you are being detained under ...yap yap yap", stopped listening because it was Thursday night (or was it Friday morning) and I was now taking up some timeshare with Her Majesty's constabulary.

Searched, strip searched, degrading but probably necessary, although the drugs were normally long ditched by this point. All laces, belts and anything else you could use against yourself removed. Then you were turned around, marched down the wee corridor just behind, "Cell 4" or whatever.

The stark light from the overhead bulb in the middle of the faded painted concrete roof ensures there is no hiding place, but where would you hide in this small rectangle anyway? A raised concrete kerb that doubles for a bed sits at the end with a with a wiry wool blanket for company. There is a window running parallel to the ceiling at the top of the wall. I sat window, but it is an opening covered over with an external grill that allows light to filter through but not sight to stare out.

In the left-hand corner as you come in the door is a toilet bowl. That's all, no sink or anything just a very basic toilet. Nothing else for it so you lie down to try and sleep, what else to do with all this time, but think. And you really don't want to do that.

Just as you feel yourself drifting off... BANG! BANG! BANG! "Are ye awrite in there?"

74

"Whit?"

"Are ye awrite?" Every hour they hammer on the door if they have to work why should you get to sleep. The alleged purpose was to make sure you had not self-harmed, the effect was it made you want to.

Early, very early on the Friday morning, (definitely not Thursday night), you are told to get ready.

Hooray. Bank holiday day trip. When I was younger, much younger than that day, it would be trips doon the watter to Helensburgh or Saltcoats. Normally on the train. Today it would be a bus, well actually a van we had nicknamed "re meatwagon".

Inside the back door of this van was a metal cage door, just to remind you how you were seen. This was no ordinary day trip though, you were going to some luxurious weekend accommodation. As Easterhouse was in 'D' Division of Strathclyde Police, you were taken to the cells at 'D' Division headquarters at Baird Street Police Station. A mainly four-storey brown, bland building just north of the city centre.

The cells had their own 'tower block' and you were all gathered together from all over the division for the weekend. Offloaded into the charge desk, I was processed (dear reader this would have happened to me quite a few times, and if I was really lucky I would go all the way up to Maryhill Police Station, a totally different divisional headquarters, as there was no room at the inn, Baird Street).

I would be taken up in the elevator to whatever floor I was staying on. As there were no rooms with a view, it didn't really matter, how high I was, life never felt any lower.

The cells were roughly the same tiny dimensions with the same concrete bed and the same utility toilet.

I would be given my blanket, walk inside to the grey coldness and that horrible clunking noise behind me. No matter your opinion of how cushy prisons maybe, a police station cell door clunking closed behind you, with the noise moving in waves around you, let you know you were going nowhere.

Neither that day nor in life.

If you were really lucky and loved, the family may drop in a change of clothes, food or even, newspapers. But, by my third time doing weekenders my family had refrained from doing this. I think the hope was that I would take stock of my situation and make the necessary changes.

I would rather have had the newspapers.

There was no recreation time unless you count the hourly, "Ye awrite in there?" as rec.

No time out of the cell.

Lying on the cold concrete grave, I enjoyed the holiday by thinking of my cold dead dreams. Non-payment of fines weekenders were straightforward, you would go to the court that issued it, and they would give you time in lieu of payment. A charge would mean that you would go to court on the Monday, or if you were really lucky like I was this time, the Tuesday, (it's a bank holiday long weekender remember), for a pleading diet and bail hearing.

That ceiling really needed the paint freshening up. That's a lot of initials scratched into the wall. EYA, DYT, GYT, Calton Tongs, Drummy ya bass - Gang tags everywhere. I wonder if anyone was ever charged with malicious damage for writing on a cell wall?

Key in lock, "Stand up, against the wall with your hands out by your side where we can see them!" roared the voice through the letter/foodbox.

Jumped to my feet. Back against the wall, hands by my side where they, (it was only a he) could see them. "Ye awrite."

"Aye"

"Ye don't have any newspapers dae ye?"

"Naw, no this time."

"Here, theres a Daily Record for ye. Ah've read it." Some of them were ok. They were guys just doing a job, and would offer a kind word, and a bit of grace. Some of them. He stood and chatted nothings for a few minutes. Then the door clunked closed, and the noise waved its sarcasm at me for a few seconds. Then back to the paintwork and history etchings. Dinner was normally a fish or sausage supper from a local chippy, too cold to enjoy by the time I got it.

Friday. Saturday. Sunday. Monday.

Weekend at Baird Street. My life at this point was like the film, Weekend at Bernies, where Andrew McCarthy and Jonathan Silverman have to get through a whole weekend, pretending their boss, (who had taken out a hit on them) was still alive.

The hitman is out to take the boss out, long story old film. But our heroes had to lump about a dead body everywhere, pretending he was still alive during an American bank holiday long weekend.

It was all to stave off the consequences of him being dead.

I was dead. In the sense that all-purpose all hope had been robbed of my life. I was dead to what other people thought of me. I was dead to any serious contemplation of how to change my circumstances. The only difference in the plot was that it was me carrying my body of death around with me.

Pretending that all was ok. Pretending that I knew what I was doing, while death reigned in my mortal body. There was no way out, either of this cell or my life. I truly was a dead man walking.

Tuesday morning, early to rise, stuff in a bag, down the elevator joining with the other guests. We swapped exciting stories about why we were here. An instant camaraderie between us – we were al in this together, unless you didn't want the other guys to know why you were in. Into the holding room, ready for our morning transport.

This morning we were off to the relatively new Glasgow Sheriff Court. I have written previously of how I had the honour of being one of the first people through its doors in its opening Monday. The cells in the Sheriff Court are probably no more than 10' by 6'. On the front is a door with a very large caged window door, and at the rear is a stainless steel toilet with a sink over it. There could be up to eight people in each cell, and hundreds in the court at any given time.

The cells were crammed, and if you had someone that was anti-social, or was nervous about disclosing why they were in court, it could be a very tense time. No privacy, no space. Be dead to it all.

Moved from one cold grey box to another early morning, but the court for the custody prisoners was always the afternoon. Pre court, the voice walks along stamping feet and shuffling keys, all noises, and calls out the names that are going in this sitting. Moved to a larger holding cell, sitting waiting on your name being called again.

Not a number yet still a name.

My turn, along another corridor, and up the stairs that brings me right into a very large, brightly lit room. Prisoner officer at my side, whispering instructions. Time for the body to be told where the likely destination is for the next part of its charade of a life. If only there truly were some way of walking out THIS prison door and entering into life.

22 - The road to nowhere (1988)
Parklife - what a trip

"Well we know where we're going, But we don't know where we've been
And we know what we're knowing, But we can't say what we've seen
And we're not little children, And we know what we want
And the future is certain, Give us time to work it out"
Road to Nowhere lyrics © Warner/Chappell Music, Inc

Blairtummock Park. It's not very large, but it is pregnant with memories for me and others that grew up in our area. As a four or five-year-old, it was Aunt Alice's office at lunchtime and the toy cars in the desk drawer in her first-floor office in the beautiful old Blairtummock House.

A wee bit older and it was how endless the road along it seemed (it's only a few hundred yards).

As I mentioned at the start of the book, we lived in Baldinnie Road for the first couple of years. Our ground floor tenement backed onto the park and it was great. As a youngster, it was like living in the country. After our back garden there was a wee red blaise football pitch and then the park road.

Buchlyvie Street was just along the back a bit and it went all the way up to Easterhouse Road, (which at the age of 5 seemed miles away). I just HAVE TO write about Buchlyvie Street at some point. The most wonderfully crazy street with some of the greatest families and memories you could ever know. But not yet. I remember how busy the park used to be in the summer. There were always families there. The two bowling greens were constantly in use by older people that would snarl at us kids if we dared to try and set foot on the most immaculately manicured lawns in all Easterhouse.

They were also fenced off with a green fence that seemed about 10' tall, but, was only 4'. Blairtummock Park was the one place where the Blairtummock part of Easterhouse could be mistaken for any small town or village anywhere in Scotland. The bowling greens faced the house itself, and we used to run around the house playing tig. There would always be loads of kids.

At one point, just to the other side of the bowling greens, a fantastic skateboarding ramp was built. It was great. There always seemed to be hundreds of kids all vying for their shot on it.

A "cinema" was set up and it was always packed with kids wanting their first taste of the big screen. Every Saturday morning in Blairtummock House I was introduced to the wonder of Flash Gordon and Buck Rodgers in the 25th Century. Both the original, black and white versions. There was always a load of cartoons on as well, and it was a treat I really used to look forward to. The house was always a wonder. Linda Shergold, one of my primary school classmates lived in the caretaker's apartment there.

We always used to think they must have been very rich. Mr Shergold always had a drawer full of sweets for visitor's kids. Different, very innocent days.

I remember how I used to stare through the gate of the garden next to the house. It was walled off but did open occasionally. What a treat it was on those days to wander around it. Around the late 70's, at the height of the skateboarding craze, the large wooden skateboarding ramp was built just after the bowling greens. It was always packed. Some kids were excellent on it.

Me? I was delighted if I could get down the ramp without falling off. One time, after skating successfully and being so excited at the thought of doing it twice in a row that I ran up the ramp, only to be belted in the face with a skateboard by someone who had come off and was on their way down.

Head split open, bit of blood, part of the fun, part of growing up - in those days. A hanky was applied to the wound, and I carried on, still determined for my two in a row.

I don't quite know when things began to change in the park. It was subtle, though, very subtle. The movie shows would stop showing. The bowling greens became quieter and quieter. The ramp was just gone one day.

More people would be drinking in the park. As teenagers, we would go there to drink with our cargo. We knew we would get peace and quiet. There was a wee bit more violence beginning to creep in there as well.

Then you blink and the House is closed, the bowling greens are closed, families don't seem to be hanging around there anymore. Just groups of local youth, at first with the drinking, and the fighting. In the late 80's, it was us with our acid trips, but this would be at night when no one else was around. That was where we named the road "*Road to Nowhere*" after the Talking Heads song of the same name. This place of family fun and frolics was different at night, under the influence of LSD. The trees, leaning over from both sides of the road TIL their tops almost touched, forming a tunnel seemed to breathe, with their branches daring you to walk past that they may grab you, like some B movie horror.

The House end of the park could not be seen in the gloomy darkness. The darkness itself seemed to possess an eerie life all its own. The distorted perspective of LSD haze. Grass was no longer grass, but long fingers reaching out for you. The buzz - that was to walk from the Buchlyvie Street end to Blairtummock House end on your own and not freak out. (Freaking out was when the LSD paranoia kicked in and you lost it).

There was always a group of us, and that heightened the fear and expectation. That was the crazy thing about LSD, though, this is what heightened the experience of the drug and made it so addictive.

It was always a fight to see who would go first, with the loser winning. I can still taste the fear that used to wash itself around my mouth and my mind as LSD induced imagination would kick in.

Each step was forced in fear, and yet eager in expectation. The surrealness of the moment captured in the leaves scraping against each other as they sought to freak us out, the grass whistling in the wind and the darkness deafening in its silence.

Euphoria! Steps of Blairtummock House. Next one up.

There were other times and other places we would go to test our LSD mettle, but Blairtummock Park sticks out because of how innocent it was in my first years.

It is only a place, but we connect memories to these places and form emotional attachments. Even this, those tarnished memories tainted by my years of addiction - even this it seems God has redeemed.

The days I was in a park facing class in college, I always stared wistfully out the window at my old friend, remembering with fondness the innocence of childhood in Easterhouse. Being reminded that God had me born into a family that would live laugh love and yes even cry here. God had me create lifelong friendships here. God would call me back to that road to nowhere and show me - with Him I am going somewhere.

23 - Silver Fine (1988)
One hair at a time

Moving from some wavy hair
All messed up, everywhere
Now I'm out in the posh west end
I need hair that sets a trend
So, uncle John, to the barbers with me
"Stuart, it needs a change, come let's see"
Into the 'hairdressers?' queue line
Four hours later with silver fine
Stuart Patterson ©2019

I sat in a barber's chair in Paisley the other day. I am a guy that keeps his hair short, so that is an almost monthly occurrence. Roberto had messed with my head by changing his premises around and moving. I like familiarity so that was slightly more uncomfortable than it should have been – barbers – number one back and sides with scissors and thinners on top. I order the same every time.

Yep, I still have enough hair to require thinners. Anyway, here I was November 2018 in the upstairs unit in The Paisley Centre with Ali snipping away at my hair. I like Ali, he is very chatty and friendly and asks a lot about Jesus and the church.

This time, as I looked at my reflection in an almost vain sort of way and I saw the silver (I prefer silver to grey) hair standing out, my chair became a time machine.

It was Partick, summer 1988 and I was in a hairdresser getting my hair done. It wasn't a number one, not even scissors or thinners. Nope, a lady was pulling my hair through a rubber thing over my head.

One hair at a time! Tugging! It took hours! Why was I putting myself through such torture? Why had I agreed to sit in this chair, surrounded by west end woman all getting their hair done?

Why? I was getting my hair dyed – silver fine. Here I was paying (a fair wee bit) to get my hair looking like it would naturally over thirty years later.

If you have got this far, then well done. You are already aware that my mid-teens were not an especially happy or productive time. In fact, I was screwed up – badly. In some memories, I talked about my mum's search for respite and a break.

Well, there is a place in the West End of Glasgow where I used to go for just that purpose.

It was like a wee piece of heaven on earth in the early days. Many times, I went to stay with Aunty June and Uncle John.

Whiteinch was council housing. It was still tenements – BUT – it was another world from Easterhouse. Bright white modern looking flats. The old railway track, the Clyde only a stone's throw away. The high flats (Curle Street) Victoria Park – and Partick and Byres Road. They were all fantastic. But that is not what the attraction to Whiteinch was. My wee cousin Paul, and my big cousins Lynn and Karen were always so good. I had a great friendship with Paul, it was not long after this though when I made one of those long-term consequences choices that included Paul.

There was Aunty June. The oldest of the Kiernan siblings, my mum's big sister. The sweetest woman you could or would ever meet – and I have her for an aunt. She would always bring me to hers from trips to nanas. I loved the bus out to the West End. Or the train depending on how she was feeling. It was like a trip to the twilight zone. Partick just seemed so different. And memory being what it is, these trips always seemed to be at night.

I remember times staring open-eyed at Partick Library's beautiful stone building. So different from the bland Easterhouse structure that was part of the shopping centre.

Then there was Uncle John. Uncle John was the man that taught me to shave. To have some self-respect, and treated me with respect, even though I did not deserve it. He got me a job with Smith & Son Haulage contractors (steam cleaning curtain side trailers – a gloriously filthy job). He gave me a bed. During a very difficult time in my life Uncle John was like a surrogate dad to me.

He was that good. Uncle John was a quiet man, which was unusual for a shipyard welder, but quiet he was. He enjoyed a wee drink in the house on a Friday night, wasn't a pub man. He enjoyed the football, especially taking Paul (occasionally me as well) and coaching him from the side lines.

John was a fiercely protective family man. For brief periods in my madness, Uncle John and Aunty June allowed me to be a normal teenager.

I could not handle it. I was just out of prison after being on remand for the drug offences when I went to stay with them for six months. I had a beard and long wavy, dark brown hair.

It was John that suggested I do something with my hair. He suggested streaks or something. Just for a change.

"A new start, Stuart. Time for a change."

So that was how I found myself sitting a barber's shop, 30 years before Roberto, Ali and Paisley. Four hours in a chair, having individual hairs dragged through a rubber cap and dye applied to them. Four hours sitting there waiting on chemicals doing the work that age and experience have taken thirty years to replicate.

Four hours and then my silver fine hair, much shorter as well, was revealed. I must admit I think it suited me.

Until today, I don't think my hair has ever looked as good as it did in that moment.

I couldn't wait to get back and show my Uncle John and Aunty June.

Uncle John and Aunt June were fantastic. They loved me and gave me a home and treated me like a son for every one of those days. I am not so sure I repaid them with similar respect.

I stayed in Whiteinch for around six months. It was a sort of happy time. I still travelled up to Easterhouse very two weeks to *sign on*, then I would head over to JW's for a fix of *speed*. After a few hours of Easterhouse I would jump the bus back to Whiteinch and my other life.

I was already way down the road to being a selfish, nasty person that would use people for my own ends. And yet I had the perfect smile that also fooled people.

In a chapter further on I talk about another, kinder episode whilst I lived in Whiteinch.

When I moved back to Easterhouse, I moved straight back into the gangs. I somehow managed to navigate being part of *Aggro* and being able to go up *Drag* for my *Tems* and *Acid*.

Back to summers spent in gang fights, day after day.

24 - The Fog (1989)
Night-time flight

Darkness hung on the phantom light
through the mystery of the impenetrable cloud.
Every movement that cannot be seen
exaggerated into ghosts graves and ghouls
groaning into phantom memories
of yesterday and of what might have been;
twisting our guilt in remembered scenes.
Our today locked with an unknown key
that leaves liberty languishing longingly
and the fog of tomorrow we cannot see.
Threatening our purpose with fears of what MAY be -
can all be set aside through
the Christ who was and is and always will be
© Stuart Patterson 2018

Out of the darkness arose a blood-curdling noise. A deep guttural cry that came from nowhere, accompanied by glints of metal; flashes in the night. All advancing through the tense tremoring fog. All heading straight in our direction.

It seemed like there were hundreds of them.

It might have been a Friday night, but this wasn't a scene out of some zombie flick.

This was Easterhouse.

This was Lochend football pitches.

This was gang-fighting at its very worst.

The usual summer gang fights had been going on all through the holidays. From the age of around twelve right up to guys in their late twenties and maybe even their thirties would gather morning noon and night for the ritual.

Normally it took place on the top pitch, set up quite a steep wee hill, with St Clare's Primary School at one end and some grass at the Den Toi end. A little dip bordered our side whilst the Drummy all congregated on the much steeper hill of St Clare's, all ready for worship on the battlefield of territorial gangland Easterhouse.

This summer seemed to be a wee bit more violent though. More drawn out as well. We had taken on the police, there had even been a stolen Lorry involved, with the mad scene of some of the Drummy trying to bounce golf clubs off the windows, as J and A raced all over the playing fields. I'm not sure even they knew what they were doing.

It was very unusual though, that we would gather here at night.

Nights normally took the form of raiding parties in each other's territories. Teams of us marauding around thinking we were the SAS and looking for unsuspecting victims that belonged to the other gangs.

However, here we were. At the path entrance was a wee brick wall, only about eighteen inches high. A whole load of us were gathered there, drinking, smoking and not really doing much of anything.

In talking with A about this particular battle, his memory is of it being late evening, but not actually dark. A talked about us watching the fog coming in from Cairnbrook Road direction, and the same rush through the fog. He shared the same feeling as me that this was very probably a life or death situation, especially in those first few seconds.

The fog really was quite heavy that night. I mean so heavy that you could only see a couple of feet in front of you. And that eerie echo that seems to accompany the old pea-souper was there.

Apart from that though, there was no sign, nothing at all, to indicate what was about to happen.

Fog is an incredible screen, blanking out everything beyond your immediate vision.

That is when that noise began, and as time stood still and we looked towards the fog, it became obvious these guys, the Drummy were already upon us.

In the sudden shattering of the quiet and the dark, chaos reigned for an eternity.

It was only seconds but felt longer. Guys darted in all directions, mostly looking for weapons of any sort. I ducked down behind the wee wall. There were others beside me. I think the plan was to let the mob get past us and the come from behind whilst others attacked from the front.

As soon as I stood up though, I was aware of something shiny flying through the air - right at me. I tried to duck. Too late!! I was struck on the right calf and I went down holding on to my leg tightly.

A metal pole, that had been thrown with enough force that the ringed end bit deep into the muscle.

I grabbed the pole and started flailing wildly at the shadows around me. Don't think I managed to hit anything though.

As the fog, (after aiding the surprise attack), begin to lift a little it seemed as though men appeared from everywhere in the tenements.

Out of closes, gable ends and even over verandas til that corner was overwhelmed with what seemed like a full-scale war.

Those of us that were caught off guard began to regroup and take our part in the main battle.

As the crowd from Aggro and Den Toi began to swell, momentum swung back in our favour, the Drummy literally began to head for the hill.

Their hill.

There ended up the almightiest battle in that area of red blaise pitch, a surface supposedly intended for young guys to play football and have fun on.

Swords, sticks, stones all flying around indiscriminately. Not caring who they hit, or the lifelong consequences that could be wreaked in those fateful futile moments.

Reactions, not decisions that would remain forever. Which was pretty much how most of us young men gathered that night had lived our lives up to this point.

Just like the fog that had been present and clouding what was about to happen, so were our lives clouded by no ability to take in the bigger picture.

The reflections of scheme life, even though it seemed to be full of light and life, barricaded in and prevented any view of a life outside the drugs and the gangs.

We lived in a fog; we just did not know it. You had to be there to believe it. Hatred borne out of a postcode, even though we all shared the G34 part.

From the gathering waiting at the wall with no purpose to the crazy stramash on the pitches was just sheer craziness. All unfolding like a scene from a very bad B movie New York gang film.

It was ludicrous!

It was frightening!

It was very real.

In minutes it was over. People nursed their wounds. I nursed my wounds. Aware of the blood trickling down the strange, three quarter circle hole in my calf, I limped down Dalswinton Path, with the rest of our team back towards where we belonged.

As the crowd cleared, the blue lights appeared. Putting on a big show of stopping the gang fighting that they nearly always missed.

Several cars descending on the crowd of teenagers and young men that they knew, just like the fog, had already dissipated.

We went and hung about another wall, in the Quad this time. Our wall, our Quad. Marvelled at what had just occurred and recognising that even by Easterhouse standards, that was different.

Within half an hour, it was as if it never happened.

Fast forward to February 2018. A hall that used to be a bingo hall that used to be community renewal space that used to be DHSS Employment Training office - now home to Easterhouse Community Church.

Again, there is a group of youth gathered. There are no drugs, no drink, no violence.

Anticipation and expectation filled the air rather than a fog of unpredictability, uncertainty and nothingness.

Youth with a purpose ready to arise and claim their lives as they are supposed to be – through Christ.

This evening the young and the old mix in a common purpose that does not involve murder death kill – but instead our Magnificent Divine King Jesus.

Instead of two by two lengths of wood, it is drumsticks. The glinting metal this time is the moving of chairs reflecting the overhead lights. The old do not fear to tread here but are active and willing partners.

No blood-curdling cries, only bold cheers of joy as the crescendo this time is of praise.

The difference Jesus makes is tangible – the only threat carried in the air is that of a loving heavenly Father for those things that seek to hinder what He wants to do through this gathering.

The fog is lifted – the way is clear.

25 – Stewarding Stuart (1988, 1991)
The Celtic Connection

"They're there, and they are always there. God bless every one of them." Tommy Burns

My history with Celtic is lifelong. It wasn't that I was at every game, and I couldn't even tell you my earliest memory of games. But I do remember many journeys from Easterhouse to Celtic Park. Normally with my elder brother Gary, and a whole bunch of other locals that pretty much make up the Easterhouse Rocket Launchers (don't ask).

It's funny how 40 odd years later we still sit beside each other at Celtic Park.

My dad would have called himself a supporter but didn't really go to many games. Gary did. No 4 up the Celtic end was our normal place, again pretty much near 143 in the Lisbon Lions lower. Half times would involve watching for the gate into the Jungle opening to sneak in. It was chaos, madness, bedlam and wonderful in there. As an early teen it's where you wanted to be. The passion, the enthusiasm the sheer energy that flowed from those steps that caused many a team to stumble.

Crowds of us on the bus, or the train or whatever to get there. Fans making their way in from all directions to gather in a small piece of land in the east end of Glasgow – my city.

It always seems to be sunny at those games, but it's funny how our memory can do that to us. The songs would be screaming out, the euphoria flying the adulation pouring forth. I remember sneaking up in the queue with Gary to get my lift over. The turnstiles then seemed to be custom designed to allow east end kids free admission so it would have been rude not to .

Before every game the jungle would roar out songs to every player and let them know how adored they were. In return the players would acknowledge the adulation with a hand wave and/or a clap. I loved my trips to Paradise, as infrequent as they could be in those days.

One of the many games to stand out was on 7th May 1988. It was our 99th season and we had just won the league. We were playing Dunfermline Athletic, who had just been relegated.

The league trophy was presented that day and there was a bit of a carnival atmosphere. I was in the jungle from before kicking off in this game and there was even more of a party atmosphere than normal.

The Dunfermline fans raised a banner saying " Jim, we'll be back. P.S. Happy birthday Celtic". (The Jim being Jim Leishman their manager).

The place erupted, the jungle singing "You'll be back" at them and the football became almost secondary. (We won the game 1-0).

1988 was a difficult year for me personally. I was 18 years old and my life had already gone off the rails really quick. I had had two jobs, cutting meat in Alex Munro Butchers, and then cutting wood in East End Sawmills, but in May I was 18 and unemployed. I was also already heavily addicted to *Temgesics*, Speed, LSD,

Temazepam, Cannabis and well basically just about any drug going. It would only be a few months later that I was arrested for my involvement in drugs.

Life was garbage. It was already one day melting into the next. Crashing from one house to another and sometimes going days without a sleep.

Anyway, back to Celtic. That game stands out as the only one I ever remember the opposition supporters saying something "nice". It was 100 years since Brother Walfrid "set up Celtic to

"*Supply the East End conferences of the St. Vincent De Paul Society with funds for the maintenance of the "Dinner Tables" of our needy children in the Missions of St Mary's, Sacred Heart, and St. Michael's. Many cases of sheer poverty are left unaided through lack of means. It is therefore with this principle object that we have set afloat the Celtic'.*"

It was brilliant and there more than a few of the Jungle surges, where, when something on the pitch was being celebrated, there was a whole press from the back of the terracing to the front . You dug your feet in and stood your ground. The excellent Celtic Wiki website has many posts on the *Jungle*

Exactly one week later I went to my first Scottish Cup Final at Hampden Park. Celtic played Dundee United and won 2-1 after Frank McAvennie scored two goals (including a last-minute winner) to cancel out Kevin Gallagher's lead for United.

At that time I was sent out to live with my aunt and uncle in Whiteinch quite a lot. The hope was a change of scenery would break the hold of the drugs – it didn't.

That day, my uncle John, my cousin Paul and, I think Scott Butterworth and I all made our way to Hampden. I don't remember much about that game, other than how my uncle John really tried to bring normality in my life and to him a Scottish Cup Final was what every young man should be doing that day.

There was a guest of honour that day but to be honest she was very low on my list of priorities. She got the red card treatment from both sets of fans, so I suppose there was a bit more supporter unity at that game as well.

Life went on and got worse but those two games, especially the Dunfermline game linger long.

"*I am now going to tell him (Herrera) how Celtic will be the first team to bring the European Cup back to Britain. But it will not help him in any manner, shape or form: we are going to attack as we have never attacked before. Cups are not won by individuals, but by men in a team who put their club before personal prestige. I am lucky – I have the players who do just that for Celtic.*" Jock Stein 23rd May 1967

I may not have been part of the Lisbon Lions that day. Heck it was three years before I was even born, but, with the above quote Jock Stein laid down what was expected of a Celtic player.

Earlier in this chapter I spoke of my earlier focus on Celtic. I grew up in a Celtic family. The team colours were all over our bedrooms.

The Irish tricolour hung proudly on Gary's wall. My room had pictures of Celtic players past and present and a cut out of Pope John Paul II taped to my desk (for the record, as I child I attended Church of Scotland services as part of my non denomination education).

Wrecked

The years in between the Dunfermline and Dundee United games had been unkind to me, maybe it was me being unkind to the years as it was my choices that screwed them up.

My addiction had gotten much worse, I had found myself in prison and I was badly screwed up. Remember as screwed up as I was, my whole family had been torn apart by my addiction and lifestyle. Me in prison was a break for them.

Released

I got out of prison in August 1990, and went straight back to what I knew. It was quite some time before I went back to Celtic Park. Mostly because paying the admission meant less cash for drugs. Yep it was that simple.

I was working as building site security guard getting £1 an hour (yes that low) and I was desperate for more cash.

Through this time my brothers Gary and Darrin, were stewards at Celtic Park. It was not as regulated at that time and the brief was to assist and to observe the fans. They enjoyed it and I had asked a few times for Gary to get me in. For obvious reasons he didn't.

My nagging eventually worked, and Gary eventually suggested me to the guys that headed it up. For some reason, wherever our Gary is, people respect him and listen to him. Strange I know.

Returned

I returned to Celtic Park – as an employee.

My first game I turn up at Celtic Park and meet with all the others the stewards in the upstairs of the old Celtic Pools Office building. It's the 25th November and Celtic are playing Rangers. What a start!

Billy McNeill is the manager.

We had not been playing that well and I don't think mulch was expected of Celtic that day. I was given my position – up at the back of the old Rangers end guarding the very steep back steps.

We lost 2-1!

At the end of the game, stewards and police were positioned down the very steep back steps. Policeman – steward – policeman -steward. All of them quite tall – except me. I was 5'7" but appeared minuscule compared to the others.

The Rangers fans were mostly good-humoured leaving, but one particularly large and obviously quite drunk guy took exception to me and lunged straight at me.

The police and stewards either side very quickly grabbed and redirected him down the stairs. To their credit the other fans shouted abuse at him, some even calling for him to pick on someone his own size. Haha.

Removed

Anyway – the result of that was it was decided I was too wee to work there so I got moved to the main stand. Celtic lost that day, but I won.

My next game as a steward as against Hibs on the 1st December 1990. A wee bit of a different time, both for the fans and for me. We routed them 3-0 that day and I got to stand in the main stand and watch it. My responsibility was to supervise the door between the main seating and the press / director's area -but only before – half time – and after games. The rest of the time I got to watch the game.

The synchronised marching up and down the stairs was introduced during my time – but not yet.

Rejoiced

It was fantastic. I loved it. I was being payed £12 a game to watch Celtic. Only a few months into my stewarding career Celtic were due to play Rangers twice in a week, March 17th and 24th 1991- Scottish Cup and league. Our performances against them had not been great. March 17th became known as the St Patrick's Day massacre. We beat Rangers 2-0 with 4 players (3 for Rangers and Peter Grant) being sent off. The papers labelled it a shame game.

We also beat Rangers 3-0 the following week 3-0. March 24th, 1991

Celtic finished 3rd that season. It was a major highlight for me in what was becoming an even more difficult part of my life. Within 12 months I would be on Methadone (abusing the programme the way I abused everything) and my life would be hell. But I kept going, at least for a while as a steward. paid to watch the Celtic.

26 – Innocent as Hell (1989)
ACYO I was there years ago

"Innocent as hell, Innocent as hell
and it's not a lot of fun being here.
I can see a few faces I'd rather see,
be a few places I'd rather be than here.

The judge says, "down you go boy,
not to be seen for five years",
he says, "Think yourself lucky,
I know it was you,
that you are sent down for five year too..."
From *"Innocent as Hell"* by Scheme on *Black & Whites* album

Down the stairs you go,
back door for the bus to Polmont YO
New label over your life ACYO,
with the cry of the con "I was there years ago"
Stuart Patterson ©2018

"Mr Patterson, on the two counts of *Possession with the Intention to Supply*, under the *Misuse of Drugs Act 1972* you have been found guilty and I hereby sentence you to 12 months on each charge, to run concurrently."

I honestly thought I would walk. It was November 1989. My guilty verdict had taken the jury all of 45 minutes to come up with three months before.

Three months in which probationary and social work reports had to be carried out so the judge could decide the most suitable punishment.

As usual, they came up trumps as I did come from a good home, and I was intelligent.

However, I had made the mistake at my trial of dressing in a suit, knowing more than the drug squad officer called to testify (he had only been with them two weeks in fairness), and was able to quote my judicial enquiry transcript better than the Procurator Fiscal.

That's not smart when you are trying to convince them you are just a junkie that needs a break.

So how on earth did I, the partially private school educated boy from the east end of Glasgow end up standing before a Sheriff in the new Glasgow Sheriff Court?

It was about one am when I heard the shout, "Paddy there's the mob comin in." I knew I had only moments but all I had on me was a couple of bags of speed and about nine 10ml temazepam tablets, not much in the greater scheme of things.

I ran to the back window of D's ground floor flat ready to make my escape, but as I pulled the curtain back, the grinning face of a DS officer was shining in the darkness. Pointing his torch in the window and shaking his head at me.

It was nearly 15 months before my sentencing. August 1988.

I had stashed the drugs, my own supply, in a matchbox under the mattress. I really was the only one in the house even remotely likely to have anything on me.

It wasn't me they were looking for.

I was just a face.

However, they were expecting J to be there and to have a lot of drugs, which was stupid on their part because John never had a lot of drugs on him.

The room has been turned upside down twice and they had even checked under the mattress, but never far enough to find my stash.

Just as they were finishing up, they came back into the room they had me in. They had kept me back from D and the others so we couldn't swap stories.

I had been careful to avoid looking at anything and just stared at the ceiling.

DS Nondescript said, "has anyone checked under here?" I said nothing. He pulled mattress back, and for the third time, nothing was found.

The shout came in from the hall to go as they were was nothing and no one of interest.

They were not happy, as always, they were convinced they would get a result it was very rare that they did.

DS Nondescript looked at me, pulled the mattress back all the way so the middle showed and looked like he had just won the lottery when he saw the matchbox.

Remember they were expecting to find drugs worth thousands, the total value of mine was about 30 quid.

I just grinned.

Nothing else to it. "Mr Patterson, I am arresting you on suspicion of being in possession of a controlled substance, do you have anything to say?"

I said nothing.

Honestly, I just looked at him and smiled and said nothing.

That bit is quite important because by the time it came to sit in my Judicial Enquiry, (a smaller private gathering with Sheriff, Procurator Fiscal, my lawyer and myself, maybe some others I cannot remember) they said I said something.

In their statements, I said, "It's just a wee bit of speed for me and my mates." I didn't, but that's an admission of supplying.

I was not stupid, and I knew the street rules when arrested. Say nothing!

That was important because denying that at trial twelve months later, and being able to recall, word for word what took place. Being able to recall my judicial enquiry transcript and especially when I was asked regarding that, came back to haunt me.

Drug addicts in 1988 in Easterhouse were not supposed to be smart. May I just point out that there was an awful lot of drugs in the 80's in Easterhouse and very few large-scale successful busts.

Stereotypes very rarely provide a foundation for good detective work.

As I was placed very gently in the back of the unmarked car, it was obvious that someone had reverse inflated their tyres, (had slashed them all with a knife).

I just groaned. I knew I was getting slapped at the station for it.

It was not unusual for police cars to be vandalized. They were in our territory and they didn't belong. We had to let them know that.

Four tyres and a very large scratch down the side of the car – all the way down the side.

"I take it I'm your payback for that?" I asked.

"Yep!" DS Nondescript replied as he got in and closed the door.

I pushed my small lock back knife way down the back of the back seat, absolutely convinced I would be pulled up for it later that evening. I wasn't. But then again, I did get 12 months in prison so there was that.

And there you have it.

A lot obviously happened in between the arrest and the sentencing, but that is for another time.

Here I was on my way to prison to serve my sentence. Sentences as it was two twelve-month sentences one for each of the charges for each of the drugs. They were to run concurrently though, which just means both were served at same time. It could have been worse, I suppose.

(ACYO is short for Assessment Centre for Young Offenders. It was located ion Polmont Young Offenders Institution and was the first port of call for newly sentenced young men, under the age of 21. Its purpose was to decide which category they should be assigned, and hence what prison they should be sent to.)

27 – Milk n a piece n jam part 2 (1990)
No rest when arrested

"It is said that no one truly knows a nation until one has been inside its jails. A nation should not be judged by how it treats its highest citizens, but its lowest ones." Nelson Mandela

December 1989, it's Christmas time, and for my parents there is some need to be afraid. I was in Castle Huntly Young Offenders Institution, and you'd think that mum and dad would be enjoying the respite.

Maybe in some parts they were, like they did not have to worry about the police knocking on the door to say I was jailed or dead, you know trivial things like that.

My first couple of months in there weren't so bad. I kept my head down, worked in their education unit on cars and really enjoyed it. I also pretty much avoided the liberally available drugs in the early days.

One of my visits though, mum and dad, and I think, Yvonne were there. I remember being excited about the visit and looking forward to it. The tension downstairs in Phase 2 (my block) whilst waiting on your visit could be unbearable. Eventually though I was called up to the visiting room which was in the actual castle building itself. Tea already on the table, sweets there as well.

"Everything awright?" my dad asked. Having been in prison himself he knew how it could be.

"Aye" I said. And to be honest, other than the extensive dental treatment I was going through, everything was fine.

"Whits that oan yir airm?" mum asked, pointing to a spot in the middle of my right bicep.

"It's a spot, ma."

"Hiv you been takin them drugs in here an aw?" she said visibly shaken and upset. If ye huv I'll no be coming back." All these years later I get that. There was no respite for her whilst I was in prison.

The stories of what went on in a Young Offenders were rife. She probably came to every visit looking for signs that I was still, as always, being me and getting high.

The truth is though, at that time I wasn't. Other than some hash, I avoided the drugs in the early days. It wasn't too long before I did start taking *Temgesics* etc again. *LSD*, *Valium* and *Temazepam* also all freely available. I never took them because my family thought I was - I took them because at that time that was who I was. I never really knew how not to.

Anyway, this chapter is about another incident. Like Seafield, it involves evening refreshments.

They served coffee in the corridor every evening. You queued and you waited your turn. Nobody really abused that, we all just waited, it was never that long.

However, one evening as I waited, DM, (a young guy in from Drumchapel for impersonating a police office by kicking in a drug dealer's door with a firearm) was behind me.

"Let me go before ye." he said.

"Naw am awrite." I said, "yir efter me anyway".

"Move it ya dafty an let me in."

"Beat it" I said. Another unwritten rule was to not let others take advantage of you. These days I would think nothing of letting someone go before me in a queue. But in an enclosed environment with a bunch of teenagers all wanting to prove they were harder than the other - not a chance.

I got my coffee and made my way to the tv room, a bland square room with generic plastic chairs and a television on a stand. I sat down and began watching "*Yellowthread Street*", a Steven Segal cop show set in Hong Kong.

Within seconds though from behind me came "Bam me up would ye" as DM smacked me on the side of the head from behind.

My beloved Celtic mug that my mum and dad had brought up for me at Christmas flew out of my hand and smashed off the wall.

I jumped to my feet and cried out "Whit ye daien ya maddy" as I reached out and grabbed DM.

When it came to fighting, I wasn't a great fighter. Our JP though, had instilled in me a mindset that you didn't give up. If you were fighting, they had to kill you to beat you.

So, DM and I started rolling about the floor. I gave as good as I got and after what seemed like hours, but was probably about one minute, DM jumped to his feet and shouted "Ye hid enough, teach ye tae bam me up."

I was as bemused as everyone else in the room at this. Clearly, he had not taught me a lesson, I had not been beaten and I was not slinking out of the room.

As DM walked out with his cut lip and soon to be black eye, I got to my feet, picked up my mug and put it in the bin and sat down watching "*Yellowthread Street*" once again.

Being in an enclosed environment with a bunch of emotionally broken teenage boys trying to prove they are hard men is not somewhere you can get a rest, never mind respite.

With incidents like these, no respite for mum and dad whilst I was here.

28 – The Great Escape (1990)
I'll no be back

"As a dog returns to his own vomit, So a fool repeats his folly." Proverbs 26:11 (NKJV)

August 1990 I was released from Castle Huntly Young Offenders' Institution. I was dropped off at the local train station with the admonishment of "See you soon." From the prison officer tasked with dropping me off.

As I sat in the train station waiting to return to Glasgow with my £30 *lib money,* I already knew what I was going to do.

It was a nice morning as I made my way up Easterhouse Road, from the train station. Anyone looking on would not think much. I looked healthy, hadn't been taking much drugs, eating regular meals, going to bed at reasonable times – why wouldn't I *look* healthy.

As I made my way up to our top floor tenement in 4 Duntarvie Quad, I was already wondering how long I would have to hang about before I could get out for a fix.

Mum was cleaning and *Dirty Dancing* was on the tv. I sat down and had a sandwich with a cup of tea.

"You're gonnae have tae sort the buroo (Unemployment Benefit) oot pretty quickly as yiv nae money."

Obviously, I never told her I had £30 in my pocket. I could not believe it. Mum had given me the perfect excuse to get out. I knew she would be stressed out at the thought of me back, but to be honest all I cared about was feeling that rush as I injected the *Temgesic* into my veins.

"Aye ma, ah'll go aer the noo an see if they will see me".

"Don't be long an don't dae anything stupid."

"naw ma." Already halfway out the door.

I made my straight down Baldinnie Road to F's but I had to be careful as he lived close to my sister. In I went, he had, so I had a fix.

All this was within ONE hour of getting home from my prison sentence.

Not much more to add to this chapter.

THIS is MY life!

29 - Bittersweet Symphony (1992)
I'm here in my mould.

"I'll take you down the only road I've ever been down
You know the one that takes you to the places
where all the veins meet, yeah.
No change, I can't change, I can't change, I can't change,
but I'm here in my mould, I am here in my mould."
From "*Bitter Sweet Symphony*" lyrics © Abkco Music, Inc
Songwriters: Keith Richards / Mick Jagger / Richard Ashcroft,

Congratulations, you have got this far. If you have read the preceding chapters then you may already know that I grew up in Easterhouse won a scholarship to Hutchesons Grammar and had good opportunities.

You may even know that I threw it all away for many reasons and that I started with the drugs and gangs at age of fourteen. In this chapter, though, I want to talk to you about my experience with *Methadone*[xvii].

After leaving prison in August 1990, I ended up very quickly back in the cycle of addiction. My very own desert of despair, where one day seemed to melt into another and prison etc ended up on methadone for the first time at age of twenty-two (1992). I went through my drug counsellor to the doctor in order to get a prescription. I couldn't believe that if I said the right words, I could get free drugs. (Note to those working with people in addiction – manipulation is a major part of this lifestyle. The goal is to get what you want and let the target think it is their idea.)

I still remember the first day I collected my prescription. I was on my way to a building site, where I worked as an overnight security guard. At this time, I was based in Scotstoun, mentioned in a previous chapter. I went to the doctor's almost in passing and could not believe it when I left with a week's worth of *Methadone* and a week's worth of *Nitrazepam*, in two very large bottles. It was before everyone had to take their script orally in front of the pharmacist, daily.

As good as it seemed, initially, getting all these drugs for free, I very quickly found out that I needed to dramatically increase my heroin intake to get a stone out of it. The very nature of the methadone made it harder to get a buzz. I was an addict. I took drugs because I wanted to get high. The *Methadone* interfered with this, so I stopped taking it within a few months (I did keep collecting and selling them, though).

Even though I continued taking *heroin* at this point I still went through withdrawal because of the *Methadone*. It was not a good time. My addiction continued, but I tried *Methadone* a few years later and this time I insisted on detoxing with it. Every day I would religiously collect my script at Easterhouse Health Centre pharmacy, and by this time you had to take it in front of a pharmacist.

I took NO other drugs during my ten-month detox and ended up on two millilitres a day put into a wee funnel-shaped glass to make it seem more. Think about how small that is and you may get an idea how strong addiction can be.

At the end of my detox I called my drug counsellor and asked him what was next. At that point, I had been on drugs for around ten years and EVERY waking thought was about my next fix. My nine thirty am daily appointment just became my next fix. Nobody had taught me how to live, how to make decisions that did not involve getting a fix. Nobody taught, me how to cope with life's circumstances without running to get a fix.

The scene in *Trainspotting* when the baby dies, and the mother just goes and has a fix is one of the most accurate depictions I have seen of addiction. Having a fix is your coping mechanism for everything.

My dependence on drugs was my go-to for everything. When my drug counsellor AND my social worker could offer no further advice on how best to proceed in a drug free life, and as I did not know how to deal with it – I went and got drugs.

I had been off heroin for ten months, within eight hours of my last two ml of Methadone, I had another fix of heroin. It was as if the previous ten months had not happened. I continued taking drugs.

This was MY life?

30 - That's handy (1993, I think)
A wee blue bible

How do you measure the use of your hand
Its ability to help you live out the plan
try going without one, just for a day
Tie it up, out of the way,
Or worse still restrict its use
By some form or other of drug abuse
See how much you depend on its use
When full function is yesterday's news
Stuart Patterson ©2018

Earl Street, Scotstoun. A portacabin on a residential, tenement-lined street; one side houses wrapped in scaffolding being modernised - the other fully revealed and lights flickering and flashing with the lives being lived inside.

Me? Why am I here? Well, it is back to my days as a building site security guard. I had been long term on this site for quite a while. I knew most of the residents of the street; they knew the me I allowed them to know. The one that was the polite and conscientious security guard, not just minding the building work and materials, but also policing their street. Nothing happened on my watch.

Monday to Thursday I was on site from 4pm for my 4.30 start. There until 8.30 each morning, the first of the workers arriving from 8am. Friday it was a 3.30pm start, and I was normally on site until Monday 8.30am. This day was a Thursday. Here I was on site, me and my holdall - travelling companions.

The contents of my holdall necessary to allow me to live out this life I know found myself chained to.

There was, of course, the packed lunch. Since I was night shift though it was more of packed snacks, normally curry Pot Noodles and Weetabix.

There was the wee portable tv - requisite for any building site security guard worth his salt. It was almost part of the uniform.

There was the usual assortment of books, I liked to read. In amongst those books was the wee blue bible my granny Patterson had given me years before. Opened only to scrawl a drug fused inscription on the cover calling out my undying love for it; but never read further than the contents page, at least in those days.

Then there were my essentials. My works. This consisted of my one ml syringe, my Abdine, my spoon and filters. It also contained a small bag with whatever drugs I had secured to see me through the night.

This night it had heroin, hash and a couple of temazepam.

I had some friends on the street. There were K and his wife on the first close. I got on well with them. Family on top flat facing K and A and a few others dotted about. K knew more of my real story though than any of the others. Anytime I never had enough hash for a joint, K would give me some. I liked K he was a good mate.

This night, however, K was away for a holiday with HMP. I was alone in the cabin and it was a bright summer's night. I had taken my heroin; the site was quiet and so I fancied a sleep.

This was why I brought the Temazepam. It was a tablet, that in the normal world, was prescribed to help with sleep. In our world, it had ridiculous effects. For those of us that chose to inject, we had to manipulate and prepare it. Wyeth, the company that made it, was constantly in a battle of will with addicts that came up with ways to abuse their gold mine. In the early days, just like a hen's egg you could pierce it with a needle and empty its contents. Now we had to empty its contents onto a spoon, heat it, pour it into the syringe and inject before it returned to its very thick gel-like formula. I was an expert in all our areas of our craft, and, despite my rapidly diminishing circulation, administering this to myself was never, normally an issue.

This night, as usual, I injected into my left arm, into the median cubital vein, just below my bicep at the joint of my arm.

I got the usual rush from it. Everything felt normal. (please understand my use of normal here as I describe drug misuse, this was my normal).

It was only as the night progressed that I was aware of increasing pain in my hand and wrist area.

"Sierra 32 call in please!" crackled my two-way radio, as I sat staring at my hand and wondering what was going on.

"Sierra 32, all in order," I replied. Although I felt anything but. It was not unusual in these days of diminishing circulation for there to be some discomfort and pain after a fix.

"I know," I thought, "I'll go and do a patrol and grab a quick sleep, that'll sort it." Sometimes a quick nap could do away with the negative side effects of some of the drugs.

I wandered up and down my portion of Earl Street, checking scaffolding, doors, windows and plant machinery. All was in order.
Temazepam had the amazing ability to let you think you were straight and rationale, while all the while anyone that met you knew that you were out of your head.

As I went to step back into the hut, keenly aware of the increasing pain in my left hand, I was stopped by a local. "Stuart can you just check the backs, thought I heard someone there."

"Of course," I mumbled and then went into a drug/pain fused waffle. I thought I was coherent, but the strange look and quick departure of the local probably said otherwise.

I went to the backcourt, and there was indeed some activity. Some young guys had been on the cycle path, that ran along the old railway track running parallel to the south of the street. They were up at the doo cabin there. Drinking. There was no reason for them to be in the backcourt, but the sight of me and my torch was enough to make them scarper.

Unfortunately for me, it meant I couldn't sleep. To drunken youngsters, a security hut on the street was like a magnet. I knew the potential for them to come back and try and cause hassle. I had to fight the effects of the Temazepam and the desire to sleep. I had to try and ignore the still increasing pain in my left hand, and I had to watch.

Not mentioned earlier, but one of the first actions of a security guard in a well-windowed, well-lit portacabin on a public street, is to try and cover up the windows. For me, obviously, this had a double purpose as it meant I could get high without the whole street seeing it. Normally this would be newspapers and coats.

Down they all had to come so I could see all sides.

Around one am, it had remained quiet, but I was keenly aware that my painful left hand was now becoming very discoloured. A sort of reddish-pink yellow hue coming over it.

I was a bit worried. But there had been times before when this happened after a fix.

I kept going.

By 6.30am, my hand was black. The pain. Imagine the worst possible toothache pain, except in every bit of your hand. It was that bad.

"Sierra 32 to Control"

"Go ahead Sierra 32"

"Control I hurt my hand earlier on the site (well I wasn't going to tell them it was an injection) it's really bad."

"Sierra 32, be advised, Supervisor is very busy just now doing site pickups, you will have to wait."

"Control, I need Mick (the supervisor) to come now. You also need to cover the site".

"Sierra 32, can't do it, you have to wait."

"Control I need Mick to take me to hospital, a guard on site in twenty minutes, or I will need to get a bus"

"Control to Supervisor, Mick channel 2." (this meant Tam on control wanted to speak to Mick on a channel the guards could not listen in on.

"Control to Sierra 32, Supervisor will be with you in 20 minutes" crackled the radio seconds later.

I was a good guard, I did not cause much hassle, so they knew I wasn't at it. But to be fair to them, it was still a highly unusual request.

Despite the severe pain, I prepared for my hospital visit. I knew my mum would probably have to come up, and if I was kept in (obviously by now I knew this was bad). Any drug paraphernalia had to go. All my syringes etc were put in a bag, mixed with other rubbish, put in another bag and then put in the skip on the street. I know it was not very safe and fair for anyone that may have to handle the rubbish and I offer no excuse for that. I was in damage limitation mode and I knew my mum would go through my bag - forensically.

Mick picked me up, said nothing whilst the replacement guard was there (one that had finished earlier on another site and would have been heading home).

In the car, he asked me what I had done.

I got on well with Mick. "I fell asleep lying on it and woke up with it like this." I do not think for one minute he bought that, but he never questioned it.

We arrived at Glasgow Royal Infirmary Accident and Emergency (it was the old entrance at that time), and Mick left me at the door.
I went up to the armour-plated reception window. Gave my name and mumbled very quietly in the mayhem of the Friday morning crowd what had really happened. It was 7.30 am and the place was packed.

"What did you say you did?"

"I had an injection and I think I have really damaged it.".

"Sit down over there, someone will be with you shortly."

"I'm in a lot of pain" and I was, by this time I was weeping with the pain. My hand was a very greyish black.

I waited for ages before I was called into a cubicle. A doctor had a look, asked me to describe what I had done, what drug I had taken.

Very quickly I was told I had to go up to a ward.

Still no pain relief!

Eventually, I was taken up to a reception ward in the old buildings.

I remember that that was also very busy. I had to sit on a seat whilst my bed was made ready. I was in absolute agony, and I remember asking a nurse if I could go and have a cigarette, believing this might bring at least a little relief.

"If you have a cigarette, you are getting no analgesic!" she said in the most condescending voice I think I have ever heard.

"What's an analgesic," I asked.

"Your painkiller!"

That did it. I passively sat still, slave to the pain and the hospital procedures. Able to do nothing except concentrate on the extreme pain in my left hand. Hoping that they would call me soon to relieve my pain. Beds pushed past by porters seemed to be mocking my pain as the squeaks of the wheels agitated my already overworked central nervous system Every low whisper at a bed side was a scream in skin. All the while my hand looking at me asking what it had done to deserve such cruel punishment.

It was nearly lunchtime before I was finally put in a bed. And still, sometime before I finally got medication.

The nurse asked, "Where do you want your injection, stomach or thigh?"

Eh, why did it matter? I wondered. "In my thigh, what is it?"

"Morphine[xviii]"

Talk about split emotions. A drug addict's dream, free morphine. But because it was the only painkiller strong enough to alleviate my pain. A measure of how bad my hand was. Almost instantly I felt the relief crawl through my vascular system. As I looked down at my hand through a drug-fuelled haze, this time legally given, I could not believe how bad it looked. My hand was almost black.

The doctor came along and described to me what had happened. My temazepam injection had started solidifying again in the veins in my hand. He expressed that a split second was the difference between my hand and my brain. He said that, to all intents and purposes my hand was not receiving any blood and was, in fact, dying. All they could do was fill me with morphine, a lot of morphine, and regularly. Every two hours. It sounded great. All they could do for my hand was put it in a sling and suspend it from an IV drip stand in the hope that the circulation could repair itself.

My hand was hung up on an IV drip stand. How ironic!

I fell asleep, to be woken very soon by mum at my bedside, with my sister Yvonne at her side.

"Look at your hand, what have you done?" she cried.

So, there I was, my left hand slung from an IV drip stand, my body saturated in morphine, my mum at my bedside, my sister Yvonne at my mum's side.

I knew I was stoned out of my head on the morphine, you'd think I would be in heaven, right?

All I was aware of was that my hand was still sore, despite the morphine, and it was black.

Mum was visibly upset and angry. My sister was angry. I tried to lie about what I had done, as far as I knew though the doc had already told them.

The ward was very busy and there was a lot of commotion going on.

I got a new, very high dose, morphine injection every two hours. They did what we called muscle popping it. That is the needle was stuck into the muscle in either side of my stomach, or one of my thighs. It was quickly absorbed into the bloodstream that way. I had very little in the way of circulation due to years of damage as an addict.

My friend, Angie Marshall came up while they were there as well. She asked how I was getting on, but never stayed long. To be fair it would have been awkward. But it was nice to see a friendly face.

I was very quickly moved to a Cardiovascular ward in what was then the new building. Ward 66 seems to stick in my head but not sure if that was correct. The ward was very modern and spacious. There were ten beds, normally occupied by older patients with circulation problems. This day it had four pensioners and, including me, six much younger addicts, all dealing with varying effects of injecting Temazepam. One guy had lost his lower arm.

It wasn't me.

Even at the time I had great sympathy for the older guys, for the most part they were there due to their bodies wearing out. Yet they had to put up with much younger, foul mouthed guys caught up in addiction but boasting about how much drugs they could consume and how wild their lives were. I lay in my bed, soaked in morphine, thighs and stomach now beginning to ache with all the injections, and hating every second of it.

The constant and very heavy morphine high was too much for me.

I remember, on the 4th day, begging the consultant to take me off the morphine, and give me Methadone instead, (well they were unlikely to give me heroin and I was still an addict). He kept refusing, insisting that I would be in too much pain. As unlikely as it seems, though, I genuinely had had enough of being that out of my head so constantly.

By now, the skin on my hand was all dead. It was black, and if you tapped on it, sounded like plastic. On the inside, I was told, that it would still be fighting hard to recover itself. I am always amazed at the human body's capacity for taking deep levels of abuse and injury. It is almost as if a loving Creator knew how cruel we could be to ourselves and built in many safeguards.

My index finger was already showing signs of even deeper injury than the rest of it, if that were possible. Very tip is still missing, and my nail just looks weird.

Eventually, due to my constant moaning, pleading whining I was taken off the Morphine and given a dose of Methadone. The Methadone did deal with any withdrawals, but not the pain. As soon as the last of the Morphine began to wear off, the pain began to force its way through. It was as if it my nervous system had been lurking in the shadows waiting to get me back for the damage inflicted on it. There was no creeping of pain, it mugged me, hijacking my thoughts my focus and all my attention. Every nerve in my body screaming out in defence of my hand. Toothache in every cell below my wrist.

Tortuous, nerve shredding toothache – in my hand. It was that bad!

Lying in my bed all the time did not help. The pain was constant and consistent, but I refused to go back to the Morphine.

It was broken only by joining the other guys in the smoking room and smoking hash. No one ever complained about us. Would you?
They just avoided us.

I did get plenty of visits from family. All of them revolved around what I was to do. How I had got away with it this time and something had to change. I always nodded compliantly, whilst tasting that first shot of heroin I would get as soon as I got out.

After 7 days, the pain had subsided enough, and the injury had settled enough that they felt I could leave. Remember, medically nothing could be done for my injury other than hang it high and let my body do what it could. No surgery could stop the damage.

My fingertips all looked like they had been badly burned, which the doctor told me was pretty much how it was. Deprived of circulation, they had begun to decompose. It was the same story with my plastic skin. It would eventually be replaced with new skin.
Creator God and His design methods.

I was checked out with a Velcro splint with a metal bar in it to help my very weak hand. The physio gave me very strict instructions on the physio I had to do, and I got strong painkillers to do me until I could go and see my own doctor. Oh, and about a thousand different creams that I had to constantly rub into my still dead skin.

As soon as we got home, I made my excuses about having to go to Ark's office, to see about going back to work.

The look on my parent's faces said it all. My dad - anger, my mum - despondency.

It is amazing how addicts learn to push all this aside in the quest for the treasure we seek. I had not had heroin now in over a week. My mind was doing cartwheels in anticipation. One week after I could have died through a Temazepam injection, fresh from sleeping in a ward with guys even worse off than me with the injuries, I had a fix of heroin.

THIS is my life?

My hand never did fully recover from the injury. My index finger is missing its tip, and the muscles in my hand are all fibrosed, which means it is in a permanently distorted, swan neck, position.

I do not have full use of it and acts as simple as picking up a can of juice, once so subconscious, now must be done with the help of my right hand.

In the Gospel of Mark, chapter 3, there is a story of Jesus going into a synagogue and meeting a guy with a withered hand. Despite the hostility of the onlookers, (I know who would think people would be annoyed at the potential for Jesus to bring healing, right) Jesus tells the man to stretch out his withered hand, and Jesus heals it.

Every time I hear a preacher read those verses, I always think, "is this the time?"

Whilst my hand may not, yet, have been healed, the cause of my hand being injured has been.

31 - Vague recollections (1990's)
Day of the dead

My name is Heroin – call me smack for short. I entered this Country without a Passport.
Ever since then I've made lots of scum rich. Some have been murdered and found in a ditch.
I'm more valued than Diamonds, more treasured than Gold,
Use me Just Once and you too will be sold.
I'll make a schoolboy forget his books, I'll make a Beauty Queen forget her looks,
I'll take a Renowned Speaker and make him a bore.
I'll take your Mother and make her a whore,
I'll make a schoolteacher forget how to teach, I'll make a Preacher not want to Preach,
I'll take your Rent Money and you'll be Evicted,
I'll murder your Babies or they'll be Born Addicted.
I'll make you Rob, and steal and Kill, When you are Under My Power, you have No Will,

Remember, My Friend, My Name is "BIG H", IF you try me one time you may never be free,
I've destroyed Actors, Politicians and many a Hero,
I've decreased Bank Accounts from Millions to zero,
I make Shooting and Stabbing a common affair, Once I take Charge, You won' have a Prayer,
Now that you know me , What will you do?, You'll have to Decide, it's All up to You,
The day you agree to sit in My Saddle, The decision is one that No one can straddle,
Listen to Me, and Please listen Well, When You ride with Heroin you are headed for Hell.
ANONYMOUS

My day to existence during the nineties was pretty much the same day after day – for me. For my family it was a different story. Whilst they were all dealing with their own problems and issues, there is no doubt my lifestyle choices wreaked havoc on them.

After my first attempt at Methadone my drug taking became more selective. I used mostly heroin, with hash to wash it down. I would sometimes have a bag of speed, but very rarely since an episode in which I suffered real and sever hallucinations. One night saw me chasing an imagined foe away from our front door, down the stairs and through the Quad whilst I was holding a steak knife. It was around midnight, and my poor mum chased after me. Despite my protestations that he had been at the door, my mum screamed that there was no one there. To me, there was.

Back up the house, mum pleaded with me to get help, but I just screamed about how he needed it, not me, and that she must be blind if she didn't see him.

Other times, I would inject *Temazepam*^{xix}, a sleeping tablet directly into my veins. This was NOT good!

The problem with *Temazepam* was that it would make me to act in a ridiculous manner, all the while thinking I was completely straight. I would have an injection, go to the kitchen to clean my needle, hide the needle then completely forgot where I had hidden it.

Many times, my poor mother would confront me with blood stained hypodermics that she had found. I would deny all knowledge of them.

At other times I would go out to make a cup of tea, or something to eat, and fall asleep standing up at the counter. It would not be uncommon to sleep standing like that for hours on end, then wake in blind panic that my drugs etc were still sitting out in my room.

When I did take drugs at home, by the time we had moved into the converted bottom and middle Ervie Street flats, it would be straight in through the downstairs door, up the stairs in the middle of the hallway and into my room. Then I would get my swab, spoon, my *Abdine* and my needle out and sneak into the bathroom with them all wrapped and stuck down my sock or my boxers – my heroin secure in my pocket.

Hours I would be in there, just as well there was another bathroom downstairs. By the mid-nineties, my veins were quite badly damaged, and I would struggle to find one suitable to take the drugs. Speed had wreaked most of the damage, well not so much the speed as the garbage that was cut in with it to make more money from it.

Injecting speed became a nightmare for me, that still scars to this day. Once again, because of the garbage cut in with it, it could be very hard to dissolve, and most of the time, the liquid in the hypodermic would resemble a heavy snow flurry. All the white bits looked just like the snow falling. To this day, when I see snow like that, I still taste the speed in my mouth.

Horrible!

The hunt to 'complete the tenner' that is get ten pounds for a bag of heroin, would have me do ridiculous things, steal ridiculous things and say ridiculous things. All the time oblivious to the damage I was causing in my own home. All the arguments raging, and my siblings begging my mum to kick me out before she could not take it anymore.

It wasn't that I didn't care, it just could not interfere with me getting my next tenner.

At other times, I would sell drugs. Unusually I did not do it for the money, but for the kicks, and it kept me supplied. Many times, I could be found hanging around Duntarvie shops, sitting near one of the two-foot-high bricked grass areas that used to sit out front. My drugs would be hidden in a bag under the concrete lip of the wall, while I stood a bit off. When I was given the cash, I would get the drugs, all the while checking for police.

I was quite brazen when it came to carry large quantities of drugs and thought nothing of walking down the street with them in carrier bags, whilst others sneaked about suspiciously through the back courts.

The mad thing was this meant I was far less likely to be stopped, as I never looked like I was carrying.

I always made a point of befriending suppliers, as this meant far more likelihood of me getting drugs or being able to do something for drugs. I wasn't a very good thief or anything, so I had to devise other means of supply.

There wasn't always that sort of provision though, and that meant there were times I would steal direct from the house.

One time, my parents had gotten wardrobes for one of the bedrooms. Whilst the five flatpacks lay in the hallway, ridiculously waiting on me putting them together (yep I still did some things) I decided that no one would notice one missing.

I dragged it down the stairs, out through the back door to the close and across the massive Easterhouse common back court. It was pouring down with rain, so it wasn't long before the cardboard got all soggy and I had to drop it in the grass.

Ridiculously I still went and knocked on a few doors and tried to sell this wardrobe, now in a soggy piece of cardboard in soaking wet grass. No one was stupid enough to buy it, obviously knowing where it had come from, they wanted no part of it.

There would be times when my body was so done in with all the drugs, and going days without sleep, that I would take a fix and wake up, sometimes, days later. I hadn't overdosed, my body had just shut down on me.

One of the times I had been arguing with my dad, he kicked me out. I slept on a few sofas and never went near the house. I bumped into JP (my eldest brother) a few times and he would tell me to get up and see mum.

I didn't. This time, after three days, I was outside my friend Katy S's ground floor flat at the top end of Aberdalgie Road, when I heard my mum call me.

It was like an electric shock. No matter what is going on, no matter how far away I was, my mum's voice was instantly recognizable. "Whit dae ye want?" I shouted as I turned around, oblivious to how hurt she was.

"You no coming hame?"

"Ma da kicked me oot."

"Never mind that, whaur huv ye been stayin?"

For my mum, on this warm spring day (I remember that much) this was a heart-breaking conversation to be having in the middle of the street. It was obvious I just wanted to getaway to all the onlookers and curtain twitchers. IT was just as obvious to everyone that mum was going nowhere until she got what she came for – me back at home. She gave me a good face saving getout.

"Yir dinner will be ready in an hour. I'll see you then."

Dinner in the Patterson household was nearly always served at five thirty pm. No matter the size of our tenement flat, there was normally a dining room table in the living room that we all sat at. Dinner was important to my mum.

That day, at five thirty I sat down at the table and ate my dinner. Conversation was strained, dad was seething, I was oblivious (you know I am saying that a fair bit at this point). I ate my dinner, went to my room and had a fix.

The search, not just for a tenner, but *Heroin* itself could be very difficult in Glasgow those days. For many reasons, there would be times of scarce availability. In those days, as soon as it was known who had supplies, there would end up being a gang heading to whatever part of Glasgow it was. At times, it must have resembled to onlookers like a scene out of a zombie film. Large crowds, eyes to the ground, not much interaction, all heading in the same direction. The drug ravaged, pale bodies and broken skin given a deathly appearance. Many times, I was in one of those groups of young men and women robbed of all sense of real life by stupid choices and their consequences.

Around 1996 I was sure that I was going to die.

I didn't know how, but I was convinced that I wouldn't see my thirtieth birthday.

I didn't know if it would be an overdose, a beating, whether I would get shot or stabbed or something – or if my body would just give up on me.

I spent nearly every waking minute, trying to complete the tenner, and convinced that death awaited me on every corner.

It was a dark place.

Darker still was that my family, who never had the benefit of a drug induced stupor to hide behind, also probably thought I was going to die. My mum worried that every chap at the door was going to bring the news that I was dead.

I was oblivious to their pain.

Sometimes, though, sometimes through the dark reality that my life was, another reality would kick into the middle of the mess. Sometimes.

Not often, but it would happen. A sight, a sound, a smell, or a touch would trigger a long dormant memory of a life lost and take me back.

At this point in my life, my hair was shoulder length, and unwashed; my shin was in bits through lack of nourishment. People avoided me as if I had leprosy.

Only my mum was there, always there.

I was a thoroughly dislikeable person. Incredibly self-centred and totally ignorant and oblivious to what chaos I was wreaking on those around me.

32 - Airplane Gaze part 1 (1997)
The sky above...

Just setting the scene for how it went down
Looking back on my past and the life that I found
Standing on a playing field, looking up at the sky
Knowing it was imminent, I was gonna die
As the plane flew over, the tremor was real
But not from the engines this shaking I feel
Gut wrenching shaking from deep deep inside
My last vestige of hope had just been denied
Resignation reigning with a tear and a sigh
My life now over, I'm not gonna lie
Hopes and real dreams of a hyper young lad
Wasted away by choices I wish'd id never had
The moment now over, eyes down again
Left foot, right foot, same after same
Over to the doctor's, collect the meth
My life now covered in the stench of death.
By Stuart Patterson ©2018

As a young boy growing up in Easterhouse I was always fascinated with satellite images (young people this was way before Google Maps). I longed for the moment I would get to look out an airplane window and see the earth spread out below. It was not the flying itself that captivated me, but what flying offered – the beauty of the earth below. I consumed maps. Ordnance survey maps, photo maps, any kind of imagery I could get as a youngster

Since you have gotten to this point then you know that life and bad choices took over. Around my twenty seventh birthday I remember the strong pull of withdrawal gripping my stomach and I needed to get a fix. I wasn't long in from my shift as a security guard on a building site. Normally I would go to bed for a couple of hours and try and grab a sleep. I had gone to bed, but the leg kicks had kicked in, and the sweats were pouring out. I tossed and turned and tried to escape my mind, hoping to find refuge in even an hour's sleep.

It was no use. The more I tried to escape, the stronger the pull of the pain got. I dragged myself out of bed, dragged the clothes over my head and dragged myself downstairs and out the door in our house in Ervie Street. I made my way up Ervie Street and onto Easterhouse Road, I knew I was going to the shopping centre, but if I went around the long way, I might bump into someone that could end my torment more quickly. It's hard to describe that feeling of withdrawal pain gnawing at you, your whole body done in and screaming out, but at the same time your mind and your eyes alert - like a wolf looking for prey – to any possibility of relief.

105

As I made my way down Aberdalgie Road, past Blairtummock on the left and St George's and St Peter's Church of Scotland on the right – no hope in either place - I eventually found myself on Westwood pitches. Approaching the slope at the end, the unmistakeable drone of an airplane distracted me, and awakened those long-buried memories. I stopped and stared up at the sky above. Th airplane seemed to stare back down at me, mocking my boyhood dreams. It all came rushing back, maps and photos and satellite images, the Amazon, the Nile, the Himalayas all staring up at me from pages and books and maps. I remembered that longing to be staring down at them. I remembered that desire, for a moment, stronger even than the withdrawals torturing my body.

Standing staring up at an airplane flying overhead, I cried with resignation that I would probably never get to fulfil that childhood dream. After thirteen years of drug abuse and addiction any hope of any sort of life was gone. My greatest need was to get my next heroin fix. This was one of those defining moments, when life itself seemed to be shouting at me to wake up. When the right choice could make a difference. As the plane moved out of sight a single tear rolled down my cheek, then my gaze returned to scanning in front of me. The moment had passed, I did what I always did – off to complete the tenner and get my fix.

After all, THIS is my life!

33 - An 'L' of a place (1997)
An 'L' of a day...

In May 1997 the Labour Party, under the leadership of Tony Blair ended eighteen years of Conservative rule in Britain. Garry Kasparov begun a chess match with an IBM supercomputer, the computer won after eight days. "Jurassic Park: The Lost World"debuted.

In May 1997 my life was lived through a drug induced haze, where the only thing I allowed myself to care about was getting my next ten pounds, the price of a bag of heroin.

No one and nothing else mattered to me!

16th May 1997 I was sitting in the front passenger seat of a four-wheel drive Isuzu Trooper. The guy behind me stuck something in my back and the started shouting that the gun had jammed, the gun had jammed. He was a wee bit more colourful than that with his language though.

How did I get here? How did I get from being the wee 11-year-old boy with the world at his feet, starting Hutchesons' Grammar School to be a 27-year-old heroin addict, working as a building site security guard for £1.50 per hour, and the boss wants to shoot me?

If you have read this far, then you will know part of that journey. I want to talk about what was going on around this time. I had worked in building site security for a few years at this point. It was the ideal job for a heroin addict. I spent fifteen and a half hours on a building site, not having to deal with people. I hated people by this point, but only in the sense that being around normal people reminded me how far I had fallen. So yeah, this suited me.

My journey started with Ark Security Services, which was part of Barlarnark Community Business, a local east end initiative aimed at employability. I remember speaking to Tam Logan, the security controller at the time, and Mick Weir, the supervisor in an over the phone interview.

The following night I was sitting at home in Duntarvie Quad, in my room watching *Trespass* starring Ice Cube. A call came in on the house phone (no mobile's commonly available at that time) asking to speak to me. It was the other controller, who's name escapes my mind just now) asking if I was available to start work.

Thirty minutes later and I was away to start my first shift in security. Friday evening to Monday morning at an old janitor's house in Knightswood. I remember thinking, as I walked around the house making sure no one else was hiding there, "I am getting paid for this wow." By the Saturday I was calling our old family friend, Betty Smith, asking if she would bring some sandwiches and cigarettes up to me. For the record, I did not like dark isolated buildings.

I worked for ARK for a couple of years and even ended up getting to being security controller. This was always done from a site and it involved me making sure all the other guards were ok. I used to do their nuts in as I was quite conscientious and would hit out with the "Sierra 12 call in please" (Sierra was just site and that would be followed by whatever site number you were calling). Every hour on the hour all night long whilst they were trying to sleep. If they never answered I would get Mick, the supervisor to visit them. This might have been early 90's but the pay was still only an average of £1.25 per hour.

As controller, I got £1.50 per hour. I would do an average of 128 hours in a week with a full weekend. I would do my shift, come home, sleep for a couple of hours, go score my drugs and then go to the site.

By the time I was working for D.... O... my addiction was at its worst ever. I had already damaged my hand via a *temazepam* injection, and my life was heroin and cannabis. Everything revolved around my next £10, (£10 being the price of a bag of heroin).

Security companies in Glasgow at that time were never off the news. There were allegations of gangster involvement at every turn. I may say that none of these allegations was ever aimed at ARK security, in fact, they ended up going out of business due to the increase in extortion etc that was going on against construction companies by the new security companies springing up.

D.... O... was one of these companies. Run by an ex-policeman who, apparently was kicked off the force, and someone who claimed to be ex SAS. They wanted to show they could cut it amongst the others and be ruthless in their business dealing.

I did, however, seem to get on well with them. When one or the other used to pick me up to take me to a site, I used to wonder why a baseball bat was always visible, that did not seem to be there when they did not have to go near my house. I asked one time and I was told: "It's in case your da starts anything". It seemed my dad's reputation had reached even their ears, to the point they were wary of him.

Ironically my dad ended up working for them and only once did his site ever encounter trouble, but that is another story.

Anyway, near the time that my time was up, Glasgow city centre was experiencing loads of office building construction and I was normally put there. The hours were always a wee bit different.

A few weeks before the fateful night, I remember going around to a site between Duntarvie Road and Easterhouse Road to get picked up. I had not had any drugs so was a wee bit wary and a big bit strung out. There was a bit of a dry up on.

As I was waiting, I heard that one of my friends, who lived not far away and was a dealer, had heroin, as I ran off towards his house I shouted, "Tell them I'll be back in five".

I was later to find out that, going to this guy's house made my bosses think I was involved in trying to rob off their sites (I wasn't, and he wasn't involved anyway as it wasn't his thing).

There had already been the talk of these guys threatening another local guy (C) that worked as a labourer on this very site with a gun. The guy in question was never really involved in the drugs or gangs and was probably the most unlikely person that you would think someone would pull a gun on. He has confirmed that it is true, and they did indeed point a gun at his head and threaten him.

I made my way back after scoring, safe in the knowledge that as soon as all the workers had gone, I could have a fix. It is incredible how withdrawal symptoms can decrease just because you have the drugs in your hand. I got picked up by an irate supervisor (glorified driver in this company(and off I went and thought nothing more of it.

About two weeks later, I was a late pick up for a late start in the city centre, ironically in a building, the Teen Challenge bus would sit outside every Friday night only a couple of years later. Both P & F were in the Isuzu, and I never even thought it strange that I was told to sit in the front. P said that we had to go and check the site of an agricultural show that they were responsible for. It was in Lenzie or Lesmahagow or somewhere starting with an 'L'.

It was an 'L' of a place.
As we pulled up in a field at the perimeter of the site, F sitting behind me mumbled something, and I remember feeling a jabbing on the left hand side of my back. He then started cursing and shouting and saying that the gun had jammed. I somehow managed to stay very calm. I think I was maybe a wee bit unaware of how bad this was.

Then P started firing questions at me about the Duntarvie site. I genuinely knew nothing about any theft from it so I couldn't answer.

He screamed that I went up to the f*&£$$s house from the site to get paid by him and I must know. They insisted one of the other guards told him that's where I had gone and that was what it was for. Everybody there knew I had gone to score heroin, the rest even I was amazed at.

It was about 12.30 on the Friday night / Saturday morning, it was very dark, and it was very heated. To this day I am still amazed at the calmness and the answers I came out with. Somehow, I think they believed me, but we ended up making our way into Glasgow to drop me at the site.

I was straight back into autopilot mode. Just doing whatever was in front of me.

Since then many people have questioned whether there were any bullets in the gun. My response has always been, when a gun is pointed at you, you do not think to stop and ask them that first. I was 27, I was in a field, and someone was pointing a gun at me. That was bad enough. Guns were not an everyday part of Glasgow scheme life, although there had been moments.

So, on we went to Glasgow city centre where not much else was said other than "don't tell your da!" As ridiculous as that sounds it is true. Gun totting gangsters scared of a Glasgow father of six in a fight!

They brought me into the office building in Glasgow, that was almost finished. There was another guard on with me who they had a word with, in quiet and was then on the phone to F & P all night). I thought he was weird because when I went to make the coffee, he insisted that I put no more than four granules of coffee in as anything else was too strong. That is weird, isn't it? What is the point of coffee, if you cannot smell it never mind taste it?

I did not sleep that night and relished the opportunities that the hourly patrol afforded of going and checking the site. It was already way after one am when we got there, but the night still seemed to go on forever. So much rushing through my mind.

The next morning, on the pretext of going to the shop, I left at 9am. I was going home to get a fix, and I wasn't coming back. I called them later and quit. After all, when your boss tries to shoot you it probably is time to go.

This is my life!

As a footnote to this story, one of the two bosses of the company passed away around the twentieth anniversary of me entering Teen Challenge. I have never borne any animosity or ill will towards him and was sorry I never got the opportunity to share what Christ had done in my life.

What did transpire after my escape, was how his need for Jesus was shown in how thoroughly corrupted he was in certain areas of his life and how other episodes with him (which I probably will never go into) showed that I truly did have a very narrow escape. I am always wary of phrases such as "Obviously God was looking out for me even then" but He was.

When Mark McGivern, a journalist at the Daily Record, interviewed me in October 2016 regarding my interaction with Methadone, (Bittersweet Symphony blog), we spoke about this event, and Mark asked who the bosses were. I agreed to tell him on the basis that the names would not go to print as my purpose is always to share the consequences of MY choices, not to name and shame others. I am thankful that Mark respected that. He did know the people involved and had guessed it was who I said. He expressed that he asked only to authenticate the story, as was his right as a journalist.

34 – Completing the Tenner (1997)
Get yir tea

Many are the choices we deem to make
in the hope of a different path we might take.
And most often the fruit not what we need
with choices often steeped in selfish greed.
But - one day it comes, a crossroads is reached;
confusion, bewilderment - what way is the breach?
One choice and life's journey alters its way
I set out for a tenner, but eternity made
By Stuart Patterson ©2019

In the previous chapter I recounted of the build-up to finding myself in a car with a gun in my back. As I said then, I got out of the situation and quit my job (felt that was the right thing to do given the circumstances).

We lived in Ervie Street at the time, Fitzgerald's next door, Bruen's upstairs and families we had known our whole life in almost every other tenement in this small street. I honestly cannot remember much about the Saturday, but I do want to, first, talk about the Sunday afternoon. I had got a ,fix of smack (heroin) on the Saturday, but I was feeling quite strung out by Sunday afternoon.

I remember going in to have a conversation with my mum. One she had heard many, many, many times about how I had had enough and wanted to stop. I was half serious, and half doing the addict thing of manipulating the conversation towards my desired outcome, £10. I promised I would call Jimmy Barr, my drug counsellor in the morning, but I still needed to get through the Sunday. I remember the look of defeat in my mum's eyes as she handed over the money.

I don't want you to think my mum enabled my addiction, she fought against it whilst loving me unconditionally every step of the way. It was unique for her to give me money that was asked straight out for drugs. As events will show, it was also the last time.

My family were also, blissfully, unaware of what had happened on the Friday night, I just lied and said I had no shifts. I knew there was a massive dry up in Glasgow at that time (extreme shortage of heroin) but I knew where to get it. I had to make my way down to Carntyne, and as I left the house, I was all psyched up for the long journey between scoring and using. As I walked out of our close and up to the corner between Ervie Street and Easterhouse Road, there was a gathering of other friends, all probably wondering where to score. I did the decent thing and stopped to chat.

I did not let on that I knew where to score as my source in Carntyne was very secretive and would stop selling me if I told others. One of the groups (P that had given me my first injection funnily enough) asked me if I wanted Valium instead. Valium wasn't my normal drug of choice, although I had abused it in the past and indeed there had been times when a dealer, I hung out with had access to ridiculous amounts of genuine blue Valium (10mg). It was strange because I remember standing there with the £10 in my pocket thinking, if I go for the heroin I will never stop. I did not want to really stop, and I was quite lazy. So, I went off with P and scored about £5 worth of Valium. The strange thing with Valium is that, when you are strung out, it numbs your head enough to get a sleep, even though your body is still going through the motions of withdrawal.

I went home and went to bed. My legs doing the usual free kicking etc and it seemed like an eternity where I was standing up and lying down (I am not even going to try and write what heroin withdrawal is like). Eventually, I drifted off to sleep.

Waking up very early the next morning after quite a restless night, I was very aware that I had only £5 left and my mind was racing as to how to complete the tenner. My life was broken down into £10 lots. Every conversation, every thought was about completing the tenner. I came downstairs and went into the kitchen to put the kettle on, very, very quickly followed by my mum, Heather. "Right what time are you phoning Jimmy at?" man she had the bit between her teeth.

"No one there until after 9" I replied, my mind trying to work the angles. How could I turn this around to complete the tenner?

"Right get yir tea (yep those of you that know me, that's right I was a tea drinker then) and then get the number ready!" Man, this was going to be a tough sell.

At 9.15 am I tried to call the Social Work Dept Drug Team to get a hold of Jimmy Barr, my drug worker. I knew their number off by heart, as I said in an earlier chapter if I said the right things to these people, I could get free drugs. No answer! Again, and again, I called, my mum called, but still no answer. This was a Monday morning and it was highly unusual for there not even to be an answer at the reception desk. Secretly part of me was relieved because I just wanted a fix.

"Do you want to go next door and see if Jeannie has the number for that place Jim was in at Christmas?" Jeannie being Jeannie Fitzgerald our next-door neighbour and. Mum to Jim, as well as a few other kids. Jim and I had been friends since we moved to Duntarvie Quad nearly 16 years previously. Many times, we had walked the block together, done drugs together, built dens together, done gangs together, you get the point we had spent an awful lot of our lives together.

I said no and suggested my mum went. Which she did, without a moment's hesitation. Jim had been in The Haven, a Christian Rehabilitation Centre, at that time part of the International Teen Challenge organisation. He had stayed six weeks and we had spoken often about it. He said that he had an experience with God there, but he found the programme too difficult.

Jim told me many times in the time leading up to this morning that after his Teen Challenge experience and his God encounter, he just could not get stoned (high on drugs) the same way anymore. This was backed up by how often I would see him sitting in his front garden looking totally fed up. I always just nodded, not really taking it in.

Jim always said it was a mistake to leave. My mum came back and said Jeannie did not have the number of the Centre but had a card of one of the guys somewhere and would look for it. My face smiled but my heart sank. I really wanted a fix. About five minutes later there was a chap at the door. I opened it and Jeannie was standing there with a business card in her hand and a warm smile on her face. I reluctantly invited her in, but she declined and said, "Can you give that to your mum?" And handed me the card. Now here was a problem. I closed the door with the card in my hand, choices - choices - choices.

Moments and choices! If I hand it over, we call the number. If I don't there is no way on earth, I am getting £5 to complete the tenner. We called the number; it was an Assemblies of God pastor called Ken Persaud who worked alongside Teen Challenge. He dropped everything and within an hour was sitting in our living room.

This is NOT my normal life!

35 – The Phone Call (1997)
Look at him, he's different

[23] *The steps of a good man are ordered by the LORD, And He delights in his way.*[24] *Though he fall, he shall not be utterly cast down; For the LORD upholds him with His hand.*
Psalm 37:23-24 (NKJV)

In the previous two chapters, I recalled the events leading up to me sitting in a car and getting a gun stuck in my back, and how I ended up on a Monday morning in May 1997 with an AoG pastor, Ken Persaud, turning up at my door.

I want to talk a little bit about the next couple of days and how one phone call changed the course of my life. Ken came out to see me. We were sitting in the living room, Ken, my mum and I, and Ken asked if I wanted to speak to him on my own. I said no as I was still trying to complete the tenner and thought that if my mum hung around, I would have more chance of making that happen. My mum, on the other hand, decided to leave me too it. I was frustrated.

Ken began to talk about Teen Challenge and how he was going to get me in, but I was not really taking it in. At every step, it seemed I was being outmanoeuvred in my quest to get another £5. I do remember him promising to get me into rehab within a week and he would keep me informed as to how that was going.

We said our goodbyes and Ken promised to keep in touch. That was that. When my mum came back in, I recounted as best I could what had been said.

There was no chance I was getting my £5. Remember I had not had a fix of heroin since Saturday by this point, prior to that I had not gone a day without in about four or five years. That evening, even though I never felt physically strung out, my mind was screaming for a fix. I had tried everything, and nothing had worked. It was like every single thought was screaming with loads of voices all crying out "I need a fix!" I had begged and pleaded with my mum, even saying that Ken had said I would be gone in a week, but she was not for breaking. She then asked if I wanted her to call that guy that was out to see me. Yes, I thought, I will go on the phone and talk to Ken, I will convince him to tell my mum to give me the cash as I was going away.

I remember going on the phone and giving a sob story about how I was not able for this. It was too hard. I needed a fix. Couldn't he just tell my mum to give me the cash? Man, I was working hard on trying to complete the tenner.

Addicts can be the most manipulative people on the face of the earth. We can convince you to give us what we want, whilst all the time letting you think that it was your idea. I was normally pretty good at it. Hence the long period I had gone without missing a day.

Today was different. Ken listened patiently whilst I moaned and complained about how tough this was. I told him I wasn't able and he just...listened. Then, instead of what I expected to hear he said, "Stuart, can I pray with you?" Eh! What did he say? That is not how this was supposed to go.

However, like a good sat nav, it was as if my mind began "recalculating" to bring this to my outcome. "I'll let him pray and then he will tell my mum that it was ok to give me the cash."

Ken prayed. I honestly could not tell you what he prayed, and in a way, I am glad as I would probably pray that prayer verbatim with every person, I knew who was struggling with addiction. I have often wondered how I can have perfect recall of everything over those few days, but not the prayer. After he finished praying, Ken promised he would get Roy Lees to come out and visit me the following evening when the Teen Challenge bus was in Easterhouse.

I knew of the bus. It sat outside the Easterhouse Health Centre needle exchange every Tuesday evening. People who believed in and trusted Jesus would offer a cup of tea and a listening ear to anyone who needed it. By anyone, I mean people like me who, it seemed, everyone else crossed the street to avoid. I used to avoid the bus. I would openly mock any of my friends who would go on it. Even more, those that applied for a place in the Teen Challenge programme.

I, unwashed in days, hair down around my shoulders and a long straggly beard, because shaving interfered with getting money for a fix, I used to look down my nose at them and think I was better than them. I mean, imagine believing in Jesus and saying He could save me from addiction.

As we finished on the phone, I said "thanks" hung up the phone and went back into the living room, where my mum and dad were sitting.

I looked at them both and said "sorry". My dad grunted, "heard it all before." And indeed, he had, through 13 years of addiction, 11 of them injecting he had heard every trick and ploy and excuse and apology in the book. My mum just looked at me, and I am honestly sitting weeping as I type this. She said, "Look at him, he is different!" I never felt any different. I had no awareness of anything other than I wanted my mum and dad know that I was sorry. We sat and watched telly, how normal is that?

#TC20 for those who were part of that night, thank you so much. We celebrated the goodness of God in transformed lives, and I will thank Him daily for ministries like Teen Challenge, and People like Ken Persaud, who believe in the power of God more than their own words. Ken spoke that night of when I called him, I was desperate for a fix and he prayed for me.

Ken reminded me that I had called him an hour later that Monday night. I had totally forgotten about it. But as we were talking, I remember my mum insisting I call him and tell him that I was ok. She said he would be worried. She wouldn't let me away with not calling. But the very fact that an hour after I had called all agitated and craving, that I got to call him back and say I was ok is a testimony to the power of Christ and prayer to make an immediate difference to a long-term problem. And to my mum making sure that no one was needlessly worried.

An hour later... I went to bed, and I slept.

As a footnote to this part, I have never looked to stick a needle in my arm since that phone call and Ken's prayer. The next couple of chapters will describe the next couple of days. Ken never preached The Gospel to me. He never overwhelmed me with knowledge or anything. He merely offered to pray for me, rather than try and counsel me.

That was Monday 19th May 1997. I was the last addict he worked with in Glasgow as he finished up with Teen Challenge. Ken is now the senior pastor of Notting Hill Community Church, and I am grateful that he is still in my life. Ken travelled up to Glasgow in May 2017 to celebrate twenty years of freedom in my life. It was incredible hearing him standing at the front of Easterhouse Community Church recounting this story and how that church was birthed in that prayer twenty years previously.

As I shared this story with one of my college tutors, he said he would have to look at all 15 Stuarts (it was a sociology class, he was referring to all the different ways I carried myself in different settings) and investigate. My answer to him was, Colm, every single one of them will tell you the same thing, I once was lost, now I am found, I was blind but now I see."

III Religious Education

36 – Bus Service (1997)
All change for a new life

In a moment everything changes,
with a new horizon, new exchanges.
Before it slips, grab it tight
as this moment ushers in the Light.
The world before and everything in
is racked with guilt, wrecked with sin.
This moment, this bus, brings a new
destination, abundant and full
now for NO condemnation
Stuart Patterson ©2019

Previously I recounted how I found myself with a gun stuck in my back, about my final weekend on drugs, and finally my first meeting with Ken Persaud, and the phone call that changed the direction of my life. Ken had prayed over the phone for me on Monday evening when I was desperate for a fix, I had apologised to my mum and dad, gone to bed and slept all night. The Tuesday morning, I got up and, to be honest, I never even thought about having a fix. It was probably the nearest to normality (for me anyway) I had ever been since about 12 years old. We did phone Ken later that day to see if there was any news on a rehab place, but I helped about the house and just really hung out. There had been phone calls to my previous employers (yes, the ones that tried to shoot me) as they still owed me about three weeks wages. I never did get that by the way.

We knew that some guy called Roy would be out that evening after the Teen Challenge bus was parked up at Easterhouse Health Centre so pretty much the whole day was spent treading time.

Around 8pm there was a knock at the door and a guy I had a vague knowledge of came in. It was Roy Lees. For those of you that know Roy, you will know that he has spent pretty much his whole life since the early 90's being used to rescue men and women, boys and girls from the horrors of addiction and let them know how much they are loved and valued.

I knew none of that then. Roy came in, my mum hung around and listened in this time. My dad disappeared to another room. This was all a bit too much for him, I think. I can understand his pessimism and cynicism. I even got that fact that being a "Glasgow man" he was not going to be anywhere near anything that could make him emotional.

Roy talked about a girl I knew a little bit, Susan Halley, who had gone to Teen Challenge Hope House (the women's centre) just over 12 months previously and how well she was doing. Why Susan's story had caught my attention was that around this time I spent a lot of time with her brother, Gus. I liked Gus and we got on very well together. My dad also knew their dad, Gus. It was strange to hear of someone so close to me. I had been with Gus just a few days previously before this all kicked off.

I was intrigued. It is hard to say why, but I genuinely felt what can best be described as a spark going off in me. I would later define it as hope arising, but at that time I just felt a wee bit better and more optimistic about the future. Future! Wow only 4 days before someone wanted to shoot me, and even if that had not got me, an overdose or something else probably would have, and here I was anticipating a future.

Roy did not say much about the process, other than he knew that Ken was trying his best. I was later to find out he never said much as he knew Ken had promised I would be away within a week, but the Teen Challenge process was to visit the bus at least once a week for six weeks to show intent and then fill out an application form.

Thanks, Roy, for not crushing my mum and dad's hopes at that time by staying quiet. I would not have lasted six weeks. Roy left, and I went to bed early and slept all night again.

I got up the next morning and had to go and sign on. My sister, Yvonne, insisted she was coming with me. After all, they only knew me as a manipulative addict that would do anything for a fix. I was ok with that and off we went. It's hard to write all the stuff that was going through my head at this point, but NONE of it was about completing the tenner or even looking for a fix. I genuinely do not even recall thinking about drugs at all.

Later that afternoon, Ken called. My mum had answered and called me out to the hall, (remember that was where we used to keep our phones). Ken said he had me a place in the Teen Challenge men's centre in South Wales on Monday, but because of how I was they were going to take me into the Haven in Kilmacolm for the weekend.

He said he would come and collect me the next day at 2pm. As I recounted the call to my family, I remember the tears in my mum's eyes. But they still had to get me there. That afternoon I took everything I owned and had a fire in my dad's metal bin in the back garden. Everything! Needles, clothes, rare vinyl albums! Everything other than one set of clothes was burned in that fire.

Around teatime I said I was going a walk. I was honestly just wanting to stretch my legs, but my sister said, "If you go out that door then don't bother coming back!"

"Ok." I said and went into the kitchen to make tea. No fight! No argument, no moaning. This was not me. Only a couple of weeks before I had threatened to jump through Yvonne's closed living room window to get out and get drugs.

Thursday came. Anticipation (and probably a bit of dread on my family's part) built. Ken arrived and we all said our goodbyes. My last goodbye was to Susie. Susie was my lurcher dog. She was an incredibly clever dog, as well as a brilliant hunter. Susie gave hugs and smiled. (I promise you this is true). And off I went into Ken's white car.

As he started the engine, he asked if I minded if he put some Christian music on. I nodded, expecting to hear organs and tambourines. Instead what came out was this great and joyful explosion of music and voice. It was only later that I found out this was music from Hillsong Church in Australia.

That day was my dad's birthday. 22nd May 1997. No one remembered at that time. We were all caught up in getting me away. My dad never mentioned it once. No cards, no presents. No fuss!

As we arrived at the Haven, I was dumbfounded when I saw it. I had only ever travelled on this road once before. It was two weeks previously when I was doing security at a site in Weymss Bay. I needed to get home and get a fix on the Saturday and after asking one of the workers (I said I needed to get home for something else obviously) this was the route we took. He made a big deal about pointing out the Haven. The sign said something like "The Haven Men's Christian Training Centre". I asked what that meant, and he said that it taught men how to live proper Christian lives. He never mentioned rehab.

It seemed surreal that I already felt a familiarity with this place because of that drive. As we arrived, I was taken into the manager's office and introduced to the then manager, Fin Moffat. Fin was a graduate of the Teen Challenge programme and had come back to Scotland to help people like me.

"Stuart", he said "we are not going to call you a junkie or a smackhead or anything like that, as that as not who you are anymore. We are not going to call you a Christian, as you have not made that choice. But we are going to call you a student as you are here to study the Bible, whether you like it or not."

That was the last time in Teen Challenge any direct reference was ever made to "junkie".

After a wee while Fin called me back into the office and said that they were going to keep me at The Haven for my induction. This was the first, four weeks, part of the course. "No, you are not!" I said. "I have a place in Wales, and I am going there on Monday. If I stay here, I will be up the road (I will go home) as soon as it gets hard."

Drug addicts are not meant to think this way. We normally take the path of least resistance and are very compliant in search of completing the tenner.

"Ok," he said. "I'll call you back in a while". About ten minutes later I was back in his office, and he asked if I had any money for my bus fare to Wales.

"Are you serious" I replied, "I couldn't even get my second fiver for a fix."

He laughed and sent me back out to the lounge, (on reflection I was in and out an awful lot that day, hmmm). When I was summoned again to speak to Fin, he told me that they had a ticket on the National Express coach the next day. (Later I found Roy had paid the fare, don't think I ever paid it back). The next morning Steve (a Phase 3 student from Lancashire, that had been having a few days break in the Haven, and I were brought to Buchanan Street Bus Station. I bought a packet of cigarettes which thoroughly displeased Steve because, as he said, I was already on the programme and smoking was not allowed. I didn't see it that way.

It set the tone for the next 13 hours travelling on a very warm May Friday. We changed at Birmingham and headed for Swansea. We had been instructed by the staff to get a taxi from Swansea the fifteen miles to the centre and it would be paid when we got there. As the taxi was about to turn into the centre, I stuck the packet of cigarettes down the back of the seat, (what is it with me and sticking things down the back of car seats). I knew that I had had my last cigarette!

We walked in through the back door of what later come to be known as Challenge House at twelve thirty on the Friday night / Saturday morning. Exactly one week almost to the minute from when FC had stuck the gun in my back in that 'L' of a place.

Walking into the corridor of a converted supermarket, in a small village called Gorslas, in South West Wales, I was struck by how at peace I was. For the first time that I could think of, I felt that I was where I was supposed to be when I was supposed to be there for what I was supposed to be there for. I had moved from 'L' to heaven (on earth) in the space of seven days.

37 – Don't Quit (1997)
May 1997 – first day at Teen Challenge

THUD! THUD! THUD! Why were the police banging on the door? Have I got warrants? What would they want me for?

My mind raced as it was dragged out of its unconscious state by a voice now loudly calling on me to get up.

Was I back in Baird Street or something?

As consciousness finally forced its way through and prised my eyelids open, I was disorientated by the strange surroundings. I definitely wasn't in Baird Street, or Ervie Street. I wasn't in The Haven. The room I was in had two single beds parallel to each other in a long narrow shape. A sink stood in one corner next to the window, with thr door down the other end, about twenty-five feet away, and two old mismatched wardrobes next to it.

A figure stood in the doorway looking at me, half curious, half suspicious. Where was I?

Then it all came rushing back. The gun, the Valium, the prayer, Ken, the Haven, Steve Reilly and the National Express to Birmingham, then Swansea and finally a taxi with the cigarettes stuffed down the back. In through the back door, searched and bag searched and, finally, at around 1.30am up to a strange bedroom.

It was Saturday morning and I had just been woken up, quite loudly, at 7.45am (apparently that was a long lie as it was Saturday). Here I was in a bedroom in a converted supermarket in South Wales.

Rehab! What the heck?

The suspicious shadow at the door told me that I was to be ready and downstairs in the lounge for 8.15 for Quiet Time. Nope, no idea what that meant then. I was supposed to get up, washed etc, room tidied and then downstairs by then. It was all a bit bewildering.

In the crushing, crowding sound of what seemed like a million different accents, I obviously was clueless about it all.

A staff member called Neil Erskine had welcomed Steve and me in the night before. Both I and my bag were checked, thoroughly, to make sure I was not sneaking any drugs or cigarettes in. I wasn't. I had failed miserably at the start of the week to complete the tender. I had failed so badly that I was now in a Christian rehab in Gorslas, and I was not even thinking about drugs for the moment. I was then shown upstairs to a bedroom on the main landing. Two beds but on my own, for now.

At 8.30 we made our way through the adjoining doors into the large dining area for breakfast. There were about 8 large round tables with a number of seats. I just sat in the nearest chair. Most of the guys were talking about the Bible and calling each other brother and being really nice in a non-manipulative kind of way. It was just a bit overwhelming, I do not know what I thought rehab would be like, but it was not this.

After breakfast, we got ready for chapel. Chapel was a sort of morning church service. Some Christian choruses (obviously) were sung. People prayed out loud, some very loudly and then someone shared some encouragement, based on the Bible. It was all vague, new and very overwhelming.

Then it was off to house (Centre) cleaning duties. Every Saturday there would be an inspection so even more effort than normal was put in. As I was only in the door I had not been allocated a duty so was left to wander around a bit.

At some point in the morning, I remember seeing a guy (Anthony Sutcliffe) sitting at the top of the outdoor metal fire escape stairs. He looked fed up, so I went over. As I reached out my hand to say hello, a small card that I had in my shirt pocket fell out. My nana had given it to me. To be honest I had not even looked at it yet.

119

Anthony picked it up and started reading it. He looked up at me and smiled. "I was sitting here just thinking about leaving, " he said. "It's too tough and I can't do it. Thank you so much for this, this is God speaking to me."

"Eh!"

The card had a poem on it called "Don't Quit" on the other side were the following verses from the Bible:

"Trust in the LORD with all your heart, And lean not on your own understanding; In all your ways acknowledge Him, And He shall direct your paths." Proverbs 3:5-6

"Here you are, only in the door and God is using you to help people," Anthony said. He was at the later stages of Phase 3 in the programme, which meant he had been there for almost a year.

There were loads of thoughts running through my head as this happened. It was hard to process. All this God talk! The poem my nana had given., obviously for me, but had been so uplifting for Anthony; the verses on the back which were to become a sort of watchword for my life. (Thanks, nana).

We had a great chat, and Anthony began to tell me a lot more about the programme, and his own life. He was a genuinely good guy and became a great friend and encourager, not just to me but to loads of guys that came through the door.

I have no idea how Anthony's life has unfolded since then, but that meeting had a long-lasting effect on my life.

One week before I had a gun stuck in my back, here I was now apparently convincing someone not to quit.

Welcome to your new life, Stuart.

The rest of the day was a bit of a blur and a haze. Lunch, followed by dinner. The guys that had been on the programme a while went to a sports centre in the afternoon. In the evening it was a documentary and a movie. The movie was always PG and even then was carefully checked for language and themes. 9pm it was the BBC News. BBC because there were no adverts, and therefore no means of the guys getting distracted. It sounds over the top, but I will write again about why later I felt it was a cracking strategy.

This evening, though, I laughed as it seemed ludicrous.

Chapel at ten pm, no singing this time, just quiet acknowledgement and thanks (to God) for getting through the day.

Rooms at ten thirty pm (I was normally just going out at that time) and lights out at ten forty-five pm. Nobody complained about this.

My first full day in what would become my home for three years, my first proper day in what was "normal" life.

I slept.

The lyrics to the 'Don't Quit' poem are as follows:

When things go wrong, as they sometimes will,
When the road you're trudging seems all uphill,
When the funds are low and the debts are high,
And you want to smile, but you have to sigh,

When care is pressing you down a bit-
Rest if you must, but don't you quit.
Life is queer with its twists and turns,
As every one of us sometimes learns,

And many a fellow turns about
When he might have won had he stuck it out.
Don't give up though the pace seems slow -
You may succeed with another blow.

Often the goal is nearer than
It seems to a faint and faltering man;
Often the struggler has given up
When he might have captured the victor's cup;

And he learned too late when the night came down,
How close he was to the golden crown.
Success is failure turned inside out -
The silver tint in the clouds of doubt,

And you never can tell how close you are,
It might be near when it seems afar;
So stick to the fight when you're hardest hit -
It's when things seem worst that you must not quit. Anon

38 - Your new life (1997)
Jesus said, "You must be born again..."

Nicky Cruz: "I'm gonna give my life to God, David. It better work, because I damn near got killed for it." The Cross and the Switchblade *by* David Wilkerson[xx]

Sunday 18th May 1997 was the day after the day after the night before.

I woke up, strung out and desperate for a fix. I did not know how that was going to work out. I spoke more about this day in Completing the tenner.

Sunday 25th May, one week seven days, 168 hours, 10.080 secs (approx.) later I awoke in a bed in a room in a converted supermarket in Gorslas, Carmarthenshire.

Apparently, I was going to church. I used to enjoy church as a schoolkid. Blairtummock Primary would hold a service in the local Church of Scotland every second Friday. We used to "fight over" the right to hold the door open, and the biggest honour of carrying the biggest Bible to the pulpit at the front. I got to carry the Bible once and hold the doors a few times.

But I was a primary school pupil then. I was twenty-seven years old years old now, and, despite being here as a direct result of Ken Persaud praying for me, I thought I was too clever for the church.

121

We made our way in the minibus to City Temple, Swansea Elim church. This was a large, orange and yellow brick box of a building, set on a street on Dyfatty Street, hundreds of yards from Swansea city centre. The bus parked just outside on the main street, whilst we all unloaded and went in through the entrance to the rear of the building. It seemed enormous inside – and very bright. The seats were split into two rows against each wall, probably about ten wide, and a much larger row, about twenty seats wide down the middle. I think it probably seated between five and six hundred. The Teen Challenge guys were all led down to a row near the front of the right-hand side row.

I was taken aback by the range of instruments and microphones arrayed on the stage. I wasn't expecting that. The morning service was a bit of a blur. I do recall being stunned by how bright it was and how happy everyone seemed to be.

When the music started, I was stunned at seeing a full band, led by a guy I was later to find out was Chris Russon. The music was vibrant and made me feel good. All the songs seemed to centre around Jesus. I watched, bemused and could not help but look around at everyone.

There were about twenty guys on the Teen Challenge programme at that time. As well as a few, like Derek Hay and Rob Taylor who had completed it but were working there. They were from all over the United Kingdom, and from a diverse set of backgrounds. Addiction is no respecter of family income brackets or post codes.

The guys always sat here, front right of the seating as you looked down from the doors. I had been told by some of the other TC students this was because the girls (Women from Teen Challenge Hope House women's centre) sat at the back left. Under no circumstances where they allowed to talk or look at each other. I was curious to see if Susan (Halley) was there.

A preacher then got up to preach but I cannot recall any of it. The whole experience was a bit tiring for me.

Off we went back to the centre where the legend that was Mrs A (Margaret Anderson) had prepared her culinary phenomenon for our usual Sunday roast.

There was pretty much nothing to do in the afternoon, some of the guys went out a walk with staff. I stayed at the centre.

Back to the church in the evening. Same lively vibrant music. The same sense of joy on the building. I did struggle to keep my eyes open as my body was beginning to adjust to its new regime. At the end of the preaching, I cannot remember what it was, the preacher started talking about those that had never given their lives to Jesus. He was doing what was known as an altar call, where you responded by going to the front of the church and someone would pray with you.

I did not really understand much of what he was saying but I recall vividly that my heart was thumping. Every cell in my body was crying out in response and I knew I needed to go out. Full of nervousness, I turned to the staff member (Phil Winstanley), sitting beside me (I was the new student so I was child-minded) and asked if I could go out.

He frowned and looked over at the other staff member and mouthed that I wanted to go out. The other staff member shook his head. No, I was told I could not go out to the front.

It was like having the best drugs ever in my possession and having no way to take them, that is how great the frustration I felt was. (To this day I still think I am the only student in the history of Teen Challenge UK that was denied responding to a church altar call).

"You can go and see Pastor Hughes when we are at the centre," said Phil.

"Who is Pastor Hughes?" I asked.

"The centre manager."

The full fifteen miles back to the centre I could not speak to anyone. I was furious but expectant, angry but excited. My chest was still thumping.

After church on a Sunday evening, chips were bought from a local chippy and the guys could make chip sandwiched (piece n chips, chip butty, depending on where you are from). This just annoyed me as it meant I was delayed in getting back to centre.

When, FINALLY, the bus pulled up in the car park, I asked Phil where I could find Pastor Hughes. He told me to hang on until all the other students were sorted.

I was not happy. Eventually, Phil led me all the way down what seemed an even longer corridor than usual. Through the glass door into reception, and he banged on a door clearly marked *Centre Manager*.

"Yes."Phil opened the door, gave a brief explanation to Pastor Hughes, still hidden from my sight, and then told me to go in. Sitting facing the door, behind a very clean desk, was an older, immaculately dressed, white-haired man. "Sit down, Stuart. What can I do for you?"

I genuinely did not know where to start, so I fumbled through a recall of what had happened. My anticipation was through the roof at this point. "So, you would like to invite Jesus into your life, is that what you are saying?"

I did not have a clue what that meant. I just knew that my heart was thumping, worse than it was in the church and I was really, excited, but did not know why.

"Yyyessss!" I mumbled. Not quite sure what I was agreeing to.

"Would you like to pray, or would you like me to pray, and you can repeat after me?" asked Pastor Hughes.

Pray? The only other experience I had of prayer was when I tried to convince Pastor Ken Persaud over the phone on Monday (was that really on six days ago) to tell my mum to give me a tenner. Look what happened there.

I was now actually, just a little bit fearful and uncomfortable at the thought of more prayer. All these new people seemed to talk about and practice praying like it was the most natural thing in the world to do.

They prayed as if they believed that their God could hear them and was answering them. My interaction with Ken's prayer and how I had been since, came rushing home. I was nervous and yet, a little bit excited.

"Will you say it, and I will repeat." Things just happened.

As Pastor Hughes began to talk about asking Jesus to forgive me for my sins and to come into my life and help me live life on His terms, I found myself repeating the words he was saying. It was crazy, but as each word stumbled out of my mouth, I began to be more confident.

By the time we both said, "Amen", something had changed.

Long my imprisoned spirit lay,
Fast bound in sin and nature's night;
Thine eye diffused a quickening ray;
I woke, the dungeon flamed with light;
My chains fell off, my heart was free,
I rose, went forth, and followed Thee
From 'And can it be' by Charles Wesley)

Those lines describe better than I ever could what had happened to me. It was like a burden had been lifted. I felt lighter and better than I had ever felt in my life.

Pastor Hughes smiled politely at me. Told me that I was now a child of God and the angels were rejoicing.

I did not understand any of that, but I felt different. I ran up to the Phase One landing and would tell anyone who would listen that I was now a Christian. There were nodding looks, (apparently, it was normal for guys to make that decision, but remember addicts are manipulative and, like a chameleon, will fit into any background to get what they want.

This was different though. I was different. I knew it. The preacher in the church that night, I was later to find out, was Pastor Phil Hills. Pastor of Swansea Elim. He was and is still, chairman of Teen Challenge UK.

He became over the years a great influence in my life, and one of the best communicators of the God of the Bible and Biblical ways that I have ever heard. Pastor Phil seems to pop up at strategic times in my life and I was thrilled that, for the first time as a Pastor myself, I was able to invite him to speak at Easterhouse Community Church in February 2018. Our church celebrated seven years of ministry to the community then.

Phil is a great believer in discipleship, following Jesus and becoming someone who leads and disciple others to follow Jesus.

In my case, 18th February 2018 was full circle. Almost twenty-one years since 25th May 1997, I was able to introduce the guy that set out to disciple me, to those I have set out to disciple.

Still the small, in ward voice I hear
That whispers all my sins forgiven
Still the atoning blood is near,
That quenched the wrath of hostile Heaven.
I feel the life His wounds impart;
I feel the Saviour in my heart

No condemnation now I dread;
Jesus, and all in Him, is mine;

Alive in Him, my living Head,
And clothed in righteousness divine,
Bold I approach the eternal throne,
And claim the crown, through Christ my own
Amazing love! How can it be,
That Thou, my God, shouldst die for me?
Charles Wesley

39 - **Ring of smoke (1997)**
Ring of smoke

Taking a puff on a cancer stick
Not really thinking of being sick
The momentary relief of the tar and 'tine
Peace in my life, through poison unseen

Years pass through with no noticeable news
Of the dreaded demand of its dirty dues
Not knowing of the constricted tightness of breath
That would hurry intimacy with the angel of death

Then one day an infection makes itself known
Showing its teeth, tormenting what's sown
by the damage done from years long gone by
Lungs now crippled and crying out "Why?"

Slowly I take in a breath, now so pure
Through an oxygen bottle, because there is no cure
If only I had listened long ago to the folk
That warned of the danger in that ring of smoke
Stuart Patterson ©2018

It was sometime around 1986 (it seems all the major stuff was). I am not exactly sure when, but probably, if I was not a procrastinator, I could find out.

Anyway, I digress, I was sitting in a cold damp cell that was the old Airdrie Sheriff Court building. My crime this time was opening a lock fast place; the lock fast place being a newsagent in Bargeddie. It was one of those things that, as young people in the gang we thought was cool, and a quick way to get money. The effect it had on the owners, parents court systems etc did not occur to us. Like so much we were involved in.

I was sharing a cell with four others waiting to be taken up to the courtroom. I cannot for the life of me remember anything about my "roommates" except they were smoking rolling tobacco. Other than cannabis, I did not smoke currently, (many hash smokers did not consider themselves smokers).

I remember asking for one, and one of the guys looking at me and asking if I smoked. I said that I did not but since it seemed I was going to prison it might be a good time to start.

They all shook their heads, but I was passed one anyway. And thus, it began.

It is amazing how quickly smoking gets a grip on you. How acceptable it is (at least on those days) to be puffing and drawing what is basically poison gift wrapped in a special paper.

People often ask how many I smoked, it's a stupid question in a lot of ways, because like my drugs, the answer was always as much as I could.

For the next eleven years, it was one cigarette after another; especially when I was at my worst with speed (amphetamine sulphate). The lengths we would go to at times, and some of the dirty habits and ways we would indulge when there was no cash for cigarettes - well!!!!

In my short remand sentences, as well as when I finally got my BIG sentence for the drugs, it was always about having a smoke.

When I got out of prison, I was always tapping (borrowing) cigarettes as If I was going to pay back that debt.

Some days I must have smoked around 60 - 70 a day, others not much less.

Right up until my entry to Teen Challenge Wales, smoking was as much a part of my life as the drugs.

Upon entering Wales, after leaving my last pack in the taxi seat, I have never smoked since.

Oh, there were times. Like when David "Packie" Hamilton came to visit with a guy the week after I came in. It was a guy he was working with to help beat addiction. Saturday afternoon, great May day. Most of the students were at leisure centre but because I was still on induction I couldn't go. I was sitting up the back, behind the volleyball court when this guy came up and sat beside me.

He asked me if I wanted a cigarette, and automatically I said, "Nah mate I've no smoked in a week, and if I take that noo, its a week wasted'"

Five minutes later, I was desperate for a cigarette, but try as might I could not get the guy on his own again.

Two weeks later it struck me what I had done then, saying "No" in the short term as it was more beneficial in the long term. Or - postponement of immediate gratification for long-term benefit.

There were other times, like every single meal. Part of the normal habit of smoking was always a cigarette with a cup of tea after eating something.

I was in a place where I could not do that. Many times, in those first few weeks I would find myself automatically reaching for a packet of cigarettes, usually in my pocket but no longer there.

Instead, I got myself a wee Gideons Pocket New Testament and Psalms. Very quickly I developed the habit of reaching into my pocket and, instead of pulling out a cigarette, I would pull that out and read a few verses from the Bible. It was great, and the temptation to smoke quickly passed.

It's amazing how temptation goes when you look to God to help you beat it.

I have not smoked since that last taxi journey. I am glad I never managed to get one from Packie's friend. I never gave the memory of them much thought until my mum and dad were each diagnosed with COPD and seeing the damage done to them.

I thought that as I had smoked for a relatively short time that I had escaped the consequences of it.

In January 2018 I struggled with the same chest infection that seemed to be taking everybody out then. Antibiotics and inhalers had no discernible effects, and the doctor escalated the medication.

After about six weeks of it, I was in with the practice nurse. We did a few tests and she suggested that those short years had maybe wreaked some damage after all.

The chest infection may have exacerbated it and my restricted breathing, lack of energy and coughing fits might just be down to that fateful day in Airdrie Sheriff Court and having that first roll-up cigarette.

What else do we take in that seems good in the moment, but in the long term can wreak havoc?

The Bible says that, *"There is a way that seems right to a man, but its end is the way of death."* Proverbs 14:12 NKJV

40 - Let's do this! (1997)
THAT first morning

"You only get one shot, do not miss your chance to blow
This opportunity comes once in a lifetime you better..."
From *Lose Yourself* by Marshall B Mathers

So here I am in a former supermarket, in a foreign country, free from heroin. Eh??????

The Sunday night, after being with Pastor Hughes and repenting of a life full of sin lived, and loved outside Christ, I went up to the Phase One landing where my room was. Having told the guys of my decision to follow Jesus, I went into my room and went to bed. At this point the other bed was empty.

I woke up the next morning, unsure of what the routine was as I had never been there on a weekday. As I was in a room on my own, I had to deal with some hang-ups and try and find out. I still did not know how to speak up for myself. I still was very uncomfortable in strange surroundings.

127

Drugs were not on my mind?

What I had to do was. Entering straight into the very disciplined structure of the Teen Challenge programme helped.

Your steps really were ordered for you. Ecclesiastes 3 talks about a time for everything, in TC parlance that was:

a time to rise,
a time to shave,
a time to read,
a time to pray,
a time to eat,
a time to clean,
a time to learn,
a time to praise,
a time to mix,
with time to play,
more time to learn,
more time to pray,
a time to sleep,
thankful for each day.
Stuart Patterson ©2018

It was a very coordinated place, designed to help build structure into unstructured lives. Especially in those early days it helped me grieve for who I used to be, but also consider who I was now and what to do.

It's not easy going from the cloud and fog of addiction, where senses are filled and thought processes are aligned to completing the tenner.

The hyper-awareness of God and love was very overwhelming.

My mind raced between blind acceptance to analytical questioning.

"How does this go? Am I on a bad acid (LSD) trip? Does this make sense?"

It is easy to throw around clichés about forgiveness etc without really understanding the reality of it.

You see, my pain did not revolve around what others had done to me, my pain, my guilt and my shame focused on the wrong I had done to others.

I spent a lot of time alone in the personal graveyard of my mind, coming to terms with a lot of the destruction I had wreaked on lives.

The destruction of my own potential and the havoc wreaked amongst family and friends.

My quest to complete the tenner had not allowed me to process the damage that I had caused to others, whilst I was causing it.

But now I had to process it.

Now I had to take ownership of that whole world of hurt. If I didn't, then I couldn't move on from it. In the words of that great prophet Bono, I would be *"stuck in a moment I can't get out of"*.

The underlying fact that God forgave me completely and unreservedly though, gave me the courage and the strength for the days ahead.

I knew part of this new life would involve seeking forgiveness from others that I had hurt.

I knew that it meant facing up to a whole load of issues that I had avoided.

I knew that it was not going to be easy.

It was funny though, that at no time did I miss the solace of the needle, or the comfort of the heroin or hash. It was a painful time, but it was also a genuine rebirth.

If I wanted to move onto this new life, I had to excise some of the ghosts of the old.

These truly were birth pains of a whole new world. As much as I feared them, I was also excited to face them.

My problem was, though, that I did not really know how to face or deal with the pain. I would go into the morning chapel times totally bemused by the guys with their hands in the air praising God.

They seemed to have no trouble praying out loud. I could not even speak out loud to people I could see.

They seemed to have no trouble singing the songs.

I did!

I knew that what I had experienced on Sunday evening with Pastor Hughes was real.

I knew the Monday morning when I woke up and the first thoughts in my mind were about Jesus.

Sure, I had questions, doubts and fears, but never about the reality of what had happened.

There was all sort of emotions racing through my head. That poem card "Don't Quit" that my Nana had given me and the bits of the Bible that were on it seemed to form a protection around me. Not the "*don't quit*" bit, but the verses, almost pleading with me to "trust in the LORD, with all my heart," to not try and work it out. I got it. I knew I was committed to whatever lay ahead, not behind, but I also knew I had to confront those shadows from my past in order to move on.

Ok, I thought, let's do this!

This is MY life!

41 - Jailbreak (1997)
There it was...

"For I know the plans I have for you," declares the Lord, "plans to prosper you and not to harm you, plans to give you hope and a future. Then you will call on me and come and pray to me, and I will listen to you. You will seek me and find me when you seek me with all your heart. I will be found by you," declares the Lord, "and will bring you back from captivity. I will gather you from

all the nations and places where I have banished you," declares the Lord, "and will bring you back to the place from which I carried you into exile."" Jeremiah 29:11-14 NIV

Two weeks I had been in Teen Challenge now.

Two weeks that seemed to promise so much, and yet I was feeling so down. From the initial elation of THAT Sunday evening to this Thursday morning.

It was the fifth June 1997. I should be filled with hope at the thought that I had not taken ANY drugs for three weeks, (since a week before coming into Teen Challenge). The first time since I was fourteen years old that that happened.

The problem was, though, that as the fight for the next fix subsided, it was replaced by the awareness of what my life had been through the years of addiction and trying to complete the tenner. It wasn't that I had never been aware of the hurt that I had caused, I just could not allow it to get in the way of getting the next fix. The pain was real, but the craving for a fix was more real

Now I had no cause to distract and no stone to hide behind. I was, to all intents and purposes, as naked as Adam was in the Garden of Eden, my fig leaf had been removed, nothing to hide behind, no Eve to blame and standing before God aware of the effect of the forbidden fruit.

My choices had got me here. I was ashamed. I was drained. I was still aware that I was seeing life differently, and that God was there. I just had no concept of how I stood in those moments.

It was a frightening place, and yet at the same time there was a comfort and a reassurance that I could not really make sense of or understand.

Anyway, morning tea break on that day I made my way to the chapel. This is a room set apart for the praise and prayer times for the staff and students, as well as a place of solitude and reflection.

We would start and finish each day with a chapel time a and the chapels in Teen Challenge were very uplifting, my counsellor, Pastor Kerri Jenkins was fantastic.

So, in I went. I found myself sitting on the front row, with a tatty blue cardboard covered NIV Bible that had probably passed through the hands of several students before me.

I thumbed aimlessly through pages and words that seemed to have no relevance to me, the way they did to students that had been around longer than me.

Nothing jumped off the pages. Nothing made sense. There were many verses that had been scored over with highlighter pens, obviously significant to other enquiring hearts at other times.

My heart cry that morning was simply an "I don't get this!"

I stumbled upon the brightly coloured verses above. Someone had stopped at these verses before, and so I stopped to see if I could see what they saw.

Often quoted verses, I was soon to discover, but I had never heard them before. No one had read them to me as a promise from God.

"For I know the plans I have for you…to give you a future and a hope" yeah yeah, there seemed to be a lot of talk in TC about that.

However, in my haze of the present, the future was too untouchable; too intangible.

It could not be seen.

How on earth could I get through the mess I had made of my life, and of those, I had trashed with my addiction?

On I read, *"In those days when you pray, I will listen…"* yep, I had done that was doing that, I sort of get that.

"If you look for me wholeheartedly, you will find Me…" I really was putting as much energy into seeking God as I had into my addiction.

Every spare moment was spent pushing aside the gravestones of the past to try and find Him.

There it happened! I discovered the power of Scripture to make eternity relevant to the present.

In the next few moments, it was as if God Himself jumped off the pages of a printed book and spoke personally to me. He got my ears. He got my mind. He got my heart.

You know when you hear somebody talking about you, but it is good stuff, in the sense that you know it is right, and it leaves you with a sense of direction. That is how I felt when I heard the following verses.

"I will be found by you," declares the Lord, *"and **will bring you back from captivity**. I will gather you from all the nations and places where I have banished you,"* declares the Lord, *"and will bring you back to the place from which I carried you into exile.""*

That one word. "**captivity…**" I got it.

That was how I had been feeling. Existing in the present but trapped in the past. I had not been able to describe it, but that word jumped out at me in a way that made me want to look at the other words it hung out with.

I knew I was captive, but I did not know who held the key to the door.

*"I **WILL** be found by you…"* wow.

It is hard to get across how the weight that had been pressing me down seemed to be lifting at the very sound of these words.

It is almost impossible to reflect in words the feeling of rising like helium in me.

God was promising that if I kept looking, I would find Him. In a mad sort of way, I knew what it meant, without any effort on my part.

In years gone by I had walked the proverbial five hundred miles in the search for a fix.

I had knocked on doors and confronted fears to satisfy that itch.

It was like that, but it wasn't.

It was as if I knew that the search for a fix was the complete counterfeit and opposite to what I was hearing here.

I could not wait to hear the next part of this conversation. *"and will bring you back from captivity."*

There it was.

Keep going, Stuart.

You are going the right way.

Keep going.

The illusion of captivity will pass into the reality of freedom.

The shackles of the past, the torment of the present will find their purpose in the promise of His future.

Only minutes had passed since I walked into the chapel.

Only minutes since I had opened a book, without much hope, but a glimmer was apparently enough.

Only minutes since a conversation with myself became an audience with the King.

Eternity could have passed.

It might have been years.

Time had stood still for just a few seconds, and yet it was long enough to raise this dead man to life.

I had spoken before about how my perspective and outlook changed as I sat with Pastor Robert Hughes and asked Christ to change me.

I had mentioned the immediate elation of those moments. I had honestly spent the next week and a half looking for God. Now I was so aware that He had always been there.

He had always been at my side.

He was just waiting for the moment to speak in a way, and at a time where I would "get it".

This was that moment.

As far as defining points in my life go, this was right up there.

It was not so much that I heard an audible voice, but the feeling in my gut as I read those words made it seem audible.

The words came alive in a way I had never known my hearing to work before.

I could almost believe it was like hearing a whisper in my ear, speaking to me directly.

I knew, in that instant, that no matter what I was to keep going forward, trusting in a God I did not really know and placing myself on a path I did not understand.

I knew I had to keep looking, in His Word, around His people open and attentive to know God more.

One day short of it being three weeks since I had felt the gun in my back this was massive.

This was different.

This was bigger than anything I could ever have asked or imagined, and since all I had asked or imagined was a fiver to complete the tenner…

All a sudden certain piece of the Bible I had already heard, like the ones on the "*Don't Quit*" poem card my nana gave me made sense.

The book of Proverbs encourages me to trust God with all my heart and not try and figure things out. Again, the promise that this would restore me.

John 3:16 told me that God loved me so much He gave Jesus for me.

This was like a low blow torch to my low self-worth.

If God thought that much of me, then surely, I was worth the work and effort it was going to take to see my life rebuilt, but on God's terms.

It was as if Christ Himself was with me in the chapel that day.

It was like He was telling me that the addiction that I had been locked into and held captive by, He was taking that captive so I could move out in freedom.

Jesus Christ was taking my captivity captive. I stood up and walked out of the chapel and into the rest of my life – more confident – more hopeful – more expectant freer than I had ever been in my life. That was twenty-two years ago. There have been moments but thank God I am still free.

This is MY life!

42 – Hands On (1997)
Power from on high

'When you strip it of everything else, Pentecost stands for power and life. That's what came into the church when the Holy Spirit came down on the day of Pentecost.'
David Wilkerson, The Cross and the Switchblade

One of the questions I was asked most often by students in those first few weeks in Teen Challenge was whether I knew a guy called Jay Fallon. He was from Drumchapel, another housing scheme in Glasgow. Jay had graduated Teen Challenge a few years before and seemed to have a bit of a reputation as a preacher, and more importantly, as being on fire for Jesus. I did not know him.

One of the first Sunday mornings at City Temple, though, a fellow student pointed earnestly at a guy standing outside the coach as we pulled up. Standing not much taller than me, with a bit sallower skin, was the guy that was going to play such a big part in my early Christian development. Neither he nor I knew that when I stepped up to say hello to him when I got off the coach that day.

Being a new student, I was very quickly ushered back into line with the rest of the guys and we went into church. As we arrived back at the centre, though after the service Jay was standing waiting when I got off the coach.

"Come here a minute," he says, "you been baptised in the Holy Ghost yet?"

"What? Whits that?" I asked bemused. My only reference to the Holy Ghost was asking my dad years before at a wedding or a funeral or something in a chapel what in *Spirito Sancto* meant. "It's when God gies ye power for being a Christian" Jay answered as he told me to follow him.

He took me into the classroom at the back of the Teen Challenge centre, placed his hands on my head, and began to pray earnestly. I am not quite sure what he was praying for as I could not make sense of the 'words' he was using. It seemed to be another language, yet it did not sound even familiar as that.

Jay persevered for a while, but it was obvious that nothing was happening. He stopped and began to explain to me, and as he did, I was a wee bit annoyed about nothing happening. Jay asked me to go and speak to Pastor Hughes and to get him to spend time with me on it. Jay then left the class, walked out to his car and drove away.

That was it! My first encounter. Jay had come all the way back to the centre just to pray with me over this. I went immediately to Pastor Hughes' office and told him what happened. Pastor Hughes sat and explained to me about Pentecost, and how God equips and empowers us to live as His witnesses. I think most of it went over my head at that point to be honest, but like on that first night, I began to feel a stirring in my gut. I was curious and I was hungry for whatever Jesus had for me.

Funnily enough, not long after that in one of the evening services in City Temple, there was another altar call (opportunity to respond for prayer ministry). This time I could go up to the front of the stage, along with dozens of other people.

Pastor Ken Robling, one of the elders in the church came over to me. He asked if I wanted to be prayed for, to be honest I already felt a bit 'weird'. Pastor Ken was a six-foot-tall, slim man with silvery white hair. Always immaculate dressed in light coloured suits. Just like Jay a few weeks before, he placed his hands on my head and began to pray. Almost instantly I felt a power wash over me. It is quite hard to describe , *better felt than telt* as they say. But it was real, and it was incredible. I could not help but fall back, gently as weird as it sounds.

Pastor Ken knelt down and continued to gently pray over me, as I felt my tongue, on fire as it were. I had to open my mouth and what came out was the most unintelligible babble possible, and yet it felt right. I was aware of everything going on around me, but I did not want to move. The babbling seemed to make sense to part of me, it was almost like the way a toddler not yet formed its speech right speaking to a parent. It was wonderful, beautiful, peaceful – and right.

After what seemed like hours, but was only a few minutes, I got back up to my feet. Pastor Ken was still standing there, smiling over me. He gave me a hug, and asked "Were you just filled with the Holy Ghost?"

I could not speak, I just smiled back. Probably the biggest smile I had managed in a long, long time.

Back at the centre, I wanted to read my Bible and any book that would tell me more about what I had just experienced. I could not get enough.

After a few weeks Jay was back at the centre, and I had to tell him. The biggest smile covered his face as he said, "Do you see why you need it noo?"

"Aye!" says I "a dae."

Jay, and his wife Fiona were to play a massive part in my life on those days. Anytime he was around, he was around. The guys loved it when he took chapel. The messages he spoke were always challenging, and yet at the same time – encouraging. When he prayed, it seemed that heaven moved.

There were other times on the programme where I had to trust in this new, implicit goodness and love of God that I wasn't sure of. After a few months, I was diagnosed with *Hepatitis C,* which was a relief in one way, as I was expecting it to be HIV, as that was what was always on the news etc. I was convinced, even though I almost always used the needle exchange (an official drop in for exchanging old, used needles for new clean ones, in Easterhouse Health Centre) that I would be infected. There had been many times before the introduction of the needle exchange where I had used whatever was available, regardless of where it had come from. The immediate desire for the fix much stronger than any other piece of wisdom, like preventing disease.

Anyway, in Teen Challenge we had Tuesday afternoon main prayer times. We would use these for praying on behalf of others and greater needs outside centre. I had spoken to then manager, Mike Rankin, about my *Hep C* and said that it was cool as I would get the guys to pray for me. Mike expressed his misgivings about this and said that he was not so sure the guys would be so understanding, and that it could cause problems. I knew though, that if I had to learn to trust Jesus with the big stuff – then this THIS was big stuff. I was told that I had been set free, then why should I feel imprisoned by the very knowledge of being sick. That did not make sense to me.

Over thirty guys were crowded into the chapel that afternoon. Only one wee window to the front of the right-hand side wall, it seemed more claustrophobic than ever. I had never in my life felt so nervous as I listened to the guys, one after another, offering up various prayers for various things.

"Father God, I thank you that now you have shown me that I have *Hep C* I can start to appreciate the new boundaries that are in my life. LORD, will you please bring a speedy healing, but also let us know, that even though we have consequences to our former life – we also have new ways of dealing with them. In Jesus name, amen!"

I held my breath as I finished, but at the same time the relief that flooded into my soul and my mind was overwhelming. "Amen." I began to hear as one guy after another echoed the sentiments.

On a visit back to Teen Challenge a few years later, I went into the morning chapel. I sat there as one guy, offered up a thanksgiving prayer that he did not need to hide his *Hep C,* and that because of Jesus he knew he had people to help support him through it. I sat through his prayer, weeping with thanksgiving. Everyone in that room was unaware of my prayer, but my prayer had been answered in an even bigger way than I thought.

My *Hep C was dealt with* through *Interferon Combi* treatment in 2003. It was not an easy treatment, and at times I was totally wrecked by it, but ever since my blood results have always come back as – *Hep C not detected.*

43 - The ghost of Christmas past (1997)
A tale of three doors.

"Men's courses will foreshadow certain ends, to which, if persevered in, they must lead," said Scrooge. "But if the courses be departed from, the ends will change."
Charles Dickens, *A Christmas Carol*

Waking up in my room on Christmas morning was strange. It was a Thursday; I now had a wee guy from Lancashire sharing a room with me.

He was a few years older than me and had a couple of kids. He had struggled in the build up to Christmas, and I was no use to him. I had woken before lights on, which was to be later as it was Christmas.

It was dark and as my eyes grew accustomed to the lack of light, I looked around to see if Jimmy was ok. He was still sleeping. The rapping on the other doors on the landing, and the approaching feet took me back to a moment in my past.

As a kid, Christmas was great. I remember very early on, probably about seven or eight years old going out with mum and dad on my own.

There were five of us at that point, with youngest Neil not being born yet, so it was very rare, and I loved it. We went down the Barras, it was Christmas Eve and it was snowing (it might have been rain, but I am writing this, so I get to wrap it in nostalgia).

The Barras was the "world's largest indoor market" so the legend went. In the 70's in Glasgow it was world all of its own; full of life and lights – lots of lights. With the famous Barrowland Ballroom and its neon starbust signage making this evening even more special. The Barras was pure dead brilliant, especially at night, especially at Christmas – and here I was with mum and dad.

Passing the shopfronts just down from the famous ballroom, we stopped and gazed in at a shop window full of toys. My eyes lit on a Scalextric set. The packaging with a full colour image of the track and the two wee plastic racing cars. My imagination already seeing them racing around the magical figure of eight track.

I'd love to have that and couldn't believe it when mum and dad both asked me what I wanted for Christmas. Speechless, disbelieving, I pointed at the Scalextric.

"Ah we'll need to see if Santa can manage that" said dad.

My mum grabbed me then and said "c'mon over here wi me" as she took me over to a clothes shop. Can you believe it?

From a shopfront full of toys and THAT Scalextric set, to a shop full of clothes. I honestly could not tell you what sort of clothes it sold.

I never even copped on to the fact that my dad did not follow us, and even when he caught up, it never occurred to me to ask what was in the large bag he was holding.

Even now, sitting here typing this all these years later I am crying at the memory of such a vivid scene from my early years.

Christmas morning was always great in the Patterson house. Christmas was celebrated. It was an occasion. It would always start with baths and early bed on Christmas Eve.

John, the eldest would always beg to stay up, but never won. Apparently, there was some mystery happened in the house on Christmas Eve that children were not allowed to witness.

All five of us seemed to have synchronised body clocks that would rise around five am on Christmas morning. We whispered and cajoled each other to go and wake mum and dad. We were all cowards though.

We knew the drill. Around 6 -6.30 mum and dad would get up and dad would then let us begin the Christmas search. We had to find the handle from the living room door. It was always removed the night before, as this was part of the mystery dad would say.

Obviously, it was because we were a bunch of nosey, impatient kids and we probably would not have waited until they were up.

We knew whoever found the handle got to go in first. I am nearly convinced that Gary, second eldest, discovered it this time, buried beneath a pile of scheme blankets (coats and jackets) in my parent's wardrobe.

As dad attached the handle, we all wondered, in pent up adoration of what was behind the door.

Who's pile of presents would be biggest?

Who would have the best present?

Where would my pile be stacked?

Mine and Darrin's were always next to each other, so I would always look on with a very critical eye to see who had the largest pile.

Up to when I turned 18, they were always the same.

So, the door opened, and in we went, led by Gary. Our living room always looked like a treasure house on Christmas morning. Despite never really having much, mum and dad always went way out at Christmas to spoil us.

As you moved in through the living room door, as soon as the light came on it dazzled off the myriad decorations hung everywhere.

Paperchains and crepe decorations, mostly made by mum, made it seem like a treasure grotto – made even more like that by the five piles of present.

As mum began to tell us where our pile lay in the explosion of colour and mountains of presents my eyes were transfixed on a pile over by the sofa, with a very familiar shaped box, its contents concealed behind wrapping paper.

It couldn't be – could it?

I had never wanted something so much in my life. As I was directed to the pile, I grabbed that package first and began ripping furiously at the paper.

Yes! As the packaging was slowly revealed, so was the Scalextric name. Christmas morning. Hopes answered, fears relieved.

Here it was. I could not wait to get it set up. Didn't matter what the others had. My petty jealousy of my wee brother, Darrin and what he got was forgotten. I was not interested in the myriad of books that would be in my lot. Whatever I normally got at Christmas, I always got books.

I was in heaven. I wept.

Then my memory moves me onto a Christmas around the early 90's. Not sure which year, but it was also accompanied by a knock on my room door.

"Stuart, open your door, its Christmas. And the weans want their sweets," mum bellowed through.

It was Christmas evening, for them. For me it was just another weekend as I did not have a shift.

So, I lay in my room, pretending to be asleep and not wanting anything to do with the joy all around me. I was in my early twenties (really cannot be sure how old, that's how messed up my life was at that point) and I worked as a building site security guard for a company called Ark Security Services. They were part of a community outfit called Barlarnark Community Business. It meant I would arrive on site at 4pm and leave at 8.30am. Home for a sleep, up at three, out to get a fix and back to work.

Weekends I normally started at 3.30pm Friday and finished at 8.30am Monday – for £1.25 per hour. I hated people. Being around people reminded me of how far gone I was so I'd rather not be around them. I did my job, took my drugs and that was that. Anything else interfered with getting a fix.

At this point in my life I only felt tolerated, even by myself. I wasn't working this weekend as I had been given a choice of Christmas or New Year and had taken the latter, although I had begged for both.

I lay on my bed, my eyes screwed tightly shut, hoping it would block out everything going on outside the door. It was no use though, as another voice joined the demand. With my big sister, Yvonne, now calling I knew I was going to have to give in.

All the sweets and treats for the younger kids were on top of the wardrobe in my room. I had been out with mum to get them in one of my more lucid moments and had naturally put them up there as no one came in my room. Probably more out of fear off what they might find.

Yvonne was screaming at me and calling me all the selfish *&^^%$ in the world. She was right and I knew she was.

I opened the door, feigning a yawn, took the stuff down and gave it to her. Then promptly closed the door again, making sure to lock the catch I had placed on it. The purpose of the catch was to stop being interrupted when I was having a fix. Door locked I lay down and slid back into my own oblivion, my own private hell.

I wept.

Only a few years later and here I am now back in this present. In my room with the light now on, and Jimmy quietly thanking God that, although he could not physically be with his kids that day, for the first time in around fifteen years he was sober. For the first time as a parent he was looking forward.

As we went through getting ready and having breakfast (no cleaning duties this morning) we were waiting on being allowed through yet another locked door, (this time the Teen Challenge lounge). The glass door from the dining room down the four steps to the large sitting room.

The lounge door was locked in Teen Challenge at night as some students had gotten into the habit of sneaking down late on to watch TV. Why that was not allowed is for another time?

After battling (with my own emotions and thoughts) to remain in Teen Challenge since entering in May that year, here I was. It was Christmas and the old apprehensions were still there. I knew of Christ, knew OF the real reason etc, but the ghost of Christmas past came back to taunt me that morning, or so it seemed.

The buzz around the Centre was unreal, around 20 guys all enjoying and enduring their first sober Christmas. I had never known a sober Christmas as an adult.

I was aware of my family back in Glasgow, that for them they did not have to worry about locked doors, and stoned son / brother.

I was aware of aunts and uncles and cousins all delighted that I was getting myself sorted. I was aware of an awful lot, which in fairness I had used drugs to numb the awareness of before.

I was aware and it hurt. It was not just the ghost of Christmas past that taunted me, but the present and the future.

In real terms, I was seven months into adult life at the age of twenty-seven.

My past had cast a long dark shadow over my present and my future, and this morning it seemed a little bit too much.

I longed for the shop window and the hidden door handle and mum and dad to myself and my brothers and sister fighting over each other's presents and Christmas dinner and visiting nana and granda and going to sleep on Christmas night. I longed for THAT Christmas.

For me though, it set up the memory of the ghost of Christmas past.

Some of the guys around me had kids, and families of their own. Some were banned from contact with their families, others were only a few weeks in the door.

Staff members that had completed the programme were buzzing and told us we were about to find out what Christmas was about.

There were no work duties, other than the basics. It was downtime all day and carefully selected and censored Christmas movies.

However, I remember the same dread that I experienced on that night a few years before.

Unsure how to approach this moment.

Unsure of my newfound faith in Jesus and how it would work out through this day.

My next memory is sometime that day, Paul Evans, one of the kindest men I have ever been blessed to know, and his wife Pru, one of the kindest ladies I have ever been blessed to know, walking in the doors with their young daughters Leeann and Bethan.

I was confused, it was Christmas. Should not they be with their family at Christmas instead of in a rehab (it's funny because this is the ONLY time in my whole TC journey that I thought of it as rehab).

This confused me. The Evans family celebrated with us as if we were their family. The games, the sweets, Christmas dinner. Everything. The whole family!

At the earliest opportunity I asked Paul. I knew he was on duty, so I knew he had to be there. I will never forget his answer.

"Stuart, you guys are our family. This IS what Christmas is about . It's not just all you that Christ is restoring but all your families and even communities. Hope starts here for you all. Why would I not want my daughters to see the real reason for Christmas?"

I was in heaven.

This is my LIFE!

44 - Airplane Gaze part 2 (1998)
The earth below...

Sometimes, flying feels too godlike to be attained by man.
Sometimes, the world from above seems too beautiful, too
wonderful, too distant for human eyes to see ...
Charles A. Lindbergh, The Spirit of St. Louis, *1953*

In the chapter *Airplane Gaze part 1,* I recounted my love of maps and satellites etc, and how I longed to stare out at the earth below from an airplane window.

I told of the resignation I felt in February 1997 when, through being distracted by an airplane flying overhead, I resigned myself to that never happening.

Yet only a few months later, through an unbelievable sequence of events I found myself here in Teen Challenge. An organisation of men and women full of faith in Jesus and His ability to raise hope and victory where there was only death and defeat.

I gave my life, wrecked as it was to Christ and Teen Challenge taught me how to live life all over again in the light of God's love for my life. The Teen Challenge programme was made up of fourteen group studies and countless personal studies. The aim was to prepare me to live this new life of love and value from God through Jesus Christ.

Here is how the introduction to *Group Studies for new Christians* describes the purpose:

We teach principles of living the students can apply to their lives immediately. The students learn to deal with their problems and to successfully change their way of living. We teach them how to get rid of bad habits and how to develop new habits. For example, we teach them how to overcome anger, how to get rid of boredom, and how to manage their feelings. Many students need freedom from guilt. We teach that guilt is caused by sin, by disobeying God's laws. Only God can remove this guilt when one admits he has sinned (disobeyed God). The only way to properly deal with the problem of guilt, the student learns, is to ask Jesus Christ to become the Leader of his life. With Jesus as Leader, he can now do what Christ wants him to do. He no longer does his own thing. Our curriculum instructs students that only after beginning a relationship with Jesus can people successfully overcome their problems,

God is the only One Who can give us the desire and the power to properly respond to each situation we face in life. Almost everyone can make a few changes in his life for a few days. But it takes the help of God Himself to successfully overcome all the problems a person faces. Therefore, we place such a great emphasis on the study of God's word.

David Batty and Don Wilkerson.

The *Group Studies for New Christians* fourteen courses were designed to form a comprehensive, Biblical life application course. Their titles pretty much describe the ground they covered and, along with counselling and personal Bible study plans, formed the basis of the Teen Challenge programme, so successful in over one hundred countries.

They did not teach us how to stop taking drugs, but rather, how to start living life – life with the ultimate value of God's love seen through Christ. The studies were as follows:

1. *How Can I Know I'm a Christian?*
2. *A Quick Look at the Bible*
3. *Attitudes*
4. *Temptation*
5. *Successful Christian Living (includes studies on the ministry of the Holy Spirit.)*
6. *Growing Through Failure*
7. *Christian Practices (Local Church Relationships)*
8. *Obedience to God*
9. *Obedience to Man*
10. *Anger and Personal Rights*
11. *How to Study the Bible*
12. *Love and Accepting Myself*
13. *Personal Relationships with Others*
14. *Spiritual Power and the Supernatural*

It was an intensive programme, with many guys joking that it was easier to do a prison sentence than complete Teen Challenge.

Each student was also assigned a counsellor (a personal development worker) on starting the programme. My first one was a former nightclub owner from the Welsh valleys, Reverend Keri Jenkins. He was about five foot five, in his late fifties maybe early sixties. Keri had surrendered his life to Jesus and gave up the nightclub in his early thirties. He was a fireball, with a consuming passion for Jesus and for people.

You could go in for a guidance session, where you were hit with a serious discipline punishment for '*white ticket*' offences and come out feeling like the champion of the world, such was the Keri effect. I was baptised in his church, Clydach AoG, in October 1997, with my mum and our Yvonne down to witness it.

As I moved on through Phase Two, I was appointed another counsellor, Jim Stead. Jim and his wife Jean had recently moved from St Ives in Cornwall, where they had been involved in a church that was a great support to the work of Teen Challenge. Jean worked in Hope House, the women's centre.

Jim and Jean originally hailed from the north of England, and I loved Jim's no-nonsense approach. He called things as he saw them and was a fantastic sounding board for me. Jim introduced me to some of the od Christian writers such as Charles Haddon Spurgeon and would go out of his way to find reading material he thought appropriate for me. My loved for the wee Cornish tin miner, Billy Bray, was direct from Jim.

I am thrilled that all these years later, Jim and jean remain firm friends and advisers to Tracy and myself. Back to the Teen Challenge programme that began in May 1997. I talked of what my first sober Christmas was like and I could write a whole separate book on my programme alone.

In April 1998, I was invited to join *The Evidence*. This was the Teen Challenge men's outreach team. I was just coming to the end of Phase Three of the programme. *The Evidence* would go around schools and churches, and through song, testimony and preaching, we would share the hope we had found in Jesus Christ.

Another essential part of the band's work was to promote Teen Challenge and the valuable work it did. There was an average of ten members. Normally eight guys that had either completed the programme or, like me, were just coming to the end.

For some reason there was also always a musician (normally a bass player) who had never struggled with addiction but had come to work with Teen Challenge as part of the team. These guys were always of great character and quality.

The team was led by Paul Evans, whom I talked about at Christmas time. Paul had left a successful career in banking to come and start up the ministry team. He was a third generation Christian, wrote nearly all the music himself, and was at talented and gifted leader and musician. Paul became a very big mentor during those days in my life.

A few weeks before I officially joined *The Evidence* one of the then members had told me how there were rumours, they were going to Swaziland (now Eswatini) in southern Africa. He said there was talk of me going with them. A guy called Kevin Ward had been working with the most broken and disadvantaged in the former British colony and he was coming under the Teen Challenge family.

We were going out to do a tour that would testify to the power of God's love in our own lives and, officially launch Kevin's ministry as Teen Challenge. August 1998, I found myself in Heathrow Airport with some of the best people I have ever known in my life.

August 1998, only eighteen months after my tears on Westwood pitches, I was on a Virgin Atlantic airplane to Johannesburg, South Africa. Along with other men that God had "raised from the dead in addictions" and the incredible John and Anne Macey and Paul Evans our musical director we were on our way to visit Kevin Ward and Teen Challenge in Swaziland. We were on our way to join with Kevin and his family as they launched the ministry in a small corner of Africa. The irony of the flight, I was stuck in the middle of the middle aisle. Nowhere near the window I longed to stare out. So close…

Pete Ryan, a graduate from ten years previously, that had recently returned to work in Teen Challenge had a window seat. All night long, from my prison in the middle of the middle I had pestered him with "Gizza a shot, Pete."

Pete, in his Islington accent, knowing how much it would wind me up "nah little student."

"Go on big bruv." I had started calling him this, because he had acted like a big brother towards me since coming into work. He called me "little student" as his response. I loved it.

Eventually, about two am, whilst flying over the tropical jungles of Africa, he gave in and swapped seats. "I want it back when I get a nap, little student."

"Not a chance," I replied.

Pete laughed, "G'night little student, see you in Johannesburg."

You see in August 1998 God showed me that He also shed a tear that day eighteen months before. I couldn't see then what He could.

Thirteen hours on a Virgin Atlantic flight, my first view looking down on earth was dark o'clock in the morning over the jungles of Africa with the planes light showing a tiny circle at a time. I wept silently whilst watching that light drift over Africa, whilst my head remained firmly pressed against the small window..

Drifting off to sleep and then waking up to Johannesburg appearing out of the redness of the South African wildernesses. I wept that day as well as I thanked God for His fulling a wee boy dream in such an incredibly amazing way.

Through song and share our life stories we were privileged to be allowed to speak in HIV clinics and prisons and schools and churches and on the streets and in shopping malls and basically anywhere and everywhere to anyone else would listen of what great things Christ had done for us and how He longed to do the same for others.

It's why I always look on with fondness and Kevin and Helen Ward's updates.

Swaziland was amazing, and heart-breaking. We saw God moving in ways and in lives that western mindsets seem to lock out. We even shared an incredible night of ministry in Mozambique. There we stayed in a missions hut, all closed in behind razor wire, with missionaries staring suspiciously over their Bibles at the five of us that had made the trip.

That night I slept in the only bed without a mosquito net, on the window haha. This is my LIFE!

45 – Milk n a Piece n Chips (1998)
A piece n chips

As wee bites go, ye cannae wack
The awesomeness of a Scots snack
Whether deep fried Mars, or battered ice cream
Us Scots know whit eating food really means
Bit for the purpose aw this wee trip
A want tae tell ye aboot ma piece n chips
by Stuart Patterson ©2018

A wee while ago, I spoke in part 2 of Milk n a piece n jam, how a coffee queue was an excuse for pretend hardmen to try and pretend to be hardmen. It was a tiring world, being in a Young Offenders' Institution. I got out, and despite my life getting much worse, I never went back. S poke about how there was no respite for my mum and dad whilst I was in prison.

Nine years later, here I was in another institution, once again surrounded by young men from broken lives.

As we had walked across the River Clyde in December 1989 for my sentencing, the air was filled with dread. It went unsaid, (other than mum asking for my keys) but we all sort of knew I wasn't coming back.

This time it was different. As I got ready to leave with Ken Persaud to go to Teen Challenge, mum and dad were VERY excited to help me pack my bags – for different reasons.

It is hard to put into words what it meant for my parents to be able to draw breath, as they did not have to worry about that knock at the door telling them I was either dead or in prison.

Funnily enough, I have never asked them what those first days were like.

When I was writing this, I decided to ask my sister, Yvonne.

Now anyone that knows our Yvonne knows that she has never been one for mincing her words. Uh oh.

"They never thought ye were gonnae stay there. Dae ye remember the letter ye sent my ma?" Straight to the point!

"Whit letter?" I asked but knew what was coming.

"You sent her a letter, telling her you couldnae handle it and wanted tae come hame. Ye sent it tae ma ma cos she wis the weak link. You thought she would gie in, Cammy wis ragin wae ye. (Cammy being Yvonne's husband)."

"Cammy wis ragin?" I retorted, "he's got a cheek. "

"He wiz ragin thit ye sent it tae ma ma cos the rest o us wid ave telt ye were to go."

Nothing I could say to that. It was true.

My only saving grace was that I had talked over that letter, and a few other things with my mum, AND apologised for it.

It was true though, both my mum, and Roy Lees, in the early days would get letters and phone calls begging to let me come home. It got so bad that I remember calling Roy one night and saying to him just to ignore me and Ronnie (another Easterhouse boy) that used to take shots each with me at calling Roy to bring us home.

I told him it meant we were just having a tough day. "Tell us to shut up and hang up on us, we will get over it".

I did tell my mum the same thing on the phone as well, but it did take a long time and a quite in-depth chat with Jay Fallon before I really found the freedom to be quite open with those closest to me.

My favourite evening snack in my Teen Challenge days was a piece n chips. This was because you weren't allowed a piece n anything through the week. Apparently, the very Scottish tradition of sticking anything between two slices of bread proved too much, to a management staff member, when one of the guys had Bolognese (a quite tasty piece if I do say so myself) and had the favoured mealtime practice banned.

The exception was a Sunday evening. Sunday evenings we made the journey to Swansea Elim Church. We enjoyed the large gathering of Christians and the exuberant praise, led, mostly, by Chris Russon.

It was also always good to hear Pastor Phil Hills preaching there. To this day still one of the best communicators of God's Word I have heard.

He speaks with authority. We were not allowed to hang around after the services. If any guys went out for prayer ministry, we would wait in our seats for them. Then we would be ushered out onto our minibus for the thirty-minute drive back to the centre.

Remember, conversations in Castle Huntly were almost always about drugs and gangs, football or women. Most of its bravado and rubbish. On the bus back from church, the contrast between one institution and another was so obvious.

The guys would be talking about how the praise songs lifted them, or aspects of the preaching.

Now and again there would be one of the guys convinced that one of the girls from Teen Challenge Hope House Women's Centre had made eyes at him the whole time.

We were just getting used to having emotions and hormones after almost every thought being suppressed by drugs. We were beginning to experience what life was really all about, and those bus journeys were a fair measurement of how far Jesus had already removed us from our pasts.

The one part of a Sunday night we looked forward to, almost as much as church, (I have to say that) was that we would stop off at one of the local chippies on the way back from church in Swansea and get bags of chips for all the guys. A lot of bags of chips.

It was great when you got to be one of the guys that got to go in because, well going into a chippy was so normal.

145

My mum and dad did get some respite whilst I was there. I never left early, in fact, I never came home for eighteen months.

I spent my weekends away with the wonderful Sutherland family (John, Joyce and Jackie) in the stunning town of Newlyn, Cornwall.

John and Joyce were involved in the leadership of The Rock Church and had welcomed other Teen Challenge students into their home as a safe place to get used to their new lives outside Teen Challenge.

My mum and my sister Yvonne travelled down to Gorslas a few times, like for my baptism and one- or two-day visits, as well as my graduation in November 1998. I never got sucked into that trap of feeling I had to prove my addiction was gone by going back to Easterhouse as soon as I could. This suited my mum and dad as it meant their respite continued.

46 - Lifted (1998)
The most normal thing...

I sometimes have to wonder, Where I might have been today
If grace, my life, had not set out to win
And looking back, I realize it must be some great love
That saw me as I was and took me in
From 'He lifted me' by Paul Evans, Challenge Music

Around November 1998 I made my first visit back to Scotland from
Teen Challenge. It was a long journey. Train from Swansea to Birmingham, change for Crewe and then onto Glasgow Central.
Arriving at Glasgow Central, and it felt good to be back in Scotland, and yet it didn't.

There was an apprehension that had gripped me all the way up through England, that only intensified as I crossed the border.

Fear!

Fear that I would give in to temptation. Fear that I would immediately do what I had always done in Scotland, go and get a fix.

It was paralysing. I know that doesn't make sense. I had been away for eighteen months. Had seen incredible sights and my life was firmly and intensely fixed on Christ.

But fear is an incredible thing. At times the cause of the fear bears no rhyme or reason, and at others, it is rooted in mistakes or events of the past. This time it was very obviously rooted in my past.

I made my way home, and in through our veranda. My parents lived in Ervie Street, a bottom and middle flat had been converted into one house due to the size of our family and the lack of available properties.

As I walked into the kitchen my dad was standing over the cooker. "Hiya I'm making the dinner, you ok."

It was the most normal thing he had been able to say to me in years. No high drama, no emotion. You would think I had only pooped out to the shops, rather than living in another country for eighteen months.

It was also light relief from the fear. Everything was normal that day. As you can imagine, the family came around to visit and the fear was pushed to the back of my mind, but it was still there, waiting to pounce.

In Genesis, just before he kills his brother Abel, Cain is warned by God that sin was crouching at the door waiting to pounce:

> *⁷ If you do well, will you not be accepted?*
> *And if you do not do well, sin lies at the door. And its desire is for*
> *you, but you should rule over it."* (**Genesis 4:7 (NKJV)**)

It was verses I had thought about many times.

Now though, during my fear, they reverberated around inside my head as if God Himself had visited me the way He had visited Cain to warn me that this was trying to pull me down.

Although, unlike in Cain's case it wasn't my brothers in danger of death, but for me.

The temptation to use drugs was strong. My sister Yvonne watched me like a hawk anytime I moved. Quite rightly too.

As I just relaxed with my family, it began to dissipate. I even began to enjoy the company of my family, something I had never really done as an adult.

I went to bed that night and slept a beautiful sleep.

Next morning, I got up full of hope and expectation. Now I wanted to find old friends and tell them what Jesus had done in my life. I wanted to show them a way out. The seed of that poem, Role, that I had written was about to be given an opportunity to bear fruit.

Off I went, heading straight over to the Buywell. Full of hope and anticipation about who I would meet. Following the same route, I had followed so many times in the search for drugs, this time in search for ears.

Up Ervie Street onto Easterhouse Road, then around the corner to Aberdalgie Road. This time I took the detour down Duntarvie and out across the pitches.

I passed the spot that I had gazed up at the airplane only about twenty months before and smiled remembering Johannesburg.

Up the slope, along the street and across into the entrance to the *Buywell*.

Immediately I bumped into old friends, they were asking where I had been and commented on how well I looked. I had no problem sharing with them how God had changed my life.

Then I saw P. She was one of our gang. Had hung out with us. Had given me my first messed up injection, (That First Time). And I knew where she was going.

Immediately my conversation stopped, and I made my way over to P.

"Where you aff tae?" I asked, knowing full well the answer.

"O'er tae J & A's tae get some tems.

Whit ye up tae Paddy? No seen ye in ages"

"Livin doon in Wales." The fear was back. The taste of the *Tems* already caressing my mouth, along with the voice of the fear, telling me THIS is who I really was. There was no chance nor intention of sharing with P any hope or way out of addiction. That would mess with me going with her. I could taste the rush in my mouth.

I wanted a fix.

"Wait an I'll walk er wi ye."

"Naw, its awright" she replied. But I was having none of it. I had already given into the temptation. The thing I feared the most had come upon me. I had dreaded giving into temptation for a fix, whilst at the same time almost savoured it.

It is the great danger of substance abuse and habit. I never got high to escape, I got high to get stoned. I loved the feeling. I craved it. I had been free from it for twenty months, had hardly given it a second thought until that train had made its way through England, slowly building momentum until it crossed the border.

The "Welcome to Scotland" sign which should have greeted me with warmth at the promise of new memories in my country, introduced a heavy cloud.

The shadow of fear had hidden well that morning, but as I walked up with P towards the centre of the centre - only the promise of the rush seemed strong enough to chase it.

As we approached the staircase in the centre of the *Buywell*, it became, in an instant, the epicentre of God's battle with the demon of addiction in my life.

"Stuart what on earth are you doing?"

"Eh"

I stopped dead in my tracks at what seemed like an audible voice, looking over at P to see if she heard it. Obviously, she had not.

"If you can't say no for yourself, think of all those who have seen a way out because of you". God Himself, it seemed had spoken to me the way

It was clear, it was audible, and it chased the fear. I mean it is so hard to get across how suddenly, I saw clearly.

In Teen Challenge, one of the studies we do to help us in our new lives is called "*Temptations*" It helps us to understand and deal with temptations God's way.

"What am I doing?" I thought to myself. "God I am so sorry." It was amazing how quickly peace and composure were restored.

Instantly things were back in perspective as my mind worked through the plan for overcoming temptation.

That staircase is now as holy to me as it was for Jacob' staircase when he saw angels ascending and descending from heaven.

I knew in that instant that Jesus Christ was more than able to, not just keep me from addiction, but to restore me to a real hope and purpose. I did not have to spend my life living in fear of the next fix.

And I haven't.

"P, you know God just reminded me how much He loved me, and He wants you to know the same." I said.

"So, yer no comin wi me then?" she replied, a bit bemused probably by what I had just said. "That's fine I'll see ye later."

"You don't need to go either" I said, "He can help you beat yir habit as well."

"Nah Im awright Paddy, I'll see ye later."

I have never seen her since that moment. I was a wee bit dejected that she gave up so easily. But I had literally just seen Jesus work in a very real way in my life that I could never have seen in the darkest days of the Teen Challenge programme.

I knew at that moment that I was following Jesus, whenever and wherever He led. He truly did have the words of eternal life.

As I made my way back home to Ervie Street, I began to sing one of our Evidence songs. "Lifted". We sung it that often that we got fed up with it, but as I made my way across the pitches, by the spot of my airplane gaze and on up Aberdalgie Road - I sung it out loud. I really did want the world to know.

And I could never dream, could never know
How much He had to pay, His love to show
When He lifted me, I had no strength
to walk through another day
And He lifted me, I was so weak
when all I could do was pray
Right at my darkest moment, when I was drifting away
He lifted me

"He Lifted Me" from the album "*Who the Son sets free*" by Paul Evans, Challenge Music (by the way I am singing on this album. Seriously.)

A couple of days later, as I made my way into Glasgow Central for my early evening train, I had my eyes opened to something else.

It was Glasgow post daytime and pre-night-time. A tale of two cities.

47 - Talk to me mate (2000)
5' 3" blonde hair and blue eyes

I don't know what you were doing
but I was in my room
wondering what the meeting would be
we were going to soon
when a voice overheard, distracted me
I walked out and was handed the phone
"here, talk to me mate"
And with that life with Tracy begun
by Stuart Patterson ©2019

"Here will ye talk to me mate, no one ever calls him?"

And with that sort of well-intended remark began the romance of my life.

Stephen was my friend in Teen Challenge, and along with Paul Morgan, at that time we shared a house in Penygroes, South West Wales.

We were all graduates of Teen Challenge and got to travel around the UK, singing and sharing our stories of how God's love through Christ had transformed our lives. (There was also the very difficult Biblical training programme). We enjoyed what we did, and we were grateful that our lives were no longer the screwed-up mess they had been before. Instead of inflicting damage and wrecking lives, we were bringing life and sharing hope.

It was a Sunday in January 2000. We must have been in a more local church that Sunday because we were back home. Stephen was hyper. He was always like that after preaching and wanted to talk to anyone that would listen.

I had been sitting in my bedroom, downstairs at the front of the house. Quietly reading my Bible and praying, when the raucous noise of Stephen's laughter drifted through from the sitting room at the back of the house.

Curious as to what could be so amusing, and knowing that no one else was in the house, I made my way through.

Just as I walked in the door, he put his hand out, touched me on the shoulder and said the infamous, "Here talk to me mate."

Stephen had been in Dublin over Christmas and had called Anna Tormey, (at that time one of the pastoral care team on staff at St Mark's Family Worship Centre, now St Mark's Church on Pearse Street in Dublin. Anna would soon be Assistant Pastor there). Anna wasn't available, so Stephen had been chatting away to her eldest child, Tracy.

I froze to the spot. One of those awkward moments everyone hates - being handed a phone to speak to someone you didn't know.

I am sure if you were physically there you would have smelt the fear. The sweat beads running down my face and my stomach contorted in angst.

Being the socially awkward person, I was, I awkwardly waited a few awkward seconds before awkwardly asking this unknown person, with a full unknown life, in an unknown city (well unknown to me) was doing.

It was awkward.

We used words, but never really said anything for a minute or two then I handed the phone back to Stephen.

"You should write to him, no one ever does." Who needs enemies with friends like these eh? Where is the bro code? He hung up and I just looked at him.

"Seriously?"

I called my mum back in Glasgow. Whilst on the phone to her I said, "What do you make of this Stephen fella, trying to get me married off to some Irish woman."

"Ye better no," my mum replied, "it's bad enough your down in Wales without moving to Ireland"

We went about our day, thinking no more of it. We were out with The Evidence again that night and life carried as before. I did not know it then, but a path had opened in my life that would lead to the journey God has had me on the past 18 years; to a happy marriage and three wonderful daughters, to lifelong friends forged only months from that off the cuff call.

To the love of my life. If you are reading this, always be aware, you never know what God can do with even the most seemingly insignificant occurrences in your life.

Life carried as normal for a couple of weeks. As I mixed back into the Teen Challenge routine the odd thought would cross my mind about the mysterious Irish lady in the other side of the phone.

Tracy was different, though. Whether it was pity, or boredom or something else (after eighteen years I have never asked), I played on her mind.

Arriving home after my shift two weeks later, I discovered a letter addressed to me waiting. It had a Dublin postmark. I could not wait to tear it open and see what waited inside for me. Tracy had handwritten a letter full of encouragement and honesty. She shared with me her journey with God and how it had taken a few years to finally find peace in Christ.

The letter itself is still with us, as are all the others we wrote to each other in those early days. Facebook wasn't a thing in February 2000, writing proper letters was. It was nice. She wrote to the guy who never got any letters and he appreciated it.

Getting the letter itself was nice and encouraging, the contents were inspiring.

She talked about her struggles and her faith and wrote in a way that made it easy for me to relate.

It seemed obvious to reply, and to reply in a likewise manner.

Sharing my experience of Christ. Being honest about where I was in my life and wondering what was next.

Off it went in the post-box in Gorslas, to be collected at 5pm that day by the Royal Mail collector to begin its journey to Dublin.

Sorting office, airplane, collection, sorting office, postman - Lombard Street East.

I did not know how long it would take, and to be honest once in the post that was it.

There was the obvious curiosity as to whether this mysterious lady would reply or not, but beyond that it was politeness and encouragement. I honestly never really expected a response.

She did reply.

I replied again.

A few letters later, it was time for a good old Teen Challenge graduation. These were big occasions. Guys and lassies that had been in the death grip of addiction had broken free because of God's love in Christ, completed the requirements of the intensive Teen Challenge programme and were about to graduate.

In those days they were held in City Temple (Elim Swansea). They were (and still are) a very big occasion. Students were rightly made to feel that they had achieved tremendous goals in the first steps of reclaiming their lives.

The church would be packed with 5-600 friends, families and other Christians celebrating the success of Christ in these young men and women's lives.

There were some graduates from Dublin, and this meant that there would be a large contingent over from St Mark's Church and Teen Challenge Ireland. Amongst them were Alan and Barbara Sweetman.

They headed up Teen Challenge Ireland, and to this day I have yet to meet anyone better at coming alongside broken people than Alan.

He would become a very good friend as my journey took me to Dublin.

Another part of that travelling group was Tracy. She would be making her way over in amongst them all. By this time, we had written each other a "couple" of letters. Continuing the pattern of those first that acknowledged we both had nothing other than Jesus to give us hope. Tracy was the proud mum of Alisha (at that time seventeen months old) from a previous relationship that never quite worked out. I was excited to meet them both.

Anyway, the service came, I was on the sound desk, (apparently the dulcet tones of my awesome singing voice were so good that I could not continue being a singer in The Evidence). With the desk set up in the middle of the very large seating area, it was always a struggle to not get distracted. Churches can be very busy places, especially at the times people should be seated and focused.

It was a great night. The Irish team were all sitting in the seats to the left of me down the left-hand side of the large sanctuary. I did notice a beautiful wee girl given her mum and the others the run-around and wondered if this was Alisha.

Anyway, one of the highlights of a Teen Challenge graduation is when all the graduates (including those from previous years) are invited on the stage. There can be up to 100 men and women, formerly trapped in addiction, now standing as trophies of grace and living full and productive lives back in the world.

I got to abandon my position and join them all. This is significant, as Tracy told me later (years later), that she wondered if the cool handsome guy working his way up to the platform from the sound desk was her mysterious Scottish pen pal.

When the service was over, and we had finished clearing away our sound equipment I made my way down to the front of the church. Stephen was standing in amongst the Irish team and was calling me over.

"Stuart" he says "meet Tracy" as he introduced me to the beautiful 5'3 blonde hair, blue eyed Irish woman.

I had enjoyed a few minutes chatting to Tracy and some of the other Dubliners. Paul Evans then gave us the look, so we continued packing away all The Evidence gear and getting it into our van.

Stephen and I were back at our house in Penygroes before long. Stephen was keen, though to get around to the Apostolic Bible Centre where the Irish were staying. (More out of a desire to get his Kings crisps than to talk to anyone, I think).

The place seemed to be in darkness and the door was locked so we shouted up at a few windows. After a few minutes of feeling like eejits, we headed back around the corner to our house. I was tired and wanted to get to bed, but Stephen, desperate for his Kings, said: "ye not wanting to go and chat to Tracy, she's lovely". What he really meant was that he wanted to go back around and was not letting me away with it.

"Stephen, we have a meeting in the morning," I said, "we need to get a sleep". But it was no use, he would not give up.

Reluctantly and resigned I made my way out the door, up the street, around the corner and down the dark hill to the Bible Centre.

On the way down the dark hill, we bumped into one of the Irish team. They told us that the guys were all in the bungalow (a one storey annexe building to the rear of the main building).

So off we went, chapped the door, the door opened and when we were ushered in with all the usual Irish good-natured craic. They were delighted to see Stephen.

Kevin Ellis, another Dublin student, was already there as some of his family were over visiting. There was a gang in the kitchen, so, desperate for a cup of tea - I made my way in there.

I remember it being bright and quite big. Tracy was in there chatting away to someone. I was asked a question, cannot for the life of me remember what it was, but off I went on one of my monologues.

I remember Kevin coming in and trying to chat to Tracy, but she shushed him and kept looking at me, I remember her eyes transfixed on me and never shifting.

I was 30 years old, I'd had a few girlfriends, none of them serious, and none of them had looked at me the way this Irish woman was looking at me.

Tracy introduced me to her good friend Claire. Claire had agreed to come over with her. Claire excitedly shared her plans for getting married that August, (it was the end of February). She was young, very friendly and obviously very excited about her wedding.

Claire asked if there was a pay phone anywhere as she wanted to call her fiancé, Paul. (Payphones remember them). I said there was one just along from the top of our street. The girls asked me if I would accompany them.

As Claire chatted away to Paul on the phone (it was close to midnight on a beautiful February evening) Tracy began to sing. I remember how beautiful her voice sounded as: "My Jesus, my Saviour" began to fill the Penygroes air. It was a relatively new song then. I had never heard it sung so good though and I listened intently, aware of how different my life was now compared to just a short time before.

The words had never carried so much joy or meaning for me.

"I sing for joy at the work of Your hands:" sang Tracy, as I breathed out the truth of how grateful I was.

Claire finished her call and, as we made our way back to their accommodation, I asked Tracy if she would like to go for a walk.

Sorry, Claire, you are not invited. I am not sure if Claire was miffed or not, but she went back indoors, and we began a long, beautiful walk down through Penygroes.

We chatted about everything and nothing. We shared our hopes and fears and what Jesus was doing in our lives. It very quickly transpired that this was not Tracy's first trip to Wales. She had been over in 1998 for a previous Dubliner's graduation.

She remembers being picked up, along with a very large contingent from Dublin on a Teen Challenge minibus and brought to their bed & breakfast.

Flashbulb memory!

I was with Phil Winstanley that day. My mum and sister were coming down for my graduation but would not arrive until later, so I went with him to the airport to pass time. Tracy had attended my TC Graduation in November 1998, and I had picked her up from the airport for it.

Only God!

As we made our way down to the bottom of Waterloo Road, where it intersects with Black Lion Road, we stopped under the streetlight. We both just looked at each other and Tracy asked, "So what are we doing here? Are we going to do this?"

In answer, I pulled her into my arms and kissed her.

THIS is my life!

48 – Now it's Time to Say Goodbye (2000)
You are an example

In April 2000 Ruby Walsh won the Grand National on Papillon; Metallica sued Napster; Salman Rushdie returns to India, after being banned because of his book 'The Satanic Verses'; the first official success of 'gene therapy' was recorded in France. In April 2000 I also decided a it was time…

Tracy returned to Dublin, but that wasn't it. Our futures were now sealed as '*a future*'.

I called her on the Monday evening, and then just about every evening after that. The phone bills were horrendous, but worth every penny.

It wasn't long before I arranged to go to Dublin for a week. My third flight in less than a year (after the two Swaziland legs). My good friend, John Gorman, a former student of Teen Challenge as well had promised that I could stay in his sister's flat. It was in Pearse Street just around the corner from Tracy's mum and dad's house.

Another friend, and former Teen Challenge student, Kevin Ellis, picked me up at the airport with his then girlfriend.

As I made my way in through the front door of Tracy's three storey house, only yards from the banks of Dublin's River Liffey, I was hyped more than I had ever been. We went though the door and down the hallway to the kitchen at the back, with all the family standing there, curious to eet me. Tracy's dad, Leo, stood, saying not much with his mouth, but his eyes already asking many questions. Aishling, the wee sister was all laughing and joking. Jonathan and Lee, her two brothers, were out. I met them later. Again though, both of them very warm and friendly, ready to welcome this Scotsman with a sarcastic joke, and a friendly put down.

Tracy's mum, Anna, went out of her way to make me welcome. After all these years, the image of her mum and dad standing there, with different (not opposing)

154

looks on their faces, still sums up parenting to me. It was like between them they were able to see things from all sides

Kevin and the others left after we all had tea., and between them they made up the whole home.

Tracy and I had a good week. We went out for walks, lots of walks, and visited some of her family. Tracy's mum had twelve siblings. Alisha, Tracy's seventeen-month-old daughter, and already a bundle of ‚light and joy, was with us all the time. This just felt right, like it was supposed to be this way.

I also got to meet Gary and Wilma Davidson, They were an American missionary couple who had moved to Ireland in the 1980's with the hope of setting up a Teen Challenge work there. In 1987 they started what was then St Mark's Family Worship Centre. Situated in an old Church of Ireland building in Pearse Street, this place would soon become my future home.

Gary had wanted to meet me, taking his pastoral role very seriously, he wanted to make sure I was right for Tracy.

I was very nervous about meeting this tall, slender American with the big personality. After the meeting, I think that Tracy was more annoyed that Gary and I spent the hour talking about Teen Challenge and the incredible work God had done through many lives. Tracy felt that he should be grilling me, as to my suitability.

Not long after that visit, Tracy made two trips to Wales, for a week each, The first, we got permission from then Hope House manager, Audry Rankin, for her to stay in the girl's house, with my friend Angel, and some of the other female graduates. She brought Alisha with her on this trip and the girls were brilliant with both of them.

Tracy was even given permission by men's centre manager, Mike Rankin, to come cook dinner in our house, on the condition that my housemates, Stephen Hevey and Paul Morgan were both present.

It was a fantastic evening, that showed me how natural Tracy was as a host. Her natural ability at conversation and putting others at ease with themselves was refreshing. Alongside Stephen's jokes, and Paul's easy going manner, it was a fitting beginning to the end of my time with Teen Challenge (even though I didn't know that then).

Tracy came over on her own a few weeks later, and this time stayed with Jay and Fiona (Fallon). Jay and Fiona were now leading Ammanford Elim, and both were pivotal in my early Christian life. I liked the fact that they invited Tracy to stay with them. I was outworking and walking out this new found faith, and it was important for me that Jay and Fiona approved of my relationship. I know many reading this may not understand that, but it was right.

Tracy herself has told me that week with Jay and Fiona was pivotal in some breakthroughs in her own life.

After the week, I went into my then boss (Paul Evans, The Evidence) and told him I was handing in three months' notice.

"You don't quit because you've met a girl." he laughed.

The truth was, that for around a year, my other mentors, Jim and Jean Stead, had been talking to me about moving on from Teen Challenge. They wanted me to see how big their God was, and that I could only see one side of Him if I was a perennial TC person. The week with Tracy only confirmed it was time. I was ready.

"Paul," I said, "I am not asking you to agree with my decision, but I am asking you to respect it." (how grown up did that sound?).

Stephen came into Paul's tiny office on the main corridor just as I had told Paul.

"Stephen, did you hear this man's leaving because he's met an Irish woman?"

"It was Stephen that introduced us Paul," I laughed.

"No I didn't" he lied.

To Paul's enormous credit, and to my eternal gratitude, Paul did accept my decision. He even stood up for me at various staff meetings etc. But more than that, he allowed me to continue to preach when out with The Evidence.

For quite some time at that point, I had been getting to "bring the challenge", that is I got to wrap up our Gospel presentations. WE always had a time of worship, a few testimonies mixed with some of our own songs, and them one of the team would preach. I loved it and I learned so much about who Jesus really is through my preparation times.

Paul let me carry on.

On a Thursday evening in July, Jay and Fiona had me down to there house for dinner. It was my goodbye.

After a great few hours full of memories (all good), Fiona offered to drive me the mile or so back up to my house.

As we pulled up at the top of my street, Fiona gave me one of the best 'pep talks' I have ever had. She told me what my first three months as a Christian outside Teen Challenge would look like. She warned of the dangers BUT challenged me to enjoy God, and my new found freedom in Christ. Her last words I have repeated to many Teen Challenge students over the years as they prepare to move on. She told me that I was to remember that god would place me in a church as an encouragement and example to those who had not been blessed with the opportunities I had. That I was always to consider my role as a servant to His Church. She then warned that if I ever caught myself looking at other Christians who were doing their best in the day to day, with any hint or thought of condemnation, because they did not seem to have the fire I had, then at that moment I was to say sorry to God – because at that moment I had forgotten what God had called me to do – preach and carry Good News.

Next day, I prepared to go to minister in Northampton with The Evidence. Remember that place. One of my happy places from my sixteenth year.

This was my final meeting with The Evidence. Most of my stuff had already been moved to Glasgow. As we finished the meeting, with me finishing the meeting, Paul Morgan and I packed the last of my stuff into his car. Paul Evans, as I said goodbye to another man that had shown me true Christian love, acceptance and guidance said, "You're not really going, are you?"

I wept a single tear.

Paul Morgan was driving me back to Glasgow. Thirty nine months after leaving in Pastor Ken Persaud's car, I was returning, except I was not really the guy that had left. He was gone.

There was the offer of a few opportunities, but nothing definite.

Tracy and Alisha came over for a two week visit, the first time meeting my family. We had spoken many times about getting married, we both knew it was right and we knew we did not want to wait. I had asked Ryanair if I could propose on the plane when it landed but was told I couldn't because of security concerns etc.

I didn't really know how to do big romantic gestures, although I did travel through the night TWICE on the ferry to turn up at her door in Dublin, much to Tracy's surprise – for a day visit.

As my wee brother Neil and I collected them from the airport, I fingered the engagement ring nervously in my pocket. Tracy made some mention of marriage, as we sat in the back of Neil's car, and I pulled the ring out and handed it to her, with a big smile. How romantic.

I don't think Tracy, quite rightly, had ever forgiven me for proposing in such a sloppy manner. We had a great two weeks where Tracy was introduced to my mum and dad, my sister and my brothers and all the other parts of the Patterson clan.

She also discovered the enigma of JP, my eldest brother, and his desire to hoover at five am because, well it needed done. JP doted on the near two year old Alisha. He was brilliant with kids. They all doted on him. I have a picture from that trip of JP walking out of mum's street, with Alisha's tiny hand in his. They were off down to Blairtummock Park to join up with some of his friends and their kids. Magical.

Regarding work back in Glasgow, well it never happened. No matter how many interviews I went for, no matter how hard I tried, it seemed the world was just not prepared to trust a former addict. My new found faith perspective though showed me that maybe God was just telling me He wanted me elsewhere.

And so, the first week in September 2000 I went to spend a week in Dublin. Stephen Hevey had now managed to move back to Dublin, get engaged to Tracy's wee sister Aishling and start work in a company called Blenders.

He had arranged a job interview for me with the Supervisor, Deirdre Byrne, "She's lovely Stuart, and I've told her all about you. I went for my interview in Newmarket Square, part of the old Dublin. Deirdre was lovely. A lady in her late forties (I think) greeted me with a warm smile and a "Your friend has told me all about you, don't you be worrying about your addiction or rehab being an issue, it's not".

Wow!   I got the job and Deirdre asked me if I could start the following week, eh my only problem was that I still actually lived in Scotland. By God's grace with a lot of last minute planning I arranged to move to Dublin. Initially I was going to be living in Tracy's mum and dad's, until I could sort somewhere else out.

On Monday 11th September 2000 I emigrated to Dublin.

IV Life Education

49 – Dublin's Fair City (2000)
and Ballymena's so pretty

One year before the towers fell
on that day, my life was swell
I moved country, with all my stuff
cos with Tracy and Alisha
now my world, it's enough.
A new job, a new life
very soon a new wife
my foundations were sound
I had Jesus around
by Stuart Patterson ©2019

    I moved to Dublin in September 2000, and my first home was Tracy's mum and dad's sofa. My first job with Blenders. I graduated to a double room on the first floor in Tracy's mums when we got married, with Alisha's cot at the bottom of our bed.

    Workwise, I was at Blenders one of the best companies I have ever worked for. David and Robert Simpson had started *Blenders* over one jar filling machine in 1990. They made pasta sauce and mayonnaise and other such delights. Their company had grown quite significantly, and to me, they embodied perfect leadership. They knew the power of encouragement, and they knew constructive criticism. I loved my eighteen months working there.

I started, at the end of a jar filling production line, packing boxes and then filling pallets, and left eighteen months and three promotions later as a junior chargehand. A position created for me. God had indeed been very good in teaching me what I should look like in the workplace. Mark Brasil, the maintenance guy (in reality he was so much more) was a good friend. He taught me how to use the machines and a lot of other life lessons. I hope he knows what a great part he played in my life.

I left in February 2002 to start work at Jobcare. Jobcare was a Christian charity that worked, very successfully with the long term unemployed. Started by my friend, Paul Mooney and others, it has grown to be a beacon of hope in Dublin. Not just for long term unemployed, but ex-offenders, those coming out of addiction and may others of Dublin's most broken. They pass through the doors hoping to find work, and instead find value, worth and a place that cares.

My role was to teach the *Employment Preparation Course,* the cornerstone of what Jobcare does. This was a four week course, aimed at teaching people the essential skills needed to secure employment or further training. It also showed how to own your past. The Irish Government's *Community Employment* initiative is also seen at its best in Jobcare. This allowed long term unemployed, to get paid a not too bad amount for working part time hours in preparation for full time work. This was on top of their benefits and was seen as an encouragement and step back into the workplace. Many friends I now have, came through Jobcare's doors, working there because of that initiative.

After two years, working first with Pete Walker, a great friend now, then we he moved on Denis Wright as my supervisors. Jobcare also always had our Sammy. Sammy would always be standing with his rolled cigarette in hand, manager of the place and words of wisdom to those that needed it, and a kick up the back side to those that needed it. Everyone needs a Sammy in their life.

One Sunday morning, after the service, I was sitting at the steps at the platform in St marks. Sean Mullarkey., at this point transitioning to take over senior pastor's role from Gary Davidson says to me, "Stuart we were talking about you in the elders meeting the other night".

A quick search of the memory banks, the tightening of the gut and throat, old life trying to kick its way back in, assuming guilt for an as yet unknown crime.

"Ye ye yes"

"Haha don't be stupid, nothing bad. We were talking about all the work you do here for nothing, and we thought we would like to make life a bit easier on you. We want you to think about coming on staff as Administrator. You will be doing what you are already doing, but you will get paid for it, which means you won't have to work another job."

"Can I pray about it?"

I went to work in St Mark's full time only weeks later. Paul Mooney very graciously letting me only have to work two weeks' notice. My third job in Ireland, each change I had been invited to work. What a change in such a short space of time in my life.

That is seven years of work in a few paragraphs. This Jesus, whom I had known of with my ears, now I knew and had seen with my eyes. I would love to do another book that walks through some of the experiences I have had, and how very practically Jesus has guided me through them, maybe help to demystify what Christianity is about – to me.

But here I am, sleeping on a sofa in the ground floor sitting room of my future in laws, in my first days in Dublin. There are another nine people living in this house, and yet it never feels crowded.

I had tried to secure other accommodation, but Dublin was just too expensive.

Tracy and I had set a date for the 31st March 2001 to get married, a little over a year after we had first met. Her sister, Aishling and my friend Stephen had since met, fallen in love and got engaged as well. They set their date at the end of December THAT year, 2000.

As the day approached, we had to attend a pre marriage course with Gary and Wilma Davidson and a whole host of other future couples. It was hilarious, but also very worthwhile.

Thirty five of my family were flying over from Glasgow for my wedding. As I have said in other places in this book, none of my family were wealthy, so this was a big financial commitment for them all. We manged to get a really decent hostel, just off O'Connell Street Bridge, went meant only a ten minute walk to Tracy's mum's and to St Mark's.

It was so very humbling that so many would take the time and the money to come over.

Gary Davidson, along with our good friend, Noel Kenny were conducting the wedding. The reception as also held in St Mark's. Brian and Ann Kelly had arranged a team of volunteers to cater for it. All black tie, the church was transformed as two hundred and twenty of our friends and family joined the celebrations. Our church family (remember most of them I had only known for months) put on a day to remember. The whole day cost around five euros per person.

We had an evening reception in a local hotel where all our friends and family enjoyed a great party. Tracy and I went to bed early. She had over two hundred clips in her hair.

The following day, after briefly visiting the St Mark's Sunday morning service, Tracy and I headed out on what was my first holiday since Butlins Filey all those years ago. It was my honeymoon, I was flying, and I was with the woman I loved and wanted to spend the rest of my life with. Alisha was staying with nana Anna and granda Leo to be spoiled.

The following January we moved into pour very plush apartment in a new development in Dublin's Irish Financial Services Centre. Worth around half a million euros, we were able thanks to God's provision through a new government scheme that said twenty per cent of all new developments had to go to locals via Social Housing.

This also involved our first foray into media activities. Our housing association, Cluid, had put us, well Tracy really, forward to do some promotional stuff. We were in newspapers and on the telly. All the time, though I'm thinking, what if our neighbours, that had paid up to a million euros for their apartments, find out that a convicted drug dealer just out of rehab, and is anything but local is their neighbour. Cluid were well aware, and were happy with my background. Again though, God was faithful. We had great neighbours and we know that we were great neighbours. It was heart-breaking recently to see one of our old neighbours, Kelly Hommes, pass away after quite a tragic illness. Her shouting on her daughters in her raspy voice will always be part of our memories of Clarion Quay.

Clarion Quay saw us through the births of our other two daughters, Zoe Ann, February 7 2003, only weeks after my eldest brother died; and Naomi Heather (on the sofa in our living room, with her nana Anna's assistance) in May 2005. Our three daughters are the pride of Tracy and my lives. We love them and are blessed to have them.

I loved working in St Mark's, and my association with the sound desk meant that Gary Davidson was able to bring me along to the fledgling Irish Assemblies of God leadership training, long before I was formally in leadership. Some of those inaugural training days were way ahead of their time – such as Anne Rowe Monaghan with *Mental health and the Holy Spirit,* and *Conflict and resolution in the local church.* Areas that I have seen, all too often churches neglect, and yet are vitally important -as I was to find out.

In the summer of 2006, though, it was obvious to Pastor Sean, and to myself that my time as administrator in St Mark's was up. The role needed someone to bring a different level, and I needed to move on into whatever God wanted to do next in my life. People tried to orchestrate an opening for me, I loved the care, but that wasn't how God had worked in our lives.

I bumped into Pastor Gary one day in the car park of St Mark's ad asked him if he knew I was leaving. He seemed surprised, but said no he didn't.

The following day Gary and his wife, Wilma, invited us for a coffee at one of the local hotels. Within a few minutes he asked us if we had ever considered pastoring.

"Whereabouts" asked Tracy.

"That's not important" replied Gary.

The truth was, that we ran a homegroup every week that over twenty people attended regularly and consistently so we had been pastoring – just not officially. I also had been involved with a lot of the younger members of St Mark's that were involved in the sound and would take time out with them teaching them Biblical values and lessons I had learned.

We might not have considered pastoring, but we had been doing it, for years.

Gary introduced us to Pastor Derrick McCourt, an AoG pastor serving in Ballymena, Northern Ireland. He and his wife Betty had planted the church in Ballykeel 2 housing estate in Ballymena over twenty years previously. One of their sons, Andrew had pioneered a church in Derry and was held in very high regard within the church as whole in Ireland.

Tracy and I visited the church, met with Pastor Derrick on several occasions, and were invited to move up to be assistant pastor with a view to taking over the leading of that fantastic small fellowship. We fell in love with the people and the place, and Pastor Derrick was looking to retire.

On the second of January 2007, Tracy, our young girls and I moved home from Dublin to Ballymena. The next day I started in my new role, not having a clue what I was supposed to do our how to do it.

Pastor Jeff Wright of Green pastures Church in Ballymena invited Tracy and I for a time of prayer and welcome when we moved there. It was nice, and we found him to be a faithful and godly man. As the months unfolded, we also saw that he was God's angel of protection and provision when we needed it most.

We were part of the church for just under twelve months. I spent nearly every day with Pastor Derrick, and I was so grateful for every one of them.

It wasn't easy though. In fact, it became a real school of Christ. Neither Pastor Derrick nor I knew anything about transition, and many times I was asked to do things that I wasn't comfortable with – not ungodly or unbiblical – just not me.

My actions and reactions may not always have been the best. Remember, as I have said before the point of this book is my choices, my behaviour and how I learned and responded to the Holy Ghost. Pastor Phil Hills had also moved to Northern Ireland around this time from Swansea. He had come to lead Dundonald Elim church, and it was a real blessing to have him nearby. There were a few times when I leaned on his expertise and Biblical knowledge.

After our short time in Ballykeel Pentecostal Church, Eric McComb (head of Elim in Ireland), placed me in New Mossley Elim as co-pastor, with Tom McCann. I enjoyed my time there alongside Tom, who was only learning church leadership himself at the time.

Elim never paid a wage though, so in answer to prayer Pastor Jeff Wright made approaches to his family's company, Wrightbus. I met his nephew Chris Knowles and was interviewed for a position in the warehouse. During the interview, when Chris became aware of my administration and computer abilities, I got a job working in the buyer's office. My role was to work on the backlog of missing or damaged parts for the buses. The office manager, Rosemary Harte, was very like Deirdre Byrne, from Blenders and again, I enjoyed working there.

March 2009 though, the need for the job was gone (as in Wrights did not need the position fulfilled anymore), my time in New Mossley was coming to an end, and Tracy and I really did not know what the future held.

The house we were staying in at that time belonged to Trevor and Anne Grimsley, a young couple from Ballykeel Pentecostal Church. Trevor's work required him, his wife and young children to move to the United States for a year. They were unaware of our financial predicament when they offered the house to us – rent free – for twelve months. Now however, they were due to return in the May of that year.

Personally, I found this whole period very tough, and there were occasions when I had to fight off depression quite vigorously.

The pastors monthly breakfast meeting I had begun when I just arrived in Northern Ireland became a must for me that month. As pastor Jeff, Jonathan Law, Martin McNeely and a couple other guys met in Sainsburys café for breakfast, the only one that was aware of how tough life was for me was Pastor Jeff. He made it the focus of that morning to keep Tracy the girls and I in prayer.

As May, and the Grimsley's return approached, Tracy and I even had to consider declaring ourselves homeless. This is NOT what we thought we would encounter in Northern Ireland; we had arrived just over two years before full of optimism. As the time drew nearer, I had arranged to go over and spend a few days in prayer with Jay Fallon, now transitioning into head of Teen Challenge UK. I was to fly out on the Monday, Tracy and I were going into the council on the Friday before, Pastor Jeff had asked me to hold off on the homelessness, he just felt that it would work itself out. I reluctantly agreed. This was all so new to me in my journey of faith, God had never made our housing had work.

I went to wales, then flew up to Scotland at the request of Roy Lees. There they made an offer or Tracy and I to move back and 'be involved' in a few things. Roy and the team felt that July was the right time for the move. This would allow our girls to finish the year in school to minimise disruption.

As I went to my mum's (I stayed there while back in Glasgow) I sat on the phone that evening talking to Tracy.

"That's great" she said, "Trevor and Ann are back in a few weeks and we will have nowhere to live. Nobody is giving us a house for that amount of time."

As she said the words, she gasped. "Stuart, Anne has just sent an email. Something has come up and they have to delay their return…until July."

"What? That's mad, are you messing?"

Tracy read the email out to me. We could not believe, that once again our Heavenly Father was showing Himself strong and provider in our house.

We made our plans to move. David Black organised for Tracy and me to go over and view houses etc so we could find somewhere to live. As we were driven all over the Clyde coast looking at one place after another, Tracy and I both sat there thinking that this was not how God had dealt with us before over housing.

"C'mon I'll bring you up to Bridge of Weir to look at some properties my friend Robert Capper has. He doesn't have anything available, but at least it will give you an idea." By the end of that afternoon we had met Robert, his beautiful wife Caro, and their son and daughter in law. One 'coincidence'; after another came oot. As they sat and talked about rents though, I saw Tracy's face falling. There was no way we could afford the quite reasonable rents for these houses.

"Don't you be worrying hen, " said Carol in her Armagh accent. "You will have one of the two houses that will be available, and we';; sort the rent."

And they did. My friend Ciaran Buckley helped me move all the stuff over on a couple of ferry trips in June that year. Tracy, at this point, had only seen the outside of the house. On the fourth of July 2009, we left Ballymena and headed to Dublin for a family caravan holiday, in northern Italy with Tracy's mum and dad, and Stephen and Aishling and their kids.

50 - Caledonia's calling me (2009)
and I'm going home

Let me tell you that I love you, that I think about you all the time
Caledonia you're calling me, now I'm going home
Songwriters: MacLean Douglas Menzies

On the twenty fourth of July, we filled our *Fire Red Renault Scenic Dynamic* with our kids and the last of our possessions and headed back up north to Belfast. We got the Belfast to Stranraer ferry and, eventually arrived at Shillingworth Steadings, Bridge of Weir. Our new home for the next part of our journey.

Tracy and I made many friends during our time in Northern Ireland that we remain close with to this day. They are too numerous to name, but you all know who you are, and we thank you for they key roles you have all played in our lives.

Very quickly after moving to Scotland, we discovered that mum had renal cancer. I will speak more of that in another chapter, but this was devastating. Mum doted on all her grandkids and we were so looking forward to the girls getting to spend more time with her. We are grateful though, that they did get the few months between July and the following April.

Our first Sunday we went to Harvest Christian Fellowship in Hamilton. A bit away from Bridge of Weir, but Gary Davidson knew Ken and Jeannie Morris, the pastors. They too were missionaries from the USA. We went that Sunday, had dinner in Pizza Hut with Ken and Jeannie after the service, then just kept returning. Ken was probably the key person in my life at that point.

When we would go to the AoG regional meetings in Perth, he would champion me and my vision to see a work started in Easterhouse. It was also at one of these meetings that I just happened to park beside Andrew Smith. The pastor's pastor. Andrew, at that time was the Scottish Area Leader for the Assemblies of God GB. He is also a good Celtic fan.

My responsibilities in Scotland, initially involved working a couple of days a week at The Haven Kilmacolm, and a mission's week that was coming up that November. It involved Pastor Carter Conlon (Times Square Church NYC) and two hundred and fifty of his church coming over to Greenock and the surrounding areas to reach out to every area of the communities. We saw up to one thousand people in each of the meetings that week.

Andrew Smith began the process with me of transferring my probationary ministerial status from Ireland to Scotland. It would take a few years, but in the summer of 2015, I was ordained as a minister with the Assemblies of God Great Britain. He also took a keen interest in my vision for Easterhouse. We had a few friends in common, like Michael McNamee of Convoy of Hope Europe. I was intrigued to find out that Andrew was a board member for this missionary organisation that I admired so much. A chance meeting in that car park that day, followed by coffee in Costa was to lead to a great relationship and our now eight years old Arise Easterhouse outreach.

I waited patiently for the Lord to bring into my life the person that was going to start the work in Easterhouse. For just under a year I waited and waited. "Stuart you are just going to have to accept that no one else is coming to do it – it's you" said Maurice Logie, my friend and one of the elders at Harvest.

We began to pray in Blairtummock Community Hall every week and set the date, twentieth of February 2011 for our first meeting. We started and then continued to meet in the hall for eighteen months. British Land, the owners of what is now The Lochs Shopping Centre invited us to take an empty upstairs unit in the centre. This was through the centre manager, Renia Tysler a Christian that attends Riverside Church in Kirkintilloch. Renia has been a good friend and ally to both Tracy and I and the work of the church over the years.

Two years almost to the day since we moved to Scotland, we held our first service in our own (albeit rented) premises. We are still there to this day. Whilst church attendance on Sundays are not huge, we enjoy the role we have in being servants to other churches through our Arise events.

In May 2013 we had to move to a new house again. We had spent about eighteen months looking after a small Assemblies of God church in Greenock that had experienced some issues. Like every fellowship, it had its good points and bad points – but our eldest daughter Alisha was baptised there, and as always, we met people we will be friends with for life.

Housing wise it seemed again that we faced impending homelessness. This time though we were ready for the battle. Armed with a confidence in God and through prayer that He would see us ok. For six months Robert and Carol, who needed to sell the property in Bridge of Weir, were very patient. They had hoped to get the house on the market in Spring. The house next door to ours had been on the market for two years. In May 2013 we moved to a new built semidetached house in Gallowhill Paisley. When we had prayed very specifically about what we needed, re location and size wise, we could not believe how specific those prayers were answered. Our previous house sold within a month of being placed on sale, again another answered prayer.

Some of our friends that we had met in Port Ban, a caravan park run by a Christian family with a fellowship on site, lived only yards from us. Michael and Jacqui McLean have become such a big part of our life, as have their church family in Renfrew Christian Fellowship.

The girls all settled into their respective schools very well and we are proud of how they have each adjusted to several upheavals in their lives. It is beautiful to watch my daughters mature through their teen years not giving in to the temptations I faced. They are very open about their struggles (I wasn't) and we are excited for what God is already doing in and through their lives.

And yet my boyhood dream is more and more awakening in the reality of my life in Christ. As I write this in June 2019, my middle daughter Zoe Ann is preparing to fly out to Eswatini (formerly Swaziland) with her school on a mission's trip. This is why I still long for the window seat when I fly. Why, even now, after so many fights, when I beat my daughters to the window seat, I still stare silently at the earth below, tears still streaming down my face.

In these moments, Christ is closer than at ANY other time in my life. As I type this, it is hard not to shed another tear. My kids have not had to go through what I did. God has truly blessed them and is allowing them to share my dreams and my hopes.

At the time of writing our youngest, Naomi is just beginning third year at Gryffe High School. She joined the RAF Air Cadets last year because she inherited my love of ground gazing from above. She has flown with the RAF twice already.

Zoe has also just begun sixth year at Paisley Grammar School. She is a very disciplined and attentive student. Quite quiet, but comes alive when involved in any drama productions, Zoe wants to go on to study medicine.

Our beautiful (nearly twenty-one-year-old) Alisha is in college just around the corner from our house. She is one of the most caring people you could ever hope to meet and is very gifted with both the very young and the very old.

All three of them are actively involved in church and Christian life, and they are developing their own minds and faith as they journey this life knowing that they are lived by their creator God. Naomi prefers the behind the scenes with all the tech stuff, Alisha loves music and especially playing the drums, but can also strum out a tune on the guitar and / or keyboard – all self-taught.

My beautiful wife, Tracy took up the challenge at the age of thirty-seven to awaken a long dormant dream of being a nurse. She jokes that she came to Scotland for a holiday and two weeks later all her furniture showed up. Tracy has my complete admiration for how she has taken on so many obstacles and challenges in her life. Many times, we have bumped into friends and family members of patients she has cared for that give glowing reports on her care.

Life is so much better for having Tracy as my partner on this journey with Jesus. If you want to know Tracy's view of what life is like with me, buy the book *So I married a Teen Challenge Graduate,* brought out to celebrate fifty years of Teen Challenge in 2008 and look up 1998 in it.

Life with me has not and is not easy at times. Jesus redeemed me form the pit, he set me down on the firm foundation of God's love and He has shown me how to live according to His Word in His strength. But now and again old patterns of thinking and insecurities arise. It's why I have just sort of skimmed over a large part of my life as a Christian. I want to maybe develop how He has helped both myself and Tracy through some of these times in more depth. And through our experience He has helped others. Hopefully, God willing that book may help you.

Now God ALSO brought my beautiful Irish rose, Tracy into my life as my wife to guarantee a quota of ground gazing every year. Back and forwards to Dublin. Family holidays every year (we made a promise at the start of our marriage that our primary goal was to build a lifetime of memories for our kids). There are, even now, the overseas trips to minster.

Remember that single tear on Westwood pitches. Wow God looked down on me and shed a tear that day as well. He knew what was ahead and His heart for me then like you now was "If you only knew what I have in store for those who Love Me and are called according to My purpose".

Last year I even had the privilege of flying a small training plane over my beloved city of Glasgow. Flying around the Queen Elizabeth Hospital, and up and over my aunty June's in Whiteinch. It was incredible to get closer and closer to the actual joy of flying itself.

As well as my love of ground gazing from up high, my heart and my gaze are fixed on Christ, hopefully you see enough of Him, reflected in and through me, that you can dare to believe for your own childhood dreams.

51 – JP (2002)
Just Perfect

Each moment you take for granted
thinking there will always be another
But no one knows the day or hour
when death comes for you BIG brother
So, make the most and make them count
Let your blessed siblings know
the greatness of your love for them
is the purest of heaven's flows
Stuart Patterson ©2019

Christmas 2002 was tough. Tracy and I were now married and living in our own fantastic apartment in the Irish Financial Services Centre (IFSC) in Dublin. Our Christmas was great. It was the boxing day/ 27th December phone call. Three thirty am there was a ringing noise that permeated my sleep and seemed to be part of my dream. It was incessant though and eventually forced me awake.

My sister Yvonne called, "John's in hospital, he is really sick" she said into the phone. John, or JP as EVERYONE knew him, was my eldest brother. We all adored him. Not a malicious bone in his body, even all the kids of friends and family etc all loved JP.

John's only problem was that he had been really badly hurt in a long-term relationship he had been in. His partner, that he absolutely doted on, cheated on him with a neighbour. It wasn't just losing the partner, but her young daughter had been a massive part of JP's life, and she was torn away too.

JP had been the perfect dad to her, and as far as we could see the perfect partner. JP just did not know how to deal with this though and retreated into binge drinking. You would not see him all week, he would hide in his room in mum and dad's. Then at the weekend he would drink and irritate you with his niceness.

I remember Tracy being shocked at JP hoovering at 5am in the morning. He was up, it needed done for his ma so why not. Or waking Neil up early hours to ask him what time he needed woken up for work. Then there was his ability to fall asleep in the most ridiculous of locations.

Or the other side of JP. I dare you to answer mum or dad back. Or not be disruptive or disobedient to them. He would smack you.

In so many ways JP, our John, was the perfect big brother. He showed us how we should speak to mum and dad. Friends loved him; neighbours loved him. Parents of friends and neighbours loved him. There are enough stories about JP to fill a book, but I want to talk just about THAT Christmas.

Anyway, 3.30 am I was dealt with the shocking news that he was in the hospital. Yvonne also told me that the ambulance guys had to get the police to make him go in the ambulance.

JP was fiercely proud and private but was in denial over how ill he was. He had accidentally swallowed a tiny sip of antifreeze.

John had been on the prowl for alcohol and had come across a bottle stored away as it should have been. He took a sip, knew it was not alcohol and put it back.

Unfortunately, the antifreeze went onto cause a lot of damage inside. As it ate away at him, undetected for hours.

When the family were aware, he was sick, they called an ambulance, he refused point blank to go. The police came, everyone was aware how sick JP was, except JP.

Eventually, they got him into the ambulance and off to Glasgow Royal Infirmary.

Still half asleep and not really processing the news, I drifted back off. A couple of hours later Yvonne called again, "Stuart you really need to get here. It really isnae good. John's in a really bad way."

"Ok" I said meekly as I hung up the phone. The days of cheap flights between Dublin and Glasgow had only really started. I had been in Glasgow the week before with our Alisha. JP had been there, but as it was midweek, I never saw much of him. He did take Alisha out. Had her at friends with their kids etc, but until I was about to leave, had not really spoken much.

By this time Tracy was very heavily pregnant with our Zoe and only just allowed to fly. I called Ryanair, (we did have internet, but you could not book last-minute flights online) they had no availability.

I called Aer Lingus, holding out little hope and wondering how on earth I was going to get back to Glasgow. "Thirty-five pounds.," says the sales agent.

"What?" I replied. I could not believe it. Tracy and I had prayed before we called. We knew we needed a miracle. The flight was at 10.30, it was now around 7.45am. Not only did we get a flight, but at a price that was completely ridiculous for the timescale involved.

The next couple of hours was a blur. All I remember is landing at Glasgow Airport, being met at arrivals at 11.30am (I had stared at my watch the whole way over) and being told: "I am really sorry son, he is gone."

I collapsed.

Imprinted in my mind now is those last seconds from the week before, as Alisha and I were heading back to Dublin and about to leave mum and dad's, JP was standing in the middle of the sitting room. I was in the doorway and JP looked me straight in the eye, walked over towards me, hugged me and said: "I love you and I am proud of you".

"I love you too, John, thanks". It was so out of character for either of us. But little did we know that God was giving us a moment that so many do not get.

I got a proper goodbye with JP. I am weeping as I recall this. It was special.

JP would have been thirty-eight only a couple of weeks later, on the tenth of January – too young.

We all miss JP terribly, I miss him.

52 – Milk n Another Piece n Jam (2003)
Rest and be thankful

"The love of a mother is the veil of a softer light between the heart and the heavenly Father."
Samuel Taylor Coleridge

As recounted in my chapter JP, Christmas 2002 had been very tough. The fallout from my elder brother's death had not been nice. Grief is always very difficult to deal with, no matter how well prepared you think you are for it.

Christmas 2003 was a bit of a different story. Daughter number 2, our Zoe, was born in February and had been an absolute delight to us.

As we approached Christmas that year, it was with excitement, tinged with sadness. JP would not be around. Mum and dad had separated in the aftermath of JP's death and things were not the best back in Glasgow.

Mum wanted to be anywhere other than Glasgow that Christmas, so she came to Dublin. It wasn't the first time she had visited, the then very recent trend in cheap Ryanair flights had made it possible for mum and dad, and various other members of the family to visit. But this was different. This was for different reasons. My mum was coming over to escape. She needed a rest,

Alisha, now five years old, was excited. Tracy was excited as granny Heather was always a great help and good company around the house. I was excited as my mum was going to be with us at Christmas.

Tracy and my mum got on very well. Mum helped, an awful lot. She was brilliant with kids and was just great to have around.

Mum was always very content with a pile of ironing in front of her. Our house always made sure she had a great supply.

Approaches to Christmas decorations, however, were worlds apart. Tracy was minimalist, with the tree and a few other pieces. Mum wanted an explosion of colour and things to catch the kids' attention.

That Christmas, mum was very respectful of her differing view to Tracy's - until one day, whilst Tracy was out - mum said "nah ye need to have decorations!"

I gulped and thought, "I'm staying out of this" coward that I am.

So off mum went into Dublin City centre (a whole ten-minute walk from our apartment), and brought back loads of ceiling decorations etc.

They were home and hung everywhere, and I mean everywhere. Not a space on our ceilings or walls had a bare patch.

Tinsel, tinsel everywhere. It made my mum smile. She had claimed her own little piece of heaven that day. Alisha loved it. The ten-month-old Zoe stared at all the colours twinkling about everywhere.

Soon Tracy came home. Mum had started cooking the dinner and I stood just inside the sitting room to observe Tracy's face as she entered.

Tracy smiled. It was not how we did it, it was not normal for my mum to do things that way, but Tracy immediately got that this Christmas' of all my mum needed this.

It was her normal. It was her escape.

After all the years of needing respite from my brokenness and troublesome nature, the onetime my mum needed respite more than ever, as she grieved for her eldest, as she grieved for her marriage and her whole life being turned upside down in the space of a couple of weeks the year before - she found her respite in the place that God had prepared, just for her.

The fact that Jesus had stepped into my life only a few short years before, that he had blessed me with a beautiful wife, amazing kids and a home beyond our wildest dreams maybe it was so my mum could have her piece n jam there.

Finally, she found a little respite right in the centre of where, for so many years, had been the cause of the storm.

Is it any wonder that on the cross, as Jesus is dying, he looks at His friend and disciple John and His mother and says "women behold your son", and to John "behold your mother".

Jesus loves mothers. He feels their pain. He understands their anguish, their torment, their agonising over their children.

When we put Jesus at the centre of our grief, He will give us rest, as He gave to my mother. As He gave to His own.

A way forward. A "Rest and be thankful" before the journey continues.

53 – Mother's Day (2010)
Foer just one more

"Strength and honor are her clothing; She shall rejoice in time to come. She opens her mouth with wisdom, And on her tongue is the law of kindness. She watches over the ways of her household,

And does not eat the bread of idleness. Her children rise up and call her blessed; Her husband also, and he praises her: "Many daughters have done well, But you excel them all.""
Proverbs 31:25-29 NKJV

It has been great reading all the tributes on Social Media to mothers near and far. Those that are good, and those that maybe could be better but are still loved and appreciated.

In all my writings, my mum does not feature that much, but she is present in every post.

It is hard almost years since she passed away to think of fitting tributes to her tenacity, her love and her stubborn refusal to let me slide into hell, even though many around her would have pushed me just so she could rest.

My mum has hunted the streets for me, dragged me out of gang fights, put up with the worst of my addiction and resulting horrific behaviour.

She even had to talk me down one night amid a very bad episode of Amphetamine Psychosis, when I was convinced some guy (a friend lol) was trying to kick my door in. There was no one there, but she got how real it seemed to me and talked me down as I prepared to run out the door with a knife chasing shadows and phantoms.

Nearly every Christmas my mum would take on several jobs at the same time to guarantee we would all wake up to a mountain of presents and a gaze of love.

She has fought dentists (another story) and schools for me. She has gone without so we all could have.

She put up with so much, but at no time was there EVER any doubt that her love was unconditional.

When my addiction had led to guns and overdoses and needles and craziness, she was always there, calm, rational loving and kind, despite the horrendous pain I put her through.

When it was time to go to rehab, it was my mum that knocked the doors and made the calls.

The visits to Wales, despite not much cash, again mum (always accompanied by my big sis Yvonne).

My baptism - mum.

My graduation - mum and Yvonne on a twelve-hour coach journey, arriving just before the start, to head back to Glasgow the next morning.

Upon giving my life to Jesus, the calm excitement from my mum, "That's great, but you still need to sort yourself out".

My days in the boy band that was "The Evidence" my mum got all the CD"s and was always encouraging, despite never being able to see us sing and minister. She kept every Teen Challenge newsletter.

My first visit back to Scotland at the Teen Challenge Praise Night at Auchenfoyle, as I shared of God's faithfulness in Christ and how He had begun to reshape and restructure my life - my mum and Yvonne right and the front, proud and weeping and acknowledging the truth of my story, even of Ken and the prayer call.

The first time Tracy came to Scotland to visit, and we had our first argument (first not last) it was my mum that talked to Tracy on my behalf. Doing what only mum's can.

Our wedding in Dublin, my mum organizing another thirty-four of the family to travel over and celebrate with us. Her many visits to Dublin and never interfering on how we raised our kids, BUT always being supportive and massive assistance to Tracy and me.
Ballymena, through it all mum was there.

As we moved back to Glasgow, excited about the plans God had for us and the time to spend with my mum....

When Ciaran and I brought the first van of our stuff over, mum was diagnosed with kidney cancer.

She faced her own battles with the same strength and courage that she had faced down mine when I could not.

Christmas 2009 altogether in Darrin's. Loud and much fun. Kids and grandkids running riot, mum loving it.

My surprise 40th in February, mum there it was a great night and a fantastic family gathering.

The times Tracy and I would contrive for me to stay over in mum's house when I had to go to Stirling for ministerial probationary training days just so I could spend time there. Not that we needed an excuse, it was always an open door.

Only a few short weeks later, as Tracy and I visited mum in her house with Ciaran and Tracy (overspending time with us on our anniversary) mum was ill in bed. She did not like a fuss (over her) and refused to even countenance a doctor's visit. Currently, she was on trial medication to assist in the battle with what was now cancer raging within her.

She went into the hospital the next day. On the Friday afternoon, I will never forget reading through Psalm 23 with my mum on a rare few minutes when it was only Tracy and I in the room with her. As I got to "*Even though I walk through the valley of the shadow of death, I will fear no evil...*" my mum gripped my hand in that special mum way - firm but just firm enough to say, "its ok".
We prayed.

By the Saturday mum was unconscious and we all knew she was going. I had told her that I would bring Naomi up that evening.

Naomi was only due to turn four the following month.

Our girls would always sing to mum, their super gran song, and as Naomi sat on the edge of her bed that night and sung it, it was as if mum stirred.

Seconds later, peacefully she passed into the arms of Jesus.

I know many children say it, but the whole of our part of Easterhouse can testify to how totally unjudgmental Heather Anne Kiernan Patterson was. Her kids' friends were always allowed in their house because that way she could keep an eye open.

She taught us all manners and respect (My early adult life may not have reflected much of that, but it was there). Mum was fiercely defensive of her family. She had to put up with so much in her life. Married to a typical Glasgow East Ender. Mother to five kids by the age of twenty-five (Neil was a few years later).

Her friends loved her. Friday nights with them all in our house were legendary. She worked hard.

She was a great daughter, mother, aunt, friend, wife and neighbour. No one could or would say a bad word about Heather.

They had nothing on her.

The phone calls: I remember Jay Fallon challenging me to make sure I told my mum that I loved her. This was whilst I was still part of the Teen Challenge programme. It wasn't our way at that time.

The fear the first time (I know, right) but I will never forget standing in that phone booth in Challenge House in Gorslas on a midweek evening and for the first time saying "Mum, I love you"

After that I never tired of letting mum know how much she meant and that she was loved. I phoned her about everything. Good news - could not wait to call; bad news the same. If I missed a few days, there would be the call "Is everything ok?"

Mum also excelled as a granny. She was perfect. Kids came first in everything. She adored all her grandkids.

Today was a good day in church. A small gathering but reliable. Those local teenagers that have been coming around, never staying long but always coming back - how I would have loved to have called Heather tonight and told her about them staying all night and having to be "persuaded" to leave at home time.

Happy Mothers' Day mum, we love and miss you terribly. As kids go, yours are all doing pretty well.

54 - Paddy (2014)
A man's a man for a' that

"Why do men like me want sons?" he wondered. "It must be because they hope in their poor beaten souls that these new men, who are their blood, will do the things they were not strong enough nor wise enough nor brave enough to do. It is rather like another chance at life; like a new bag of coins at a table of luck after your fortune is gone."
From *Cup of Gold* by John Steinbeck

Paddy (John McGuire Patterson), was born in 1944, but I wasn't around to be aware of the circumstances surrounding his birth.

He was the son of William and Margaret.

William, my granda, was by best pal until he died in 1981. I doted on my granda. Used to love the walks he would take me on and the knowledge he would give me on these walks, real practical stuff like how to walk on a country road. And what car

173

registration numbers meant and how to read them. Maybe not mean much to you, but to me it was everything.

I also remember how I used to go to the shops for him, I'd get him his "willy woodbines" and his dinner out of the chippy when he was ill.

I can recall in vivid detail seeing him in Belvedere Hospital the week before he died. Sitting up in bed, chatting away about my entrance exams for Hutchesons and High School of Glasgow the following week and how he would be out of hospital then.

He wasn't, he passed away in between the HSoG and Hutchesons, and I wasn't told til after the Hutchesons' exam.

When I was told, I screamed and ran out the door and all the way up to Todd Coster's house. Todd's dad had driven us to the exam that day, and I just needed to run somewhere.

They were brilliant with me as I sobbed my story at them. I was very angry that I had not been told the day he had died.

I am convinced a piece of me died that day.

Mr & Mrs Coster (I think both) brought me around the corner to mum and dad's and explained what had happened.

When I shouted at my parents that granda had told me he was getting out of hospital that week so he couldn't have died, my dad calmly took me by the hand and explained that granda knew he was going to die and did not want me to be upset in the middle of the exams, so he had asked them not to tell me.

Whether he did or not wasn't really the point all these years later though.

My dad had his own grief at the death of his father so I would not be upset or distracted at such a key moment in my life.

They carried on as normal for a full day in front of me.
Man.

After reading my initial blog post on this, Todd Coster reminded me of the following as well:

I always remember your dad as such a big man massive to a wee boy like me seemed like 8 ft tall and hands like shovels. I also remember how he had this reputation of being a man not to messed with and not someone you would dare be cheeky to.

My memory of your dad is different, he was one of the tough guys yes, but would do no harm to anyone unless they crossed him or his family's path in some negative way. Then you may see the infamous Paddy but only then.

I recall we once had an argument/scuffle on way home from school one day. I think it was about the fire hydrants which we use to call free hits if someone stood on them. Anyway, I went home probably wearing a second prize as you know I was more of a talker and runner than a fighter!!

My mum, being well my mum, was having none of this and marched me down to your house. All the way down I am thinking this is not a good idea if Paddy's (my nickname as well) dad is in we could be in trouble here.

So, my mum chapped the door your mum answered and told us to come in. So, into the living room, we went. Your mum and my mum both agreed that we should shake hands and behave better towards each other.

Then your dad turned around and ushered us both over, I cannot lie I was petrified. He put one of those massive hands on each of our shoulders and said: "you two boys have brains let the others fight and knock the s*%ot out of each other don't let this happen again." And I didn't!!

Anytime I seen your dad in the passing in the years after that he would always ask me "you are behaving" and I would always of course say "yes Mr Patterson"!!

For all the stories about Paddy Patterson, and there are many, good, bad and downright horrid, there are moments when a genuinely loving and tender father could push its way through that hard exterior.

It was my dad that took me by the hand and explained that day, not my mum.

My mum was always loving towards us and that would be expected of her.

It was my dad.

It's been five years since John McGuire (Paddy) Patterson passed away into eternity, I want to indulge myself by remembering some of the brilliant moments when it was John the dad I saw and not Paddy the Maddy.

For as long as I can remember, my dad loved hunting, both lurchers (a greyhound like hunting dog) and ferrets, camping, fishing, and drinking.

They were his hobbies. They were how he filled his time when he wasn't climbing one hundred feet, or higher chimney stacks or sweeping domestic chimneys or any of the other jobs he would do.

The fishing and camping were always and as much an excuse to do the drinking part without being moaned at by my mum, at least in the later days of going, after discovering Minty and his hut.

I loved the countryside. I loved going out with the ferrets, and especially the dogs, it did not matter whether it was with Billy McGarritty or George or any of the other guys that would transport us. I loved it because out there my dad was a different guy. He was in awe of the countryside, and he was very good at hunting.

He knew how to pick the right sort of lurcher, and he knew how to use a ferret to catch rabbits in burrows.

Dad was also at his most gentle when he was out there. Still every inch the man, just kind and considerate and would go to great lengths to explain what he was doing and how to do it.

One of the greatest feelings was watching my dad watching the dogs chase down a hare and make the kill. Some people may frown on that and call it barbaric, whilst they munch on their Big Mac. It was what we knew, and it was a part of growing up.

Tiger and Susie were two lurches we had, at different times and they both excelled. It was a thing of beauty to watch nature being natural. And more hares escaped than were caught. Those that were caught were eaten by us.

The circle of life. Taught to me by my dad.

It gave me an appreciation for the countryside and wildlife that could never be got through books or college lectures.

He loved it when I started going out with Billy McG jr and friends of my own hunting.

My first time in trouble with the police was for poaching around the age of fourteen.

Gamekeepers out with their shotguns, on a hunt, decided that us boys should not be out with ferrets and dogs. They called the police and then, the whole lot of them approached a group of young teenage boys in a field with their loaded shotguns in their arms.

We were all searched and taken to a police station in the back of a van a few miles way. When I say that we were all searched, Billy McGarritty had a big hunting coat on and still manage dot go through the whole experience with a rabbit in his pocket, and not get it found. We got cautioned and kicked out of the station.

I asked how we were meant to get back to the bus stop.

"Walk!" The desk sergeant said.

"But its miles away" I replied.

"Walk," he said again 'And don't come back"

As we walked down the road, Billy pulled the rabbit out of an inside pocket on the big overcoat he wore.

We were killing ourselves laughing at that all the way home.

I think, at the time my dad wore it as a badge of honour because we were caught in an area, he had shown us.

His son was not in trouble for any bad stuff, but for poaching.

Ardmore Point!

In between Cardross and Craigendoran was the Patterson men's heaven on earth. A little piece of circular land that butted out into the Clyde.

Way back as far as the late 70's we used to go there camping and fishing.

It would be an ordeal getting all the massive backpacks loaded with old style canvas tents and everything needed for our weekend at the point.

Campbell McKnight and others would join us. Off we went on the train to Cardross, then a walking the couple of miles to the Point, often along the train tracks. I know it that would be frowned upon now, but it was just a Boys Own adventure then.

Water would be taken from one of the natural wells in the private grounds from the Big White House in the middle of Ardmore. That was always an adventure. As were the cooking apples from the private orchards and making our own jam.

One instance stands out though. I was about eight or nine years old and the usual crowd were all there.

It was night-time and it was dark, except for the light casting across the Clyde from Port Glasgow.

Stars shining brightly above and a cool, perfect evening. All the men used to boast about how far they could cast their beach casters out, with Campbell normally getting about two to three hundred feet (or maybe even yards).

I was getting to fish tonight.

My dad took his time and calmly showing me how to hold the rod and line in my hands in order to whip it forward.

Meekly I pulled the beach caster back and to cast the baited line out to sea.

You could hear the noise of it whipping through the air for what seemed like an eternity. It was less than a second and I think that it landed about 15' out.

Hahahaha!!! The laughs could be heard coming from the men as they began to slag my attempts.

"Leave him ya bunch of ...., or I'll .... batter yis".

"But he needs to get it out mair thin that Paddy, or eel no catch anyhin", said one of them.

"Shut it ah said" retorted my dad.

Only minutes later the end of the beach caster began to dance wildly, a sign that a fish had bit, as I reeled the line in it was obvious that I had hooked a fish.

A small coalfish I, as I recall.

I remember, as my dad unhooked the fish, he turned to the others with a triumphant smirk across his face, "that's ma boy" he said, genuine pride beaming out.

Not only did I catch the first fish of the night, I caught the only one that night.

Fast forward a wee bit, to my first day at Hutchesons'. It was my dad that brought me across the city on the two buses. He took me to the school gate, and he said, full of fatherly love and wisdom, "Right, I'll see ye later then." (He was a Glaswegian after all).

And he did, he was there as school came out that day, he showed me what buses I had to get and as we got home and through the door, "Yir able to dae that yirsel noo".

I was eleven years old. It was a different age, but even then, it hit me that I was being trusted with bussing myself across the city.

There were many arguments, many disagreements, and many, many, many miserable times with Paddy Patterson my dad, but my next moment was when I was in the height of my addiction.

It caused a lot of arguments between my mum and my dad as mum would never allow him to kick me out.

He just did not know what to do with me or how to deal with it. One moment, though, he allowed the hardness to melt for a moment.

We lived in Ervie Street at the time, and I was in a particularly bad way.

Only my dad and I were in the house.

I was wrecked out of my head, and I walked into the living room and asked him for a roll-up (hand rolling tobacco). He looked me straight in the eye and very calmly and gently said: "When I think of the man you should have been!"

Ouch!

And again, OUCH!

Probably the fatherliest thing he ever said to me. I knew then what he meant, and even now some twenty odd years later I still know.

He cared, and it hurt him that he was helpless.

Anyone that knew my dad will know that helplessness was never something you would associate with him.

Another quick moment, I have been with Teen Challenge in South Wales for a year and a half before I return to Glasgow for a visit. I had seen my Mum and my sis, Yvonne in that time but not my dad.

My first visit back, I walk through the opening in our ground floor (by this time we had the bottom and middle flats in 2 Ervie Street converted to one house) into the kitchen.

My dad stood over the cooker.

He hadn't seen or even spoken to me (other than the odd manly grunt over the phone) in all that time.

"Hiya I'm making the dinner, you ok." (it was one of his pots, I'm going to get our Neil at some point to try and describe them).

It was so normal; it was as if I hadn't been away. No great emotion, no hugs. Just hiya, you want some dinner.

I had never had a normal moment with my dad since I left Hutchesons' about fourteen years before that. It was what I needed.

"Aye," I said as I walked into the living room to hide the tears in my eyes. I loved that moment. I have talked about it many times.

His speech at my wedding, (we won't talk about how he got there, those that know, know.

I know why he came the way he did and why he was the way he was because I had a grown-up conversation with him about it and he told me).

He was bursting with pride, and very nervous.

And I loved every one of the very few words he spoke.

My eldest brother JP passed away in December 2002 through very tragic and ironic circumstances. For another time.

My beautiful mum passed away in April 2010, months after Tracy, the girls and I moved from Ireland back to Scotland. I want to maybe talk about that separately as I believe how God helped me through that time may help others.

Fast forward to when Easterhouse Community Church had not long started.

We were meeting in Blairtummock Housing Association's hall.

It was around summertime in 2011, and I remember feeling quite disappointed that things did not seem to be working out the way I thought they would. I always hung about outside the door, with expectation about who may come along, even out of curiosity, out of those I knew.

Once the meeting started, I did the lyrics etc, and I had decided that during the praise I would not be distracted by looking back to see who had come in.

Praise was about thanking God for who He is and what He had done and was doing through Christ's death on the cross, and subsequent resurrection.

This was now my reason for living, not who I wanted to see at a church service

One evening my overflowing, abundant faith resulted in a prayer something like this, "God who am I trying to kid with this, I cannot even persuade my own family too come"

I was genuinely very dejected that evening, but I still made the decision to praise God for who He is.

As the music finished, and I began to turn around I remember catching a strange smile on Tracy's face.

There, only two rows behind me were my youngest brother Neil, my sister Yvonne and right beside them, my dad.

It was one of the best moments in my experience of ECC. He was an ever-present visitor form that moment on. Dad and Neil used to also go to the Teen Challenge cafe in Port Glasgow after our meetings I loved watching him respond in those meetings, and even some of our conversations in his house afterwards.

When we moved to the new hall in Shandwick and his health began to deteriorate, he couldn't make our stairs.

(Note to readers, that is still an urgent problem of Easterhouse Community Church, we need to get a stairlift fitted to enable more infirm and elderly to attend if you can help please contact me).

Wesley Owen bookshop in Glasgow city Centre (it is now Faith Mission). My dad and I looking for a Christian book he could and would read, and a large print Bible.

I never thought in my wildest dreams I would be in a Christian bookshop with Paddy Patterson. So, he could buy a book!!!

With God all things are possible.

My dad's health deteriorated very quickly over the next couple of years. He had Chronic Obstructive Pulmonary Disease[xxi] and it began to take its toll.

As he moved into the end stages, Yvonne pretty much took care of all his needs. She was brilliant with him.

We used to joke about him taking up this timeshare in Glasgow Royal Infirmary he was there that often.

He was a great patient, to begin with, but not at the end.

December 2013 we were all gathered around him in Monklands hospital, convinced we were witnessing his last hours. Last rites had been said. We laughed, cried and slagged the old git.

He was out of it, his breathing was laboured and rasping, but somehow, he came around and we got an orderly.

We were kicked out of the room whilst the orderly attended to him. Dad did the toilet, (sorry but that's what happened) and was fully revived.

You had to be there to see the difference in him.

It was ridiculous what happened, and how it happened, but that was Paddy.

He got out, by some miracle, went back in (to GRI) got out, went back in and then pretty much stayed in.

By this time his short-term memory was gone.

I would get a phone call after leaving and he would say' "Thought you were coming for a visit".

179

The early frustration at his lapses in memory were by this time filled with sorrow. "I told you I will be up tomorrow, dad" which was the truth. No point in telling him I had just left. It only confused and upset him.

The night he died, we gathered around his bed.

Naomi and I had been up to see him before the football, Celtic were playing at home. He was in a very bad away and curtained off.

Yvonne was there providing all the bed care for dad and genuinely being a hero.

She did not think it wise to let Naomi see him that way, but Naomi had been promised she could. Naomi was very good with dad; we only stayed a few seconds.

We all gathered around dad's bed that night. By then he was on morphine, a lot of morphine. He would periodically wake up in pain.

I sat quietly praying.

At one point, not long before dad slipped away, he woke up, looked around us all with eyes blazing and said, "I'm still here ya b@#$%&*s" and then slipped back into sleep.

Around 5.30am on Sunday 2nd March 2014 my dad, Paddy Patterson slipped into eternity with that same stubborn arrogance that had made him a survivor his whole life.

The quote at the top of this post from the John Steinbeck novel, was about a pirate, Henry Morgan believing that men had sons so their sons could do the things they were not brave enough, strong enough or able enough to do.

I genuinely believe my dad always wanted his kids to be better, stronger, braver.

In glimpses that shone through. Most obviously for me with "When I think of the man you should have been"

Love you dad and miss you.

Thank you.

V Further Education

55 – Bored in the Winter (2017)
SWAP for an academic challenge

Everything you go through as a Christian is a training exercise behind which God has a divine purpose. He did not save you so the you could cruise into paradise on a luxury liner; He saved you to prepare you to be of use in Hs Kingdom. The moment you were born again, He enrolled you in His school of suffering. And every affliction, every trial, is another lesson on the curriculum.
Rev. David Wilkerson

Many times, through the years of our marriage, Tracy had challenged me to "go back to school". For years, whilst sharing my story in churches and schools etc I had always said that at fourteen the intention was to be a lawyer, but by fifteen I was a YTS butcher. I took umbrage at this, but deep down I knew I was awe bit wary of the challenge – was I as good at education as my memory told me I was.

I had been on the Scottish Wider Access Programme (SWAP)website a few times checking out what was needed. Once or twice I had even started applying – but I never completed it.

SWAP was set up to help prospective mature students (normally twenty-five or older) to return to further education. It consisted of a year at college to attempt to gain an equivalence grade that universities would accept.

I had always said I wanted to be a lawyer, so that was what I had investigated.

Tracy was out at a woman's meeting one evening. I had been doing some studying on my laptop, and curiosity got the better of me.

Www.scottishwideraccess.org I typed into the browser. Clicking on the link for *West of Scotland* I began the process. I was delighted to find that *Access to Humanities* the course I needed to do was available in the college campus around the corner from my home in Paisley, but also in Glasgow Kelvin College Easterhouse campus. This just happened to be on the grounds of Westwood Secondary School, my third and final secondary that I had walked out of thirty-two years before.

Part of the application process asks for a profile and why you want to study there. I was brutally honest, probably subconsciously hoping they would reject me.

I said nothing to Tracy about it when she returned later that evening.

Not too long after, I was invited for an interview. It was to be in their East End Campus in Haghill. By this time Tracy did know about it and was obviously delighted that I had listened to my wife.

On the morning I made my way over, introduced myself at reception and sat and waited, and waited, and waited. After around thirty minutes I discovered that, despite checking several times beforehand, the interview was in Easterhouse and I was late.

I made my way over, was brought to the correct room, and sat around desks with another ten or so prospective students. We were given a basic test paper to go through, whilst the interviews were conducted five feet away at a desk in the same room. I was sat next to a young guy, who also aspired of being a lawyer, but just because of the amount of money he could make (his words).

Interview over, home I went having to wait to find out. It wasn't long before I heard officially that I had been accepted onto the course which would start that August.

On my first day at college, walking through those doors was like going through a time machine – straight back to that December day in 1985 when I had walked out of a class, thinking never to return. The buildings were all different, but they stood on the same ground. My fist class, and a class I was to spend a lot of time in over the next ten months directly overlooked the Social Work building that used to contain that fateful Geography class. The first day I looked out, I could not help but shed a tear for that wee boy, ignorant of the consequences of that fateful choice.

Not long into my college course, it became obvious that my long-held view of studying law was a non-starter. Apparently, that fact that I had done a custodial sentence would bar me from practicing law.

Moments and choices. Under the guidance of my course tutor, Pam Currie, I began to focus on Social Policy and Creative Writing.   My long dormant love of writing had been awoken by my Communications lecturer, Alex McPherson. Another English teacher.

He was always very direct and did not waste time when challenging us. If we were wrong, he would say so. But his love for *English,* whether it be poetry, or books (especially *The Great Gatsby*) or even magazine articles was infectious, and I began to enjoy writing again. I had always loved my Theology stuff. I enjoyed my Bible Study and prep, but this was different. It was a different area of my imagination (remember that) and it was good to welcome it back like an old friend.

My classmates were a good bunch as well. A few of the younger ones that had started, soon left though, but the remainder of us almost all finished the course.

Maths, as it had always been was a struggle. A couple of us benefitted from collaborative study in it, and I learned to cope. Delighted when I got my National 5 result through to discover I had achieved an 'A'.

College also saw me win two awards (remember those) Glasgow Kelvin College awarded me *Class Prize* for SWAP Access to Humanities.

I also reached the final four for the national *SQA Star Award for College Candidate*.

In May 2018, I finished the course with a AAA score. I had been accepted for all five of my university courses that I had applied for, but chose University of Strathclyde Joint Honours in Journalism, *Creative Writing and Social Policy*. I added two Education modules at the last minute to make up my credits required.

Moments and choices.

56 – The Road to Nowhere – Revisited (2017)
Parks and Recreation

I'm feelin' okay this mornin' and you know
We're on a road to paradise. Here we go, here we go
Chris Frantz / David Byrne / Jerry Harrison / Tina Weymouth
Road to Nowhere lyrics © Warner/Chappell Music, Inc[xxii]

As I was saying in one of the earlier chapters - *The road to nowhere* - Blairtummock Park was a place I knew and loved in my early childhood.

It was always full of life and people. My memories of it began to change as I got involved in drugs, and *LSD* really altered my emotions of it.

It is only a place, but we connect memories to these places and form emotional attachments.

Fast forward to 2017. It's a snow-covered day. I am now a student at Glasgow Kelvin College, and some of my fellow students and I go a lunchtime walk. Andy, Jonny, Megan, Eileen and myself.

Today it is the road to nowhere. The park is empty now. The House has day-care classes going on in it. All modernised and different, no movie shows. No history in its hallways, just magnolia.

The bowling green long fallen into disrepair through neglect. No more white coats and polished bowls. No more "get aff the grass or al thump ye".

And yet as I walked through with my classmates, staring the wrong way up the road to nowhere, I heard my childhood cry out to me.

Once again, I could see the bowlers bowling; the kids playing; families picnicking. I heard the thunder of the skateboards hammering down the ramp. The monkey tree was still there, daring youngsters to clamber up its long spindly arms.

It was, once again, a joy that whistled in the grass and rustled through the leaves in the trees. Those trees, rather than the threatening pose of the *LSD* days they looked like, they were stretching out their arms to embrace an old friend.

Welcome home, Stuart.

The park itself seemed to miss the sound of laughter and the innocence of kids playing.

Even this, those tarnished memories tainted by my years of addiction - even this it seems God has redeemed.

The days I was in a park facing class in college, I always stared wistfully out the window at my old friend, remembering with fondness the innocence of childhood in Easterhouse. Being reminded that God had me born into a family that would live laugh love and yes even cry here. God had me create lifelong friendships here. God would call me back to that road to nowhere and show me - with Him I am going somewhere.

57 – Fazed at Freshers (2018)
God keeps the *peace* though

A place of useful learning
Mr Anderson had intended
But that first day in uni
My world was upended
Surrounded by girls as young
As my daughters were
Didn't look like fun
I thought that God
had a made a mistake
Me back at 'school'
was half baked
and yet, it has a happy ending
Stuart Patterson ©2019

Freshers Week, September 2018 – I turned up for my first induction lecture, surrounded almost entirely by teenage girls. As a man approaching fifty, I felt extremely uncomfortable and questioned my choices and whether I should be there.

I still, at this point did not know what my first lecture would look like or how my final timetable was going to be.

I remember standing outside the lecture hall and praying that the Holy Ghost would help me know this was right. After the lecture, I came out and checked my uni app, anxious to know, well something anything.

Timetable for Education was up, my first lecture was the following Monday at nine am. The lecturer's name though, caught my attention.

Amanda Corrigan. I knew an Amanda Corrigan led the *Teen Challenge* outreach bus in Largs, and I had met her a few times. But I thought she worked in the Royal Alexandra Hospital in Paisley.

"Amanda, do you lecture in Strathclyde Uni in Education?" says I over Facebook Messenger.

"Yes why?" came a very quick response.

"Nae luck, you have me in your class." I then explained to her what I meant.

Only an hour after being out of my depth and extremely uncomfortable; after asking for some reassurance that I was in the right place – I found that my very first lecturer, in my very first lecture on my first official day in university was a born-again Christian. Not just any though, no God was very specific, a Christian that led a Teen Challenge bus, my very transport back to life.

Onto another induction class, this time favourite pop songs and movies. They weren't very knowledgeable on the 80's. Hmmm.

The lecture was a fifty-year-old hippy, that was quite content being single and earning a lot of money for doing not much (his exact words). Not quite the inspirational talk I would have expected on my first day.

Being *Freshers' Week,* I was rather dismayed to find that it really was nearly all about where to get drunk and have a party. There seemed to be nothing much for learning. I attended very few events that week, and instead looked forward to my first day proper.

That morning I made my way into Glasgow, walked along to the Royal College Building, went in the side door and climbed six very old, very steep staircases to my first lecture. It took me a few weeks to discover that there were plenty of lifts, you just had to know where to look – or how to read the signs posted the door.

Nine am, there I was, along with just over three hundred other students, a few guys among them to my relief.

The lecture hall was massive and followed the normal pattern of tiered seats on a slope with a work area running along in front of the seats. Seating was split into two narrower rows either side of a very wide middle row. I sat about six rows back on the right-hand side of the middle as you look down.

I was amazed to see that none of these hip, young students had iPads, or MacBook, or anything electronic to use. It seemed like Hollywood had lied. Week after week, as each students grew more comfortable in the surroundings, the electronic devices all began to appear.

Amanda opened with a welcome and introduction to the module. She wasted no time in introducing her *modus operandi* of pointing out individuals and asking them questions. It was almost humorous watching people trying to hide behind their eyelashes, hoping they would not be seen,

I had already said hello to Amanda on entering, and obviously I was one of the ones she picked on for a question.

After one hour, my first ever university lecture was over.

I had survived.

Amanda has been brilliant on her guidance to me through first year. I took her class as my tutorial as well. I also discovered that some of those young people on that first induction day have an incredible heart to make a difference and that, in the classroom, it is great to hear their input.

They are also pretty much the same age as my daughters, so I get an insight into that level of thinking and understanding that has helped me at home.

Very quickly, I found my role in university amongst my much younger peers, was just to challenge them on why they believed what they believed. Not just to take everything at face value because a lecturer or a textbook said so, but to question everything and hold it up to scrutiny. I was amazed, especially in *Social Policy*, how so may lecturers' own illustrations did not stand up to even the most basic of scrutiny. I would sit in the lectures, eager to learn, but also just as eager to *test everything.*

In February 2019 – thirty three years after my sixteenth year - the year that so much happened on the back of the moment I made the choice to leave school - I got seventy eight per cent, (an A) in an essay for *Understanding Education* in university. I have done other essays (not got such great grades but have passed them all). But this A, in Understanding Education – a module I only added to make up my credits but love.

This A and the timing of it! The only thing lacking was being able to call my mum, as I always did, since a conversation with Jay Fallon. Good news, bad news indifferent news Tracy and I always called my mum.

I love my wife Tracy, but that day I would have just once more been able to pick up the phone and call my mum. "Mum, I just got an A in my Understanding Education module. A conversation that, other than that moment, she had maybe expected to have thirty years EARLIER.

The next day, in the Royal College Building in UoS, a group of friends (all around 18- 21 years old) and I, did some basic Physics experiments with primary school kids. It was my placement for *Placement and Curriculum Education* module. I am grateful to God for this bunch. They care and are kind. (I passed this module as well).

In April 2019, I accompanied the University of Strathclyde Deputy Head of Education, Amanda Corrigan, to Polmont Young Offenders Institution. I have been blessed with the opportunity to speak in many prisons in my role as a pastor and as a Christian. My *Return to Polmont* though, was as a student and a representative of the *University of Strathclyde.*

It was to speak to some young men imprisoned there about my experiences and my journey.

I chatted about being heard; of how many had assumed they knew the core issues affecting me, but no one really HEARD ME, until the day I walked into The Haven Kilmacolm, and Fin Moffat the then manager spoke to me, and listened.

My *Return to Polmont* felt like a homecoming; an arrival, just as my entry into the Teen Challenge men's centre in Wales had been.
That day, after hiding from my academic journey for decades, I got it. I saw and understood education. I saw the need for the individual to be heard, even if they are wrong, and to be assisted in their next steps in their journey.

My long walk to education has been arduous and it is far from over. But the mess I made in my sixteenth year, Jesus has stepped in and redeemed.   He has offered a second chance at so many lost dreams. He has taken me by the hand and guided me to this moment. I am grateful.

58 - We don't need no education (2019)
Understanding Education (finally)

"Holding back the years
Thinking of the fear I've had so long
When somebody hears
Listen to the fear that's gone
Strangled by the wishes of pater
Hoping for the arms of mater
Get to me sooner or later"
From 'Holding back the years' Neil Moss and Mick Hucknall 1985

At four and a half years old I had my first day at school. I went to Blairtummock Primary School in Glasgow's Easterhouse housing scheme.

Four and a half years old and I was being abandoned by mum and dad whilst my wee brother Darrin stayed at home.

This was not on. I carried on through Primary School, uneventful for the most part, but Secondary School (High School to the post-millennials) brought with it many, many challenges. Some of which I am pretty sure I still *enjoy* the fruit of even today.

After doing a tour of secondary schools, (Hutchesons Grammar, Lochend SECONDARY and Westwood Secondary) I left School December 1985, halfway through the fifth year. I was fifteen years old. I was already drinking and smoking hash. Only a short time before, whilst in Hutchesons at the age of fourteen, I was going to be a lawyer.

Instead, within weeks of leaving Westwood, at the age of fifteen I was a YTS butcher. It wasn't long before I had taken my first acid tab.

By the summer I had my own council flat, ingesting copious amounts of speed, and had nearly overdosed, on paracetamol. My sixteenth year also saw my first, second and third criminal convictions. I also began eleven years of hitting up (intravenous drug injection).

I spent most of my time hanging on street corners and in other gang members (we were really just a collection of locals) houses taking drugs. That quick.

At eighteen I was arrested and charged with being concerned with the intention to supply drugs, (I know long winded but that's what it was).

I also spent some time (only a couple of weeks mind you) in Polmont Young Offenders Institution. I was on remand but owed fines, so I did my time there.

By the age of nineteen I had been on probation twice and I went to prison – again. Well, I say prison, but it was Castle Huntly YOI (540 / 89) I was a number.

It was full of teenage guys who, for the most part, wanted to be gangsters. We were in an open prison – but it was still a prison.

I was released in August 1990. Dropped off at a train station and let go with the echo from the prison officer of, "See ya soon". Within hours I had another injection.

Between twenty and twenty-seven life really is a blur. A lot of trauma happened; I think. I nearly lost my hand to a Temazepam injection. At twenty seven I had the privilege of my real boss pointing a real gun at me and wanting to really shoot me.

At twenty seven I went to Teen Challenge and met Jesus, and, for the first time really understood love and forgiveness.

At thirty I met Tracy and understood real love in a different way. We married shortly after that and have three daughters.

December 2002, my eldest brother, JP died, weeks before his thirty eighth birthday.

2007 Tracy, my three beautiful daughters Alisha, Zoe and Naomi moved to Ballymena in Northern Ireland. We met some beautiful people that sustained us through a difficult time.

In 2009 we moved home, (back to Scotland).

Mum passed away in 2010.

Easterhouse Community Church started February 20 2011.

Tracy's dad Leo passed away in 2012.

My dad passed away in 2014.

2017 after much harassing and bullying from Tracy I started the *Scottish Wider Access Programme* in Glasgow Kelvin College's Easterhouse campus. It stands on the grounds of the former Westwood Secondary School.

My first day was in a class overlooking the building where the class I had walked out of thirty two years before stood.

September 2018 I walked through the doors of the University of Strathclyde, beginning a BA in Humanities.

February 2019 – thirty three years after that sixteenth year I got seventy eight per cent, (an A) in an essay for *Understanding Education* in university. I have done other essays (not got such great grades but have passed them all). But this A, in Understanding Education – a module I only added to make up my credits but love.

This A grade and the timing of it! The only thing lacking was being able to call my mum, as I always did, since a conversation with Jay Fallon. Good news, bad news indifferent news Tracy and I always called my mum.

I love my wife Tracy, but that day I would have just once more been able to pick up the phone and call my mum. "Mum, I just got an A in my Understanding Education module.

The next day, in the Royal College Building in UoS, a group of friends (all around eighteen to twenty one years old) and I, did some basic Physics experiments with primary school kids. It was my placement for *Placement and Curriculum Education* module. I am grateful to God for this bunch. They care and are kind. (I passed this module as well).

April 2019, I accompanied the UoS Deputy Head of Education, who is also a friend, (Amanda Corrigan), to Polmont Young Offenders Institution. I have been blessed with the opportunity to speak in many prisons in my role as a pastor and as a Christian. My *Return to Polmont* though, was as a student and a representative of the *University of Strathclyde*.   It was to speak to some young men imprisoned there about my experiences and my journey.

I chatted about being heard. Of how many had assumed they knew the core issues affecting me, but no one really HEARD ME, until the day I walked into The Haven Kilmacolm, and Fin Moffat the then manager spoke to me, and listened.

My *Return to Polmont* felt like a homecoming; an arrival, just as my entry into the Teen Challenge men's centre in Wales had been. That day, after hiding from my academic journey for decades, I got it. I saw and understood education. I saw the need for the individual to be heard, even if they are wrong, and to be assisted in their next steps in their journey.

My long walk to education has been arduous and it is far from over. But the mess I made in my sixteenth year, Jesus has stepped in and redeemed. He has offered a second chance at so many lost dreams. He has taken me by the hand and guided me to this moment.

I am grateful. The purpose of my book is to give a look at some of the moments that have made up that journey, and through it maybe some others will KNOW they have been heard, and maybe trust those doing the hearing for some guidance.

This is my story arc. Many people have shared with me, helped me and challenged me on this walk. I am thankful for every one of you. Even those at the time I hoped and prayed would go away.

Today I am thankful. It's never too late. This is just but a short overview of the moments that make up my life. Thank you for reading and getting a bit more of an understanding into the background of each of those moments.

Each of them forms the sum of my life to this point. They have brought you along with me to just after I left Teen Challenge and moved to Dublin. Each of them *completes the tenner* of my life.

Jesus completed the *Ultimate Tenner* on my behalf, when He died on that cruel cross for me, and my sin, guilt and shame. The ten commandments, the law passed down by God, was complete in Him and He offered to me a new freedom, a new hope to go, back to Eden, as it were, to that place of innocence and trust in a loving God and His ways.

Thank you for journeying with me. My intention is, later to continue the journey and show just how much a daily walk with Jesus means in the EVERY day, and maybe break down some of the mystery around it.

Blessings

Stuart Patterson

Return to Polmont was a technical term used in my Castle Huntly days of imprisonment. It referred to a serious disciplinary procedure, and normally meant your inmate category had been changed from a 'D' to a 'C' and so you were returned to Polmont. I never did return in any capacity – until I re-joined my academic journey.

Stuart Patterson

About the author

Born and raised in Glasgow's tough Easterhouse, housing scheme, Stuart's life was never the conventional. From being offered a scholarship to Hutcheson's Grammar school at the age of 11, passing through another two comprehensives before his 16th birthday, this is a life of many twists and turns.

Gang violence and drug addiction in his teens led to a prison sentence at the age of 19. Over the next eight years Stuart's family and friends watched helplessly as his life went from bad to worse, accelerating rapidly downwards. A life that seemed to offer so much, fast becoming robbed of even the resemblance of promise and hope, whilst bringing misery on everyone he touched and those that loved him.

This all changed one incredible weekend in May 1997. One incident after another that weekend led to dramatic events that would change Stuart's life, and those lives he would go on to touch, forever. Right at his darkest moment, when he was drifting away, Christ lifted him.

Stuart went through the Teen Challenge programme and learned how to live free from the stranglehold of addiction through the love and value given to him by Jesus.

Stuart has been married to Tracy since 2001, and has three daughters, Alisha, Zoe Ann and Naomi.

Along with Tracy, they now run Easterhouse Community Church, an Assemblies of God fellowship, back where he grew up. Stuart now spends a lot of time helping those suffering from the issues he used to have. He has also just completed a year at college and the first of four years university degree after thirty-two years out of education.

For more of Stuart's story, alongside other poems and media work, please visit: www.stuartpatterson.org

Glossary:

a - of
aboot - about
ae - of
ach - oh dear
ah - I
ah'll - I will
ahm - I am
ah've - I have
an - and
av - I have
aw - all
awright - alright
aw yis - you all
aye - yes
cannae - cannot
couldnae - could not
ae – do
daein - doing
deid - dead
didnae - did not
eejit - idiot
fae - from
fun - find
fur - for

n - going
' - gave
- give me
t - got
ie - home
- had
no - why not
- have
- just
- can
ny - loan
t - lost
- my
- mum
iel - myself
r - more
sus - mrs
ra - tomorrow
and
e - none
- no
- now
t - nothing
- on

o'er - over
oot - out
pit - put
ra - the
rerr - there
staun - stand
stoap - stop
sumdy - somebody
tae - to
their - there
thum - them
um - I am
wan - one
wee bit - soon
whit - what
wir - our
wis - was
wisnae - was not, wasn't
wrang - wrong
ya - you
ye - you
yir - you are

[i] https://marklowry.com/about
[ii] https://archive.org/details/EdwardMFavor
[iii] https://youtu.be/IfW3TxQhy20
[iv] http://talesoffaerie.blogspot.com/2012/01/magicians-cape.html
[v] https://www.haven.com/parks/yorkshire/primrose-valley/
[vi] http://www.disused-stations.org.uk/f/filey_holiday_camp/
[vii] https://www.nationalgeographic.com.au/history/the-80s-timeline.aspx
[viii] https://web.archive.org/web/20070916000942/http://www.newi.ac.uk/englishresources/workunits/ks4/fiction/ofmicemen/llshort/factsheet.html
[ix] http://www.robertburns.org/works/75.shtml
[x] https://www.breitbart.com/clips/2014/12/02/barkley-everyone-has-tribe-mentality-on-race/
[xi] https://www.brainyquote.com/quotes/pam_brown_402583
[xii] https://en.wikipedia.org/wiki/Lysergic_acid_diethylamide#Adverse_effects
[xiii] https://www.emmarosekraus.com/
[xiv] https://www.goodreads.com/book/show/43841262-little-arson-annie
[xv] https://www.medicines.org.uk/emc/product/1142/smpc
[xvi] https://www.glasgowlive.co.uk/news/history/easterhouse-street-gangs-history-12261102
[xvii] https://www.medicines.org.uk/emc/product/4907/smpc
[xviii] https://www.webmd.com/drugs/2/drug-148127/morphine-intramuscular/details
[xix] https://www.nhs.uk/medicines/temazepam/
[xx] https://www.amazon.co.uk/dp/B001QREWKA/ref=dp-kindle-redirect?_encoding=UTF8&btkr=1
[xxi] https://www.copdfoundation.org/What-is-COPD/Understanding-COPD/What-is-COPD.aspx
[xxii] https://genius.com/Talking-heads-road-to-nowhere-lyrics

Printed in Poland
by Amazon Fulfillment
Poland Sp. z o.o., Wrocław

58492991R00120